T0354732

Without a
Suitcase

The Story of Katie as Told to Her Son Janek (Jon)

Jon Butcher translated by Ruth Butcher

WESTBOW
P R E S S®
A DIVISION OF THOMAS NELSON
& ZONDERVAN

This book is a work of non-fiction. Unless otherwise noted, the author
and the publisher make no explicit guarantees as to the accuracy of
the information contained in this book and in some cases, names of
people and places have been altered to protect their privacy.

WestBow Press books may be ordered through booksellers or by contacting:

WestBow Press
A Division of Thomas Nelson & Zondervan
1663 Liberty Drive
Bloomington, IN 47403
www.westbowpress.com
1 (866) 928-1240

ISBN: 978-1-9736-1716-7 (sc)
ISBN: 978-1-9736-1717-4 (hc)
ISBN: 978-1-9736-1715-0 (e)

Library of Congress Control Number: 2018901027

Print information available on the last page.

WestBow Press rev. date: 03/06/2018

To write this book empowers me to bind my life with my family and the prisoners who were displaced from our homeland during the war in Europe. I will attempt to give the reader all of the material from my own experiences and observations of my life during that time. This book is my life's story of forced deportation to Siberia and our miraculous escape from that frozen land. The loss of life and living conditions in that foreign inhumane land of Soviet Siberia and Uzbekistan haunt me to this day. It is the story of our personal survival, initially in the grip of the Soviets and later in the free world traveling to Persia (Iran), India, Africa, and England. The members of these displaced families who lived in Siberia were scattered all over the world. It is my hope that this book will help the reader to understand the difficult experiences of the displaced Polish peoples and will be a valuable reminder of what they endured during this time in history.

Katherine Butcher
Janek (Jon) Butcher, Katherine's son

Acknowledgements

A very special heartfelt thank you to Paul Ryan. His dedication in editing this work made it possible to bring this story to print. Without his inspiring and untiring work, this book might never have been completed. Words cannot express my gratitude.

Thank you also to West Bow Press for all the guidance and help. A special thank you to Jordan Ling who worked patiently in helping me edit this work. I could not have completed this without your help.

Life in Poland:
My Family's History

It was a very hot summer. The air was stuffy, humid, and heavy, without even the slightest breeze, making it hard to breathe. My grandfather Frank said it was the calm before the storm. When I think about it now, I don't know whether he meant the weather, a coming storm, or maybe he sensed an impending catastrophe because of the trains sitting at the local railroad station. In actual fact, it turned out to be something that threw our entire family into the eye of a storm. It swept us out of our house, tore us away from our roots, and cast us to another side of the world, where we would be naked, hungry, helpless, barely able to survive, and sentenced to death. I've never returned to my homeland. I'm alive today, living on another side of the world, although I still think and speak in Polish. I speak little English.

My grandfather lived with Marysia, my grandmother, in Ojeżowicach, Poland, under Austrian rule. Among their ten offspring were six sons and four daughters, namely my father Joseph and his five brothers: Martin, Kuba, Charles, Paul, and Tom, along with his four sisters: Zosia, Marysia, Salamandra, and Jozia. The house was filled with these ten children, creating a never-ending and constantly joyous hullabaloo.

Martin, the eldest of my uncles, was very spiritual and wanted desperately to be ordained as a priest. He was hardworking and consequently completed his theological studies quickly. My parents were very proud of him. Uncle Martin served his priestly duties at the rectory in Husiatyn, Poland. Our whole family was highly respected in our area because we had a priest within our family.

My father decided to follow in the footsteps of his brother and also began studying theology. He was twenty-one years old when he unexpectedly got a call from the Austrian military command. He was not happy about this and did not want to stop his studies, but he had no choice. He had to appear before the military and decided to pretend to be deaf, therefore unfit for military service. The medical committee tested his hearing. He was taken to an empty room with a chair in the center of the room. A doctor and a nurse seated my father on the only chair and ordered him to stare at a designated point. They stood behind him and began to knock and stomp their feet on the floor. Father did not react. He did not pay any attention to them, pretending not to hear them. Two other men came into the room with a huge barrel. They pushed it toward my father, making a loud roaring noise. This frightened my father, and he couldn't help but turn around to see where this scary noise was coming from. The doctor just laughed. Moments later, Father left the command center, carrying a certificate of ability to serve in his hand.

My father served in the Austrian army for four years and advanced to the rank of general's understudy. From 1914 until 1918, when the First World War was over, he took part in many battles. After the war, he returned home with the intention of resuming his studies. But shortly after his return, he met Angela, the woman he called his angel. After a brief courtship, they married and moved to Yaroslav. On May 7, 1922, my older brother Tony was born.

My grandfather was also in the Austrian army and was paid in Austrian koronas. This helped him to purchase many acres of fertile farmland. By then, my grandfather was quite a wealthy man and was blessed with a knack for business. He sometimes took risks but never missed an opportunity to buy or sell for profit.

After Poland regained its independence from the Austrian occupation under the leadership of Marshal Pilsudski, the korona was exchanged into Polish zlotys as a currency. This increased my grandfather's wealth by several times. New boundaries were established on the eastern border of our country. Rumors were circulating that new colonies would be set up. There was no work in our homeland, and Grandfather did not want to miss out on such an opportunity to purchase land in the new colonies. He went on a trip to investigate these new lands, and from the first time he laid eyes on it, he fell in love with the landscape. He immediately bought many, many acres and became the owner of a beautiful, big house, stables, and an expanse of fertile land situated ten kilometers from the town of Sokal.

My grandfather was a real family man and wanted to keep the family together in the same house, including my parents. The house was actually a mansion, and it was called a *folwark*. It was huge but very comfortable, so everyone living in it was content and happy. The economy was prospering in this new land. His farmstead was so rich and fertile, it produced an abundance of crops at a very fast pace. Grandfather found it necessary to hire many local workers to help in his fields.

His home and stables had permanent employees on staff. A young couple named Fred and Hanna, whom he brought with him from his estate in Poland, were hired to manage the household duties as well as the stables. My grandfather was a very compassionate person who cared not only about his family but also about the local people. He treated everyone equally and fairly, with no exceptions.

I was born on January 10, 1924. Father would have liked me to have been a boy, but my mother was thrilled with her little Katherine.

As my aunts and uncles grew up, they started their own families and sometimes left our nest. Grandfather divided the farm property among them as they married. He helped them set up their own homesteads as they built their own new homes. We all worked hard, and our family grew not just in size but also in land holdings and prosperity. However, Grandfather wanted to buy even more land.

My aunt Sophie had read something about Canada and whined that she wanted to visit and get to know this country. Finally, Grandfather and Grandmother agreed to finance her overseas holiday. Aunt Sophie liked it there so much that she did not return to the colonies; she settled permanently in the province of Alberta.

As the children grew up, they needed an education. But there were no schools in our area, and Grandfather wanted all the children to be properly educated. So he started a school for the younger children in his large home and sent the older ones to larger cities so they could get a better education. We had a huge dance hall with a stage in our home, which was remodeled into a classroom. Grandfather hired a teacher who came to us every day. Word soon got around the area, and soon even the neighbors sent their children to be taught in our school.

Our school became so popular that there were more applicants than space for students. Grandfather agreed with the neighbors that the school needed to be moved to a separate building. So, funds were collected from all the residents of the surrounding area. A short time later, a new building was built about a kilometer from our house. Tony and I attended this school regularly. Our classes were conducted in two languages: Polish and Ukrainian. Knowledge of both these languages would be useful to the children in the future. However, another problem arose. Once a week, a Catholic priest came to the school to teach religion. Since the Ukrainians were not Catholic, they demanded to have an Orthodox "Pop" to teach classes also. Eventually, everyone came to an agreement, and on Wednesdays, we had the Catholic religion lessons, and on Thursdays, the Orthodox lessons.

The floor of the hall was finished with beautiful oak planks that were varnished so they were like a mirror. Tony liked to go there quite often with his friends, especially in winter, sliding on the floor as if it were ice. They competed to see which one was the fastest. As they slid with their boots on, they scratched the floor. When Grandfather saw the scratches, he yelled at Tony and his friends and chased them from the room.

The stage in our house was large enough to have professional performances. We had plays in which the children sang and acted. We also had performances for children to enjoy. One memorable performance was a comedy that we waited several weeks for. Songs and dances were performed by a woman and a man with a wooden leg. They made the room full of people laugh till they cried. I could not understand how a man could move around without a leg and still make us laugh with his jokes. Our theater was popular and always attracted large crowds, at times with standing room only. Many people started to buy land and housing in the neighborhood. The population of our district grew so quickly, a new name was needed. One of the names suggested was our family's surname, but the name finally chosen was Romosz.

As my family continued to grow, despite the roominess of Grandfather's house, my father decided to build a new home for our family. He hired builders and constructed a new house for us, with the help of my uncles. I loved our new house because it was so spacious, but I loved the huge basement most of all. We filled it with lots of fruits and vegetables for the winter.

Soon, Josephine was born, followed by the three boys: Chester, Godfrey (also called Fred), and Alexander.

Every Sunday, our family went to church in Świtarzówce. To get to church, we had to walk on dirt footpaths for several kilometers between the farms. We had to leave early in the morning and didn't get home from church until late afternoon. One Sunday morning as we were walking to church, we met up with a girl named Stella and her five siblings: three girls and two boys. Stella was the oldest girl and was my age. From the moment we met, and as we walked together to church, we got along well and became good friends. We made plans to meet every Sunday morning to walk together to church. She lived in Stanisławówce settlement and said the settlement was named after her godfather. Although twelve kilometers separated us, we become such good friends that we visited each other quite often during the week.

Stella had to do a lot of work at home, helping her mother. Since she was the oldest, she had to help with the house and look after her younger siblings. Her father was an officer in the army, and when he returned from the war, he was thirty-two years old. He purchased some land in the colonies and built a house there. They owned two horses and a few head of cattle. Rumors circulated that her father owed some money but refused to pay his debts. Stella said that he was invited to a reception and presumably given poison in a drink. He came home very ill and soon died. Stella was only three years old when she lost her father. She confided to me that she missed her father very much. She said her stepfather was very bad and abused her. I hope her friendship with me eased some of her domestic troubles.

By now, Uncle Kuba had married and built a house for his family. As time passed, he and his wife were happy and had a daughter and two sons. But one day, three tipsy Ukrainians looking for trouble started a fight and beat Uncle Kuba, leaving him alone only when he lost consciousness. Passersby, seeing him lying on the pathway covered in blood, picked him up and carried him home. As he recovered, Kuba said he'd had enough of this hatred and prejudice between the Ukrainians and Poles. He did not want to live in fear for himself and his family. He revealed to us that he would move his family to the vicinity of Czestochowa. Grandmother and Grandfather did not like his plans; they wanted the family to stay close together. They tried in vain to persuade him to change his decision, but soon, Uncle Kuba and his family moved away.

Aunt Marysia always wanted to teach religion as a catechist, and she also left us. She moved to Uncle Martin's presbytery. Since they both lived nearby, they often came to visit or to help with the harvest. During one of these visits, while he was working in the fields, Uncle Martin asked me for a glass of buttermilk. I ran to the kitchen and asked for the milk. Mother poured it into a pot, and as I was on my way back, I spotted a small frog. I don't know what came into my head, but I caught it and threw it into the pot with the buttermilk. I gave my uncle the pot and couldn't keep from giggling, watching him as he drank the milk, with my surprise inside. Only when he finished did he realize that something was watching him from the bottom of the pot.

He asked, "What is this?"

I continued giggling and answered honestly that it was a small frog. After he picked it out of the pot, he started to chase me with it. I ran all over the field without getting caught. My godfather was a forester by trade and looked after the forests in our area. It was his job to cut down trees and to plant other trees. His house was located on the outskirts of the forest near our house. I often visited him, and he showed me where to gather wild strawberries, blueberries, and other berries. He showed me the best places where the bushes were so laden with fruit that the branches bent under the weight. Once, when I wanted to impress my friends, I took them berry picking, showing off my knowledge of the best fruit-laden bushes. My godfather found us and became furious. He screamed at me, asking if I was out of my mind showing our favorite places to pick berries. I never brought my friends there again.

A Very Hot Summer

The peaceful, harmonious, and industrious life of our family was broken the first of September 1939, and although I did not know it at the time, it was broken for the rest of our lives. That evening, I was attending a dance with my friends, when suddenly the lights went out. The hall was plunged into darkness and then silence. Then we heard a voice announcing the startling message that Germany had declared war on Poland. I heard sobs coming from everywhere in the room, with the sobbing getting louder and louder. I left the dance and returned home, terrified. Thereafter, each new day brought more and more uncertainty. We asked ourselves meaningless questions about the future, questions no one could answer.

Within days, a knock came to our door from officials with papers, indicating the conscription of able-bodied men to serve in the army. We read the names of all seven of my uncles, who were to appear immediately at the police station. The next day, already dressed in full uniform, the young men marched off to war.

The chaotic information we received was that Germany, after crossing the western Polish border, moved quickly east, and in its wake left the country as though it had been hit by a devastating hurricane. We received an order not to cross the river Bóg. As I looked around, I saw the first casualties of war, people fearing for their lives and crossing the river to get to our settlement. I was frightened as I looked at the people running around in a panic, not really understanding what was happening. These were the first refugees from the west. Every day, more and more people arrived. After crossing the river, they stopped at our house to stay with us for a day or two. We gave them some food, and after a short rest, they left. All I knew was that they were fleeing from the Germans.

We often saw German Messerschmitts in the distance, shooting and bombing different estates and houses across the river Bóg. Every day, the roar of their engines came closer and closer, louder and louder. I was afraid of them. I believed that sooner or later, they would reach us with their bombs.

One day, while working in a field picking cabbage heads, I heard the sound of an aircraft engine, only this time, it was louder than usual. I looked toward the sound and saw a plane flying straight toward me; I was his target. He had crossed the river Bóg. My only thought was that I must escape. But where? I was in a field of cabbages, but the rows of cabbages could not hide me from the plane above. The plane was getting lower and lower, and suddenly, I heard the sound of death: ratatat, ratatat, ratatat. Dust rose up in the air, mixing with the chopped cabbage leaves. I didn't know what was happening, but I was very scared and started to run blindly, running away like a startled animal, leaping to the right and then to the left.

I heard the plane get even closer; I felt a strong blast of air as it passed over my head. By the grace of God, I spotted a field of colored lupine in the distance and rushed across the field toward these plants with tall spikes, praying I could hide among them. I knew he was aiming for me because he turned around and headed to where I was hiding. Relentlessly, he kept coming in my direction. I fell to the ground when I reached the lupines, knowing that only God could save me now. The roar of the returning fighter plane began again: ratatat, ratatat, ratatat. He shot at me again, the bullets flying and chopping the lupine. I lay quietly, without moving; my heart was in my throat and shook me like it was going to pop out of my chest. I was so frightened, I did not know what to think or do. I was not even sure if I was still alive. I could only feel the painful thumping of my heart. I lay still without moving for a very long time. Finally, it was quiet. I realized he was gone.

I didn't know how much time passed until I heard screams. I tried to get up but couldn't. Although I tried to raise my head to look around, I was not able to move; I lay frozen to the ground. Slowly, I recognized the form of my mother and the children coming toward me. When they found me, they helped me to my feet and asked if I was hurt, but I was not able to answer. I waited for Mother to look me over and tell me I was all right. What a relief; this time, there were no injuries. I started to recover slowly as we made our way back home. German aircraft flew overhead from time to time, but now everyone was trying to stay in more sheltered areas, away from the sight of the planes.

Seventeen days after the outbreak of war, the Red Army crossed the river Bóg on the eastern borders of our country. We were convinced that the Russians were coming to our aid. We had not heard that Hitler and Stalin had agreed to divide Polish land; the Ribbentrop-Molotov Pact was signed on August 23, 1939, in Moscow. It stated the whole of Poland would be divided and annexed by the two countries. This secret agreement placed the territories of Romania, Lithuania, Latvia, Estonia, Finland, and our beloved Poland under Russian and German control.

Each day that passed, we felt more and more vulnerable. The Ukrainians took advantage of the situation to show their hostility toward the Poles, who were now in a weakened position. Almost every day, I saw plumes of smoke floating in the sky from the burning Polish mansions. Parents whispered news of the discovery of dead bodies found in fields or forests of the owners of these mansions that were now in ruins.

The rumors that our Polish troops were fighting for our freedom brought us some hope. But our illusions were shattered when my uncles returned home, one after the other, dirty, ragged, and hungry. They told us the enemy army was so strong, they barely managed to escape with their lives. That spring, the NKWD killed twenty-two thousand Polish military officers and other intellectuals in Katyn, western Russia, by shooting them in the back of the head and then shoving them into mass graves. It was hard to believe that we were once again in bondage. The Russians began distributing their Marxist constitution, depriving us of the right to freedom of expression, freedom of religion, and the freedom of our ordinary daily lives. Now we had to work for the glorification of the October Revolution.

Poles, especially the more educated ones, could see what was happening and tried to oppose the Russian government, with the result that they were recognized as enemies of the people. The Russians began to arrest the intelligent Poles, the most prominent citizens in the cities and villages, the priests, teachers and professors, doctors, lawyers, and other nobles, as well as Jews, and sent them to a military industrial building complex, where they were shot dead. Soon, all the jobs held by the Poles in the area were eliminated.

One evening as dusk approached, Mother asked me to help her in the kitchen. She told me we had guests in the basement, something I already knew. My guess was that these were Polish refugees fleeing the enemy. When I went down to the basement, I could not believe my eyes. It was so crowded that I could not move. We were hosting about sixty people, and Father told them they would all be properly fed. I asked Mother whether we had enough food for this number of people. She assured me that thankfully, this year brought a great harvest; the harvest season was coming to an end, and our granaries were filled to the brim.

Autumn arrived and turned ugly and grim. What's worse, a very harsh winter was predicted. Grandfather noted that empty freight wagons had appeared at the railway station in the last few weeks. He wanted to know why and asked among the people, but he could not find out anything about these empty wagons. There were strange rumors because the officials either avoided answering or, less convincingly, tried to assure us these wagons were for agricultural crops and cattle. In the evening, our whole family sat down at the table, and everyone tried to find out more about these wagons. But it was all in vain;

no one knew anything. This situation increasingly bothered Grandfather. He recalled that the Russians were able to export the Poles to the Far East more than once. He talked about what had happened almost a hundred years ago. In the czars' era, many thousands of Poles were captured and deported to Russia as prisoners of war. My grandfather was increasingly worried as the days went by; he said he sensed this may be repeated again.

I finished primary school, and Father sent me to school in Sokal, about ten kilometers from home. I arrived home for the first winter holidays just before Christmas. But at the end of the school holiday, he stopped me from going back to school; he felt bad times were coming and wanted the whole family to be together at this uncertain time.

We Have Gold Spoons

That year, the winter was very severe, as predicted, producing piercing cold and waist-high snow. On February 10, 1940, a loud banging on our front door woke us up. It was five o'clock. My mother, who was already up and busy in the kitchen, hastily composed herself and opened the door. There on the threshold stood an armed Russian soldier. He started shouting at my frightened mother. She already knew what was going to happen. This was the moment everyone dreaded. The Russian soldier gave us an order to move out of the house and to sit in the nearby sled that was waiting in the deep snow. Our house was surrounded by Russian soldiers; Ukrainian volunteers wearing red armbands glared at us with hostile looks.

Father and my eighteen-year-old brother, Tony, tried to talk to the intruders. They calmly asked why this was happening and where they were going to take us.

"Get out!" the soldiers yelled, brutally throwing Father and Tony to the floor and handcuffing them with their hands behind their backs. Mother started to carry on like a crazed woman. This frightened us so that the rest of us screamed and cried too: seven-year-old Josephine, five-year-old Alex, eight-year-old Fred, fourteen-year-old Chester, and myself at sixteen

15

years of age. We cried, and I wondered if this was a brutal end to our childhood.

A Russian officer seemed to show some pity for us and allowed Mother to quickly feed and dress the children in warm clothing, especially the youngest children. He said we only had a few minutes. There was no turning back now, as the sleighs were waiting and would not move without us.

"*Narzymaj! Paskarie!*" (Hurry up! Come on!) the enraged soldiers yelled outside. The Ukrainians were laughing and yelling, "For you *Mazurians*, everything has already ended. You no longer live here. You have to go with the Russians; if not, we will butcher you ourselves right here, right now."

Clearly and happily, the Ukrainians told us that we would never return here because the Russians would deport us far, far away, and the children would be made into *Komsomols* (converted forcefully, without a choice, into Russian residents). Mother was so scared, she could not move. She was not even dressed, even though she was already awake and working in the kitchen. She was preparing to bake bread because there was only one loaf left. If she had known about our home being invaded that day, she would have been prepared with more loaves of bread for the long journey.

Mother suddenly moved in the direction of the living room. There was a beautiful mirror with a lot of tiny drawers under it where my parents kept treasures of gold and silver: rings, chains, and foreign gold coins. There were also lovely golden spoons that my mother had told me would be in my dowry when I grew up. She rushed into the living room, grabbed a bag of spoons, and deftly hid them in her bosom. She went to grab the rings and chains, but someone else was even faster. A Ukrainian burst into the room and ripped the jewelry out of her hands. He looked into the drawers at our worldly possessions and stuffed them into his pockets with a nasty smile. Mother screamed and pulled off her babushka (head scarf) and threw it on the floor. She ran wildly around the room, ripping out chunks of her hair. In the end, weeping bitterly, she grabbed a flower pot next to the mirror and smashed it to smithereens. Those beautiful flowers had taken years to cultivate and grow.

One of the Ukrainians caught Mother, who was now almost comatose in her rage; he picked her up, pushed her outside, and threw her into the sleigh. My siblings and I were almost without clothing; we ran after Mother into the sparkling cold snow. A soldier grabbed us and our few bundles of clothing and threw us into the sleigh. The Ukrainians smugly informed us that we could not take anything with us. But a compassionate Russian officer brought a comforter from our house, and Mother quickly used it to cover the youngest children. This Russian also gave us the last loaf of homemade bread and told me to go back into the house to get a fur coat because I was sitting in the sleigh in the cold, half-naked. Mother whispered in my ear for me to grab two holy pictures, one of baby Jesus and the other of our Lady of Czestochowa. When I ran to the house, crazy thoughts went through my mind. This was very serious; we were not able to do anything to help ourselves or change the course of these tragic events. We could only pray.

I ran into the house and got my sheepskin coat, and out of the corner of my eye, I saw my beautiful *krakowski* (colorful native costume). I was so heartbroken that I could not leave it behind. I hid the costume under my coat, took the pictures out of the frames, and wrapped them in a blanket. Still looking around, I reached for a fancy pillow from the couch, knowing it would be useful to one of the children. I hurried out of the house in my boots, making loud, creaking footsteps in the frozen snow. I ran toward the sled, and just before I got in, the Russian officer walked away for a moment, and one of the Ukrainians grabbed my sheepskin coat and took it away from me. My family sat in helpless silence, too frightened to get my coat from him.

The Russian said we would be going far, far away, and it would be a very long journey. He looked at us for a moment and went back into our home; he took a few pieces of clothing and threw them into the sleigh, shouting, "*Pojechali! Dawaj, pojechali!*" (Go! Get going). The Ukrainian driver repeated the command and cracked the whip several times. The horse jumped and broke into a run. With horror, we looked back at the quickly receding image of our beloved home. We didn't know if we would ever return.

The sleigh glided quickly as the horse rushed forward; from time to time, we heard the whip crack. It's not enough to say the winter was severe. It was freezing, much colder than usual. I was cold, so cold. I looked up at the sky and the twinkling stars. As we glided through the snow, my eyes picked up some shadows, but I did not want to believe what I saw: there were four bodies hanging from a telegraph pole, with hooks pierced through their throats, dangling like meat hanging in a butcher shop. *Dear God, what was going on?* I repeated over and over again in my mind, unable to comprehend the meaning of the events of this day.

As we glided along the road, we saw the military loading more sleighs with our neighbors. We were quickly approaching the local train station in Romosz. There were already hundreds of people being pushed and beaten by uniformed guards into the freight wagons. I shuddered to see how the Ukrainians mercilessly tugged and kicked the more resistant people. Now we understood why these trains were here and what they were waiting for. Grandfather was right: we were the cattle.

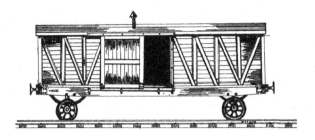

Several soldiers circled our sled. *"Na shalon,"* they shouted, forcing us to get out of the sleigh and move quickly toward the wagons. We were pushed into a dense mass of people huddled near the tracks. I felt the blows on my back from the butt of their guns. People were whispering nervously about something, and as I listened more closely to them, I heard it was something about the horrifying sight of people hanging from the telegraph pole along the way to the waiting trains. They said it was a family. He was a Pole; she was a Ukrainian. She was told to murder her husband. Because she would not do this, the punishment was that the whole family was hanged with hooks on the telegraph pole.

We reluctantly got into the wagons. No one spoke, not even a word; even the small children cried quietly, afraid to make noise. I looked around inside the wagon but did not see much because it was dark and stuffy. I knew it was a cattle wagon and began to realize we were the cattle and would be treated like animals. The guards pushed more and more people into the wagon. Only one side of the car opened; the opposite side door was boarded closed. It was impossible to escape.

I saw four small, barred windows: two in front and two in back. There were compact two-tiered bunk beds running from wall to wall made of crude, rough-cut boards. Attached to the floor in the middle of the car was a little woodstove with a chimney going through the roof. They had given us a few small pieces of wood lying next to the stove. Between the stove and the boarded-up door stood a bucket. I learned later that this was to be used as a toilet (it is called a *parasha* in Russian). I could not believe these primitive conditions. There was not even a little bit of straw to lie down on, or anything to cover ourselves with, only bare boards.

Mother unwrapped the two pictures and used the blanket to cover the younger children. Their quiet and sad faces stuck out from under the blanket. They did not understand what was happening. Mother rolled the pictures up and hid them. We covered ourselves with the small amount of clothes we managed to bring along with us. Dad threw some of the wood into the stove, kindling a fire.

I lay down against the wall, feeling exhausted now from this ordeal. It was icy cold. I saw frost sparkles on the ceiling and walls. Inside the dark wagon, I could slowly make out the different silhouettes of people lying on the bunk beds and the floor. Like us, no one had anything, except for a few pieces of clothing and a little bit of food. No one had been aware this forced journey was coming, so no one had been prepared. People were driven out of their houses with only what was on their backs, holding in their hands what they could manage to grab at the last moment and what they were able to hide from the Ukrainians, who would have taken it all from them before they got into the sleighs.

Soon, everyone needed to use the toilet, but no one was allowed to leave the wagon. The guards laughingly pointed at the bucket. Everyone was embarrassed at the thought, but the urge to empty our bladders and other bathroom needs surpassed our embarrassment. A young man tried to cover his wife to give her some privacy. In her young and innocent eyes,

I saw how humiliating this situation was. After the realization set in that this was the way it would be, a queue formed for the bucket.

We waited inside the wagons at the station, as the hours passed slowly on this freezing day. The sun finally set, and night fell. As the darkness set in, the guards at the station started fires. Two of the guards approached the wagon and slammed the door shut, making certain the latch was locked. It got even darker inside the wagon. Only a little light came through the four tiny windows, creating a few pale shadows. My eyes slowly grew accustomed to the darkness and began to distinguish the faces of fellow passengers. I was scared, but I saw that they were too. Some of them were so frightened that they were not able to control their nerves; they shook uncontrollably and burst into tears.

As this dreaded day came to a close, we heard the train whistle blow and began to move slowly. We did not know which direction we were headed. Actually, I still had not come to terms with my situation. But I knew it was a time of war, and I remembered the Russian officer's words that were stuck in my mind, that we were going to a distant place, far, far from here. But what bothered me was, where?

From time to time, the train stopped, and we heard them putting more people into the wagons. We heard the banging of doors opening and closing and then the wagons colliding against each other as the train started to move again. I could not fall asleep. I don't think anyone could sleep in those conditions.

Eventually, the night ended, and dawn broke; the rising sun brought a little light into our cold wooden cage. Every bone in my body ached from lying on the frozen boards during the long night. Father pushed his way to the window and looked out for only a moment. He said we were going in a northeasterly direction. I hear someone say they were taking us to Russia. Was this possible? And for what? My head was full of questions as I listened to the clacking of the train on the tracks. The wagon got a little warmer. I think it must have been because body heat had warmed the air, because the stove was not putting out any heat. Every now and then, someone burst into tears. And we could not get used to the embarrassing bucket. People tried to cover themselves as they used it; some tried to help cover others, but their facial expression showed their humiliation. The smell from the bucket became unbearable. I felt nausea rising up into my throat, so I rushed to the open window and breathed in fresh, crisp air. It helped.

The train slowed down, pulling and pushing the wagons, and we finally stopped. The Russian soldiers opened the door and ordered us to empty the bucket. There were no takers for this dirty, disgusting job, but eventually, someone took care of it. The wagon got fresh, cool air, and we could finally breathe after so many hours spent in this sickening stench.

Someone at the door yelled, *"Kipiotek!"* (hot water with a sugar cube). I saw people coming out of the wagons apprehensively to fill a mug given to them by the soldiers. We needed something hot to drink after being in the freezing wagon all night. The Russian soldiers pointed their guns at us and said they would shoot anyone who tried to run away. Steam rising from the mugs made me realize how cold and hungry I was. I walked nervously over to the field kitchen, hoping for some broth. The guard poured a ladle full of kipiotek into my mug, and I eagerly took a drink to fill my stomach and quench my thirst. What a disappointment. It was just plain hot water. Hot water and nothing more. The guard pushed a sugar cube into my hand. Dissolving it in the hot water, I greedily swallowed the so-called soup. My stomach was a bit warmer, but hunger persisted. I hoped they would bring us something to eat. Anything to eat. I felt like a cold, starving, abandoned animal. Why? Why were we treated like this?

We were ordered to get back onto the train; the door slammed and the train moved on. I was very hungry. I lost track of time and had no idea how long our journey was going to be. Once a day, they fed us with this kipiotek. The atmosphere in the wagon was more and more difficult to bear. Some cried, some lamented, others cried out from hunger pains, some prayed out loud, and yet others were cursing. Most were consistent about one thing, asking ourselves, "Have we met our end?"

At the next stop, we were ordered to get out. It turned out that not everyone was able to jump out of the wagons. Some of our elderly neighbors could not endure the hardships of this journey; they died, and their bodies had to be removed from the wagons.

Someone said we were now in Sarny, on the border with Russia. Father calculated that we had traveled almost three hundred kilometers. The guards rushed us onto another train, with cars that seemed to be much bigger. Father explained that the Russian railroad wagons were wider than ours. The soldiers took a count, and we heard we were some two thousand people.

"Get in!" the soldiers screamed. "Get inside the wagons."

Although they were wider in size, they proved to be as dark, sultry, and airless as the previous ones. I saw little difference. I scanned the people in the wagon, looking for my relatives, but I did not see any. I rushed to my father, who began frantically searching for my grandfather, grandmother, uncles, and aunts. He returned after a few minutes with a look of despair in his eyes. They were gone; only half of our family was in this wagon. He repeated with a shaking voice he could not find the rest of our family. After a while, he spoke a little more calmly, saying that they probably ended up in another wagon. He hid his face in his hands; I understood that he wanted to believe it, but I was fearful he may be wrong. We agreed to check the adjacent train wagons in search of our missing relatives at the next stop.

I kept wondering about the purpose of this journey. I felt older than my sixteen years. I felt I had aged and matured in the last few days. At my young age, life showed me how cruel it could be. I kept trying to reason with myself; this was a war, and it must come to an end. I was sure that when it was over, we would go home. When I closed my eyes for a moment, the vision and memories of my life at home allowed me some comfort.

This new wagon was roomier, but more people had been pushed and crammed into it. The decor had not changed; around the wagon were still the two-tiered bunks, with a stove and a bucket in the middle. Similarly, the temperature was the same; it was still terribly cold. Father and Tony tried to light the stove, but the wood was so wet that instead of getting any heat from the stove, we suffocated from clouds of smoke.

As the train continued, we observed through the tiny windows the position of the sun as it rose and set. We were heading east. We passed villages and towns along the way, but we could not see the names: dozens of nameless villages. Sometimes, when the train stopped, we didn't move for what seemed like hours or even days. We often passed other trains, also filled with human beings. Some shouted their names or where they came from before they disappeared into the horizon.

The soldiers did not allow my father to wander away from our wagon when we stopped, so we could not search for our loved ones. Sometime later, we noticed the train had turned, and now we were headed in a northerly direction. Some of us were assigned the task of emptying the bucket and others to the gathering of firewood.

At each stop, the soldiers asked if anyone had died, and more and more often, we saw them bringing out dead bodies. We were convinced without the slightest doubt that the Russians had no qualms about throwing the bodies into the bush or leaving them next to the tracks. There was no question about burying them; the ground was frozen. We stopped only briefly, not enough time for the Russians to dig graves for the dead Poles.

People were dying of hunger or exhaustion, or freezing to death. All we got was kipiotek and a cube of sugar. I was dreadfully hungry, and my stomach hurt terribly. I was dizzy more often now and noticed that I was getting weaker. I was young and healthy, or at least I had been before this journey started.

At the next stop, a man shouted that he recognized this place because he had been here before. This was Moscow, so we had traveled over a thousand kilometers from our Polish border. We noticed there were many plainclothes Stalin police officers, the NKWD. The soldiers told us we would get some soup. We didn't believe them; they would probably bless us again with hot water and a cube of sugar. But they assured us they would give us real fish soup. At these words, we broke out of the wagons, with a sudden surge of energy and strength, pushing and jumping out of the wagon; like hungry cattle, we ran to the promised meal. Boilers of the promised fish soup stood before the nervous crowd of people. Everyone tried to get as close to the kitchen as possible for the warmth as well as the food. We didn't know if there was enough for this huge crowd of people. I heard the clatter of the ladles dishing out the soup into aluminum bowls.

I was so nervous that I shifted my weight by standing on one foot then the other foot, as I waited to get to the front of the line. The saliva in my mouth was out of control as I got closer to the big, beautiful boilers. I could see fish heads floating in the soup. God, how happy I was. Just a moment, and then, there it was. I got it. The soldier gave me a bowl with a fish head floating in it. I was even given two noodles: the finest two noodles of my life. I swallowed the contents in the metal bowl in the blink of an eye. I divinely loved it, but I was still very hungry. I stared blankly at the exposed bottom of the bowl and felt I could eat at least ten more bowls.

In Moscow, we finally had the opportunity to look for our family, but there was not much time to search, as the guards rushed us back into the wagons. We waited on this siding for a few days. I didn't know what we were waiting for. We had a little more freedom here, so Father and I walked along the tracks to look for our family. It helped to be able to straighten our legs, and it warmed us up as we marched around. Vigilant sentries were always guarding us, watching us but at a distance. Other trains passed us. Through the barred windows, we saw pale, frightened, and starving faces of hungry prisoners: thousands of dejected people heading to the unknown. Finally, we were ordered back into the wagons, and the train started to move. We passed smoking chimneys, massive buildings, and stately structures. We said goodbye to the city that gave us a little better food and allowed us to regain some lost strength.

Once we were back on the tracks, we quickly reached a faster speed, judging by the clacking of the wheels on the tracks. Someone said we were traveling straight north, and then we heard the name "Siberia." A man standing at the window said the forests we were passing were becoming denser. The temperature, already intolerably low, was still falling.

Exhausted, I fell asleep with my back against the ice-covered wall of the wagon. Terrible pain woke me: my back was frozen to the wall. I could not get away from the ice-covered boards; even my hair was frozen to the wall, like icicles. My mother helped me, trying to melt the ice from my hair with her warm breath. She could not melt it fast enough, so as she tugged on my hair, she pulled handfuls of hair out of my head. I was desperate, hungry, frozen, and now this. I cried in my mother's arms as she tried to comfort me. She told me that we had no choice; we had to accept this fate, but I didn't understand. Why should we accept this?

We had not washed ourselves in several days, and we smelled. We were embarrassed at our body odors and the stench in the wagon. The faces all around me were extremely gloomy. No one had smiled for a long time. Not even the children smiled; they were miserable and depressed. It was as though we had all run out of tears.

The train arrived at a big city with huge buildings that were covered with black soot from the towering, smoking chimneys. This was Vologda, a city with a railroad station that resembled the Moscow station. The soldiers opened the doors, and confusion broke out. A series of shots rang out, and young boy who tried to escape was shot dead. This ended his dream of freedom and ours with it.

As the days went by, the towns and villages we passed became smaller, and the distance between them increased. All we saw now was forest, forest, and more forests. It reminded me of a green hat covered with white snow. If not for the tragedy of our situation, I could fall in love with this beautiful landscape.

At the beginning of March, after being on the train for three weeks, we got to Welsk. We were near the end of our ill-fated journey.

Posiolok (Camp) Jakodym

After leaving Welsk in the morning, the train wandered slowly for another day. As we looked through the tiny windows, we only saw snow-covered dense forests and woods. When evening approached, the train stopped, and as the door opened, we felt a gust of crisp, freezing air, which immediately assaulted and revived us, bringing us up to our feet. The guards started yelling for us to get out, and as they continued yelling, they informed us that we were now in Siberia. As everyone got off the train, it was still relatively light; there are about two thousand people getting out of the wagons. Despite the late hour, there was still a lot of daylight, and we could see quite clearly due to the Aurora Borealis, which lit up the frozen, sparkling snow.

Someone shouted, "Podwody!" (the name of a district). The Russian soldiers standing nearby pointed at sleighs and ordered us into them.

Despite the confusion, curiosity, and disappointment, I could only think about my incredibly empty stomach. And the cold. It was at least forty degrees below zero Celsius, and we were almost without clothes. We sat huddled in a sleigh, clinging to each other in an attempt to bring a little warmth.

Gliding through the frozen snow, we were introduced to the Siberian winter. This was a real winter, the likes of which I had never seen before. It was so quiet there in this wilderness, and there was an incredible and unbelievable amount of snow and frost.

Once we were all in the sleighs, the drivers raced many more kilometers even farther north. We passed by a village in the distance, and I saw flickering flames between the trees. I rubbed my eyes, thinking that what I saw was a mirage looming ahead. But as we emerged from the forest, we came into a clearing with huge fires and groups of people standing around them. Their long shadows were almost touching the extended rows of crude wooden buildings. Here the sleigh stopped.

I heard someone saying, "This is the end of your journey; this is your posiolek [camp]."

They pointed at the buildings and said, "This is where you will be living and working."

We got out of the sleigh at a turtle's pace and moved in the direction of the barracks that were to be our homes. Looking around at all the soldiers, I could tell that they were going to be merciless, and we were going to be mistreated here. It did not look promising, as we were on the verge of collapse.

"*Poskarej!*" the guards yelled. "Poskarej!" (Hurry up; move).

As I suspected, the local guards showed us no mercy, hurrying us regardless of the fact that we were barely alive. We got a little bit of warmth as we hustled, walked, and looked around for the rest of our family. We still could not find them. We saw some of our friends and neighbors, and we asked them, but no one seemed to know anything. They told us that many people got sick along the way and died. Father did not want to believe that. He said it was impossible for all of them to be gone. But the fact was that we could not find them. Fourteen of us got into the train wagon, and only eight of us were left.

We were huddled in the cold, not knowing what the next move would be. The word got around that the comrade *towarish* (friendly commandant) would speak to all of us over the loudspeaker. While everyone gathered into a group, we heard the commandant's voice coming out of the speakers. We could not see him, and I wondered if this was actually his voice.

This Russian voice welcomed us to Posiolek Jakodym (the camp name). "All of you are starting a new life, a new economic and social life," he said. "I know what you think about the Soviet regime." We were anxious and uneasy at the sound of his voice. "You are here to work for the Soviet Union. Everyone has to work, women and children, disabled and old people too."

There was a sternness to his voice; I rejected his initial greeting and pushed it from my mind. He informed us that women, children, disabled, and old people would be working in the barracks or at the camp grounds. Men, strong women, and girls would be directed to *lasoróbki* (lumberjacking), cutting the trees down and trimming off the branches. We would have one day off a week, *wychadnoj*. *"Jak nie rabotash, nie budesh kushat"* (If you don't work, you will not eat), said our lord and master, and my guess was that the wages of work would be food. He noted further that laziness would not be tolerated, and any such occurrence would be severely punished. At the end of his speech, he gave us a word of warning: there was no escape from the Siberian camps; if we tried, they would find us. He also reminded us that we were very far from our home country. With these disheartening words, he ended his welcoming speech.

Father and Tony tried to get to the commandant to find

out about our lost family. Unfortunately, they were unable to break through a squadron of soldiers, who chased them back to the barracks, promising that tomorrow they would have a chance to talk to the commandant.

Once we were inside the barracks, the soldiers handed us a box of matches and recommended we start a fire in the stove. They suggested that we put some snow into a pot, melt it, and boil it on the fire from the stove. They gave us each a sugar cube, nothing else. We drank the hot water with the sugar cube to warm ourselves up. We lay down on the bunks, which were the same as in the wagons of the train: bare, frostbitten boards. We managed to fall asleep, but the feeling of hunger was so all encompassing that I knew how a wild animal feels when it is hungry, hunting for its next meal.

We were awakened at five o'clock. It was still dark. The day began with everyone being frisked. The NKWD (Stalin's detectives) took everything they found on us: medals, statues, rings from our fingers, and they pulled the rosaries from around our necks by breaking them. They aroused in me a mixture of fear, anger, and disgust. We didn't have anything, but they combed even the smallest of nooks and crannies. I knew that Mother should have had the two holy pictures, although I had not seen them for a long time. I worried what would happen if these thugs stumbled on them. My mother certainly would not destroy the pictures. If they found them, it would be a major calamity, as these pictures meant the world to her. Praise God, it worked this time. All the knives and open razors were taken from the men, and in general, all sharp tools were taken. We stood together humbly and quietly. If someone tried to speak, the guards hit them with the butt of a rifle. They pushed us brutally and informed us that after the frisking, we had to run to the courtyard for a *prowierka* (a gathering in rows for a head count). I took advantage of this time to look around at this camp they were calling our home.

The camp was built on a large clearing, surrounded on three sides by dense forest. The fourth side was a forest that someone had already started clearing the trees out of. They took a count and again reminded us of the consequences of laziness or escape. After we were counted, they led us to the river, from which we could draw water by cutting a hole in the ice. We were warned to tread carefully on the ice. In fact, there was a stream that flowed through the camp, but in the winter, it was frozen from top to bottom. At forty degrees below zero Celsius, it was impossible to get water from this stream. We had to get our cooking water from the river.

They showed us a kitchen where the bread was to be issued daily. The first steps I took after the head count was to go with Mother and get into a line for bread. Mother and I stood in this line for several hours and finally managed to get to the kitchen barrack. The smell of the freshly baked bread was so intense and appetizing that again, as in Moscow, at the sight of fish heads in a pot, I salivated uncontrollably. I could not get my fill of this almost forgotten smell of fresh baked bread from the ovens. Finally, we got to the front of the line, and it was our turn. They asked how many people were in our family. They cut the bread and weighed it; this was how they allotted how many portions of bread were given to each family. They also gave us kipiotek and a sugar cube. Mother asked for milk for the small children. The Russian women behind the counter burst into hysterical laughter and asked Mother who she would like to milk. Mother then asked for an extra piece of bread, telling them I was older than my age, thinking that she would receive an extra portion for an older child. Quickly she learned, however, that age meant nothing to the Soviets; all rations were the same, regardless of age: *"Vsio rawno."* (Everyone is equal.)

We went back to the rest of the family with the bread. Mother said we got only two hundred grams of bread per person. She also told them how she had asked for milk for the little ones and how the women ridiculed her. Father said there was no milk here and there never would be, and that in time, the children would forget and not even remember about this nutritious white liquid.

We gazed for quite some time at the miserable portion of bread. It was burnt black and looked like a chunk of coal. When I picked it up, it was damp, like a piece of clay; therefore, they did not have to give us as much. The two hundred gram allotment did not amount to much. Mother said, throwing her hands in the air, she has no idea how to share the crumbs. In the end, each of us ate our small portions in silence, overflowing with sadness. In the evening, we tried to use the snow to scrub the bunks and the barracks, which were extremely neglected. However, we were hastened to go to sleep by the NKWD, who told us that the night would be very short because at dawn, we would have to go to work.

They woke us up bright and early at five o'clock. After they frisked us, the NKWD men rushed us outside into the courtyard for a prowierka. The commandant went over the rules again, explaining that the payment for the work would be in *tałanach* (tokens). He further explained that these tokens would be designated according to family size and the amount of work done per day. The kitchen would exchange our tokens for bread, kipiotek, and cubes of sugar. The food was prepared in the kitchen during the day. Portions were issued in the evening for dinner and had to last us until the following day at dinner.

The commandant also explained the different categories

of work, saying that children, some women, the disabled, and the elderly who were unable to work would get 200 grams of bread. But those who worked less than a full day would only get half of the full-day limit of 350 grams, and those who worked the whole day would get the full limit of 700 grams of bread. The people who significantly exceeded the established work limits could count on an extra kilogram of bread. He informed us that everyone would still get the hot water with a cube of sugar. In conclusion, he repeated emphatically, *"Nie robotasz, nie budziesz kuszac!"* (You don't work, you don't eat.)

After the head count, Father and Tony tried again to break through the crowd to the commandant to try and find out about the missing members of our family. This time, they managed to get through. The NKWD brought them into his office. Once inside, as they looked around, they realized how poor this field office was. As he talked to them, being very patient, he said, *"Ja nie znaju"* (I don't know), but he promised them that he would try to find out. By the way, he said that he particularly liked *donoszczyków* (informants).

The Russians apparently believed that since they brought us here, we were stuck here for good, for the rest of our lives. They placed an emphasis on the education of children who, although they were forced to work, also had to spend a part of the day on learning. A brigade, a forced work crew, hastily converted one of the barracks into a school. Renovation went quickly, and soon lessons began for all children under the age of fourteen. There was only one teacher. She had excellent discipline and saw that the students spent a few hours every day learning the Russian language. Every morning, school began with gymnastics, followed by the standard "prayer" to Stalin. All the foreigners who were educated in Russian learned the language and the prayer to Stalin and were then known as Komsomols. These were the future flowers of the Soviet regime. I remembered the Ukrainians who had expelled us from our home early that morning said this would happen. They predicted correctly. The teacher gave chocolates and candy to the children who progressed well in the Russian language and showed respect for Stalin.

Fred and Alex were still too young to go to school, so they stayed at home with Mother. Josephine and Chester were the only children in my family old enough to go to school and too young to work full time. Chester then announced he intended to be a poet. One of his first poems was about the huge pine trees, which the workers from the camp had to chop down. He always composed his poems in Polish, not Russian, writing about various topics related to felling the trees.

> Chopping, chopping with a little axe.
> He chopped sixteen trees.
> If you don't believe it,
> you can count them.

Josephine always came back from school very hungry. One day, she stumbled into the barracks and rushed over to Mother, who immediately gave her a bit of bread to eat. But this time, it was different. She said she was hungry, but she did not reach for the bread. Mother was shocked and asked her why she was not eating the food. Josephine told her she could not see.

Mother asked Josephine why she couldn't see and thought she was joking. Mother thought this was a very clever joke, but Josephine still insisted she could not see anything, nothing at all. Mother asked Josephine to explain why she could not see. Mother then told her she would tell Father as soon as he got back from working in the forest. My sister spent the afternoon avoiding everyone, and in the evening, I heard her crying into the night.

The next day, Josephine got up and readied herself for school, as if nothing had happened. Watching her, we came to the conclusion that she was okay and that nothing was wrong with her. However, when she returned from school in the afternoon, as dusk began to fall, she said she could not see anything again. We realized this was not a joke. We talked about this strange affliction; Father said he had heard about this mysterious ailment in the camp called "chicken blindness" or "night blindness." Josephine was in tears, and Chester, as if on cue, recited a small poem:

> Gray and sad,
> cold and hungry,
> we persevere,
> because we will return to Poland.

Chester shrugged his shoulders and recited the poem for Josephine, trying to make all of us feel better. He asked his sister to memorize it and repeat it when she felt sad and homesick.

Because my mother was busy with Alex, the youngest, I took care of Josephine when she returned from school with a group her friends, with Chester leading the way. Chester had grown up a lot since we left home. He matured quickly. He was the leader of this group of kids. He repeated this poem to them every day:

> Remember, here they teach us Russian,
> But we will go back to Poland!
> We must not forget
> our language.

Every day after school, the children's duty was to line up for the bread, hot water, and sugar cubes. But it was so very cold that one person could not withstand the cold temperature for long; we took turns standing in the bread line. The children waited in the line first, then Mother took their place. Sometimes, when I came back from work, I saw Mother still waiting in the line, blowing into her hands and stomping her feet to try to keep warm.

After a few days, the commandant remembered his promise to us. He said he was seeking news about our lost family. He checked, and it turned out they got off the train at the last station and were in a different camp. What a relief. Father asked him to try to reunite us. The commandant said that he would try to do what he could, but he reminded us about being informants. When we returned, Father was depressed and did not talk to us. I knew he did not want to be a spy. He warned us that we must be on guard at all times and watch what we say, as our friends and neighbors in the camp could be working for the commandant.

The barracks in which we lived were very old. For many, many years, each winter, they were the accommodations for the *lasorobców* (lumberjacks), who apparently were also prisoners. Inside the barracks, there were about thirty bunks on each side. There was a door at one end and a stove at the other end. The lucky ones got a place near the warm stove, and others by the door froze.

We were given a few battered and deformed pots. To tell the truth, our dogs at home had a better bowl to eat from than this. But who cared? It was more important for us to have something to eat, not what we ate from. We were given a can so we could melt snow for water to make our hot drink on the stove inside our barrack.

It was dark and stuffy inside the barracks. Tony made a broom of young birch shoots and started to sweep the barracks and clean up. The Russians demonstrated how to make kindling out of birch splinters and how to make torches from birch brush. Birch torches burned slowly like a candle and did not smoke. Other wood species were not suitable for this purpose. The flame lit up the inside of the barracks a bit, and we saw that a few small windows were so dirty and full of cobwebs that even in daylight, it was no wonder it was so dark inside. These windows did not open, so the stench inside could not be eliminated. The walls were constructed of rough-hewn logs that were not cut evenly, and thus the gaps in between the logs had to be filled with moss. In the moss, to my horror, were many colonies of live bugs.

The latrines were outside, and we had to walk quite a distance before we could get to them. This meant we were in constant danger from wolves, bears, and other predators. The warmest temperature was forty degrees below zero Celsius. No one in their right mind would leave the barracks at night because of the fear of wild animals and the freezing temperatures. The Russians understood this and handed out metal cans to use during the night. But because there were not enough of these cans, we had to improvise by hollowing out tree trunks or thick branches to use as chamber pots. Leaving the barracks during the night was now unnecessary, but the odor in the morning was unbearable. Also, it was quite embarrassing to use these chamber pots, as we lived under the same roof with sixty strangers and had no privacy. We all complained about the vile conditions and a lack of intimacy. The commandant finally gave us blankets that we hung from the ceiling to act as walls between families. The commandant said that in the summer, new barracks would be built. The announcement sounded promising; although we were not quite sure whether it was true or not, we looked a little more optimistically toward the future.

At night, these barracks took on a life of their own; the moss in the cracks between the uneven logs came to life. As we tried to catch a little sleep, millions of bloodsuckers came out from the moss of the walls and attacked us. It was impossible to close our eyes. Bloodsuckers tried to drain the last of our life after our tiresome days. Mother could not sleep. She tried to look after us by pulling the bugs off of us. The Russians then gave us some straw to lie down on and cover ourselves with. We slept like the dead in luxurious comfort, but only for one night. A day later, the straw was infested with the bloodsuckers; they furiously attacked us again, trying to drain us of the last of our blood. Someone came up with an idea to put the bunk's legs in pans of water. Bloodsuckers cannot swim, so we won this battle. Finally, we had a quiet night, but again, not for long. After several days, the hungry bloodsuckers defeated the moat and stormed at us, dropping from the ceiling and through the walls with even greater intensity. There was no solution to this problem; we had to learn to live with it if we were to survive.

All topics related to politics or religion were prohibited in the camp. We were not allowed to pray or even say a word about God. The guards said if they caught anyone doing this, those people would be sent to the polar bears, or they would kill them. People were so afraid, they did not want to talk to each other and avoided talking to friends and neighbors. Father said this was the typical Bolshevik method to increase labor productivity, to intimidate people. Everyone was afraid of their own shadows. No one knew who was who, who to trust, or who would report them. From time to time, someone would say something about the food because everyone was hungry. In this, we were all equal.

One afternoon, we learned there was a priest among us. The man did not look like a priest; he was dressed like the rest of us and was unshaven and dirty. His name was Father Joseph. He announced that he would conduct Confessions in the coming night. Later, he told us we would quietly celebrate Holy Mass in the dark. He decided to do this despite the fear that someone would tell the guards, or that an overzealous guard might hear him and take him into custody. We confessed to him late into the night, and he granted us absolution for our sins. I heard our neighbors praying the Our Father or the Hail Mary.

The next night, by the light of the moon coming through the window, Father Joseph celebrated Mass, quickly and nervously. We prayed all the words in a barely audible whisper. The priest was without his priestly garments, and instead of a chalice, in his hands he clutched a bent, deformed tin pot. We accepted Communion in the form of a tiny piece of Russian bread. After this unusual and extraordinary Mass, I felt an inner peace and immediately fell asleep.

Falling Angels

The first day at the camp, we formed into three- or four-person brigades. Ours consists of Father, Tony, and myself. The NKWD guards kept a watchful eye on us. A carpenter taught us how to sharpen the tools we were given to cut down these huge pine trees. But you never know if someone might get an idea in their head and throw an axe at one of the guards.

We started a new day with an armed guard leading us to our designated work area. There was always someone trying to escape. However, they were captured quickly and either shot on sight or thrown to the hungry dogs to be torn apart and eaten alive.

They showed us how to undercut the pine trees. They called these pine trees "angels." The undercutting had to be done in such a way that the tree fell safely in the proper direction. Later, using an axe or a handsaw, we would chop the branches off. Then we cut the log into three-meter lengths and attached these logs to a horse using chains; the horse took the logs to be stored in a pile until springtime. This was a first-class lesson; never in my life had I done anything like this. This was only theory and a demonstration, but in practice, I had no idea what I'd be doing as a lumberjack. But I had no excuses; I learned to deal with this chore. We could not get used to this cold or the depth of the snow, which sometimes reached to our waist, making it very difficult to work as well as move. Cutting down the angels, however, was quite easy. They were frozen, and as they fell, the branches broke off with a crash. We noted that the lower the temperature, the easier the job became (except that the colder it got, the colder we were).

At noon, we took a short lunch break; we ate whatever we saved from last night's bread allotment. Some of the other workers filled their stomachs with snow. The smokers used their break to smoke coarsely cut tobacco waste. But I was so tired during this brief stop that I just fell down in the snow and rested.

In the beginning, we cut down the trees closest to the camp. With each passing day, we moved deeper into the forest. The more trees we cut down, the farther we had to walk to get to our assigned site. Finally, in order to earn our normal bread wage, we had to wake up earlier and return from the forest later. From morning to night, all we heard was the impact of axes, saws, and the rumbling sound of falling pines. Once in a while, the young men picked a tall tree and climbed to the top of it, looking to see where the rest of the world was in relation to where we were. The Russians did not initially understand what was going on; they thought the prisoners were trying to escape and wanted to shoot them. Later, they realized what they were looking for and burst out laughing.

"You will see nothing," the guards said. "Only forest, wolves, and bears. The nearest village is twelve kilometers away."

Every evening after returning from work, there was a head count. We were exhausted, and all we wanted to do was return to our beds in the barracks. Suddenly, however, we got a boost of energy. We found Grandfather and the rest of our family. How thankful we were that they were alive and well, and that we were together again. Grandfather said that they were taken to different camp, but he did not know how it happened. Father said that he knew why: The commandant expected him to be a snitch. He told Grandfather life would probably not be any easier here than there, but at least we would be together.

Father and Tony usually undercut the huge pine trees with a large saw, and after the trees fell, my job was to take the axe and cut the sharp-needled branches off. Next, I threw the branches into a pile and set them on fire. I sometimes stood in front of the fire and felt the wonderful warmth spread throughout my body. I watched the multicolored flames as the branches sizzled and sent sparks flying into the sky. The sap boiled and dripped onto the snow as the smoke billowed into the sky; it smelled so good as the branches burned. But I was warned not to get my front too hot when my back was cold, or I would catch a cold in my back that could turn into pneumonia. I was so tempted to stay in front of the fire and drown myself in the warmth, but in the end, common sense won. When I came back from burning the branches, we cut the logs into specified three-meter lengths.

From my first experience in cutting the branches off the trees, I learned to trim them against the tree trunk. If I did not, the horse would not be able to haul the logs. The protruding branches would get stuck in the frozen snow. The horse had a hard enough job pulling the chained logs on the compacted trail, and any protruding branches would make it too difficult for him to push his way through the deep snow. The horse had to pull the logs a kilometer and a half to the river, which was frozen solid. There we stacked the logs into pyramid-style piles and drove wedges under them to keep them fixed in place. I was told that when spring came and the ice started to melt, the rising water would flood the area. Someone would come out and remove the wedges from under the logs so they could be floated down the river. The logs would be floated five hundred kilometers northward to the mills in Arkhangelsk. The logs classified as the best or first choice were tied together in two layers in a crisscross fashion, to form a raft. This special timber was floated down the river under the guidance of someone who was trustworthy and who got extra pay for this dangerous trip to Archangielsk, someone who wouldn't try to escape.

I got great pleasure watching the gold-tinged resin seeping from the pine bark while I worked. It brought back memories from home and the treats we had that I missed so much. I asked Tony if the resin was poisonous. He said he did not know, but he didn't think it was. I salivated at the sight of these honey candies. I really had to try it. I tore a piece off, looked at it, smelled it, and put it into my mouth. At first, it was as cold as ice, hard as a rock, tasteless, and odorless. But as it slowly warmed inside my mouth, it softened, and I started to chew on it very slowly. I liked the taste of it. I wondered what would happen if I swallowed it. I was so hungry, and this pine sap candy brought out the instinct in me to survive. And so, I swallowed it.

The next day, when I woke up, to my surprise, I was alive and not even feeling sick. After that, I made it a regular habit to chew on the delicious resin. I wondered if my stomach was deceived by my swallowing it. It was so tasty. I brought a piece of this treat home to Alex. My mother asked if it was poisonous. I confessed that I had been eating it as food, a gift from the forest, and nothing had ever happened to me. Mother gave in and surrendered. Alex grabbed the treat and devoured it with a dreamy look in his eyes. I promised that I would always bring him the delights of the forest.

After the evening head count, we went back to the barracks, and to my amazement, there hanging on the wall were the two holy pictures I brought out of our house. I thought they were long gone. I asked my mother where she had hidden them, but she only smiled mysteriously and said we had to watch out for the guards, who would surely take them and destroy them and maybe destroy us too. Then I remembered the golden spoons my mother was able to save when we were taken from our home early that frosty February morning. But I did not even want to ask her about them. I was sure they must be well hidden somewhere.

By now, we had been at this logging camp for several weeks. We had been cut off from the world and did not know what was happening. We had no news from the outside world. We heard very little about Poland, nor had our relatives heard anything about us. Unexpectedly, the commandant said we were to write letters to our friends in Poland. Although he implied he was asking, he was actually demanding that we write letters, telling them how well the Russian regime was treating us. These letters were to be very optimistic. First of all, we needed to describe how good it was here. We were to praise, praise, and praise again. Even though it was contrary to his previous command, he suggested that we ask them to send us things that we needed. My mother just shrugged her shoulders and said we had nothing and needed everything. The commandant then dictated our address:

Posiolok Jakodym
Wielski Region
Archangielsk Oblast
Russia.

So I wrote to my friend Karol, whose family was left behind in Poland because her father worked for the railroad, and railroad workers were needed. He even made good money. Sometime later, I was called to meet with the commandant. Upon entering his office, I saw a group of NKWD men digging through a parcel. They said the package was for me. After searching the contents, they gave it to me. Oh, all the treasures inside: grits and some flour, pieces of sweet candy, and one bar of elegant scented soap. When I was allowed to leave the office, I showed this treasure package to Mother. She began to cry rather than rejoice. I did not understand why she was crying.

Karol wrote in the letter that her family was faring reasonably well. Her father was still working on the railroad, except now he was working for the Russians. The Ukrainians who were working with the Russians had also been deported to Siberia themselves. She continued to tell me the Russians were using our house for dances. My heart ached when I read the letter from her. I was happy with the package she sent with the sweets and soap, but I was embarrassed about our situation here. How could I answer her? I could not tell her the truth because I knew every step, every spoken word, and every written word was monitored and spied on. I did not answer the letter to Karol.

We were getting more experienced and efficient in the work we were doing. We produced the normal work load expected of us. Our wage was seven hundred grams of bread and some kipiotk. Mother with her four children got the two hundred grams of bread. When we put it all together, we shared it equally among the family. But this was still not enough; we were consistently short of food and constantly hungry. They told us the conditions in which we lived would change as soon as the sanitary and food commission arrived. We waited day by day, but as time passed, nothing changed. The commission did not arrive, and the conditions did not improve.

Day by day, our clothes were getting worse. We had not changed our clothes since our arrival here. The logging work made our already dirty, ragged clothes worse, as they got ripped to shreds. I did not have any shoes now, as they totally fell apart in the forest. My feet and legs were frostbitten and badly cut, so that I was not able to walk. I felt that I had come to the end of my tether and could no longer work. The Russians did not care how I felt. My family could not help me at all.

One morning when I got up, I declared that I would not go to the forest. I could not. Mother complained, saying there would be less food for all of us and that the NKWD would be angry, but she ultimately agreed. I didn't know how, but Mother managed to conjure up a few cloves of garlic, which she rubbed on me to cause a fever. I lay covered with a pile of rags and pretended to be sick.

The commandant and the NKWD came flying into our barrack, shouting, "Why are you not at work?"

Mother was scared out of her wits and said I was sick. They tore off the rags that covered me and told me to get up immediately. Being scared out of my wits, I could not move.

The commandant grabbed my hand, touched my forehead,

and screamed, *"Mankierant!"* (Lazy bum). "Get up and get to work immediately. If you don't work, you will not eat."

With the rest of my strength, I raised myself from the bunk and showed them my wounded, swollen feet. I explained to them that I did not have any shoes, and I could not go outside barefoot into the minus forty degree weather, but they did not care. They spun around and left without saying a word. Only the devil knew what ideas they had. Without so much as a thought, I ran outside without any shoes, going barefoot into the snow and the forest. I worked without shoes all day. The commandant scared me so much that I felt as if I got an extra boost of energy. With every hour, I grew weaker. I was not able to withstand the pain from my freezing cold feet. I wanted to commit suicide. I did not have the strength to live like this. I considered throwing myself under a falling tree. Many people already did that.

Father kept my morale up during the day, and in the evening, we returned to the barracks. My feet looked like big, swollen, ugly wounds. They hurt so badly I could not stop crying. Mother tried to comfort me, but what could she say? We didn't have any clothes; everything was ripped and ragged, and we all looked like human wrecks.

Mother had an idea how to make me some new boots. She said we could wrap rags around my feet and then explained that we'd pour water on the rags, and they would freeze and become frozen boots. Hearing this, I was speechless. I would never in my life think of this, but these conditions forced us to do things we would never dream of.

It turned out, however, that it was not that simple; rags were very scarce. We searched all the corners and collected a few pieces and began the work. Together, we wrapped the rags loosely around my feet and lower legs and poured water on them so they would freeze. As they froze, they began to get stiff. I tried to make sure that my feet had some slack inside. Once they were frozen, I took them off and left them outside for the rest of the night. Now I had some boots; I was grateful to Mother that I could go to work with my feet wrapped in frozen rags. I didn't know how it was possible to have frozen boots keep my feet warm, but it worked.

One day, the commandant entered our barracks with a companion. They asked my parents to send me to school in Archangielsk. They said that they were looking for girls like me in the camp. They promised the government would take care of my education, and my parents would have one less stomach to feed. Father jumped up and down in anger. He said that he heard about how the Russians took children from their parents, placed them in Soviet orphanages, and turned them into Komsomols. To me, one question came to mind: How would my family survive without me? I felt I had to be there to help them.

Mother thought that it was too far and I would have no one to look after me. The commandant promised they looked after the young girls very well. The girls went to school, and the boys worked or joined the army. Finally, he could see that my parents would not change their minds about sending me away, so he gave up on the idea and left. But Auntie Josie, who overheard this conversation as she was passing by, said that since her parents died and she was alone with her grandmother, she would like to go and be educated in Archangielsk rather than live like a slave in this camp. It took no time at all for her to leave us.

Father and Tony did not shave, so their beards grew more and more. They did not get haircuts, either, so they started to look like cavemen. All the men in the camp had the same problem. Some shaved their beards using a sharpened metal spoon instead of a razor. But it was a luxury they could not afford. Only the families who brought spoons hidden on themselves had this luxury. The NKWD took them away when they frisked them because they were a danger to the Russians. They distributed only wooden spoons for eating.

Occasionally, we got a tiny piece of brown soap to do our laundry. We had to be very frugal and save this soap. We washed our laundry and used the same soapy water to wash off at least some of the thick layers of dirt and some of the sticky resin.

There were four bunks in our makeshift clinic. Referrals to the infirmary were only issued by the Russian camp doctor. They said he was a good man, but after a short time, he disappeared. In his place, they sent a young Russian woman, a hospital nurse right out of training. They gave her a bottle of iodine and showed her how to handle the patients by putting the iodine on the problem area. After a week, she also disappeared. We wondered why; an NKWD said that she was needed at the front in the war against Germany. Later, we found out she could not cope with what was happening at the camp, drank the iodine, and poisoned herself.

We realized all the Russians who worked here had problems with the law; every one of them had committed a crime and were sent to Siberia. Many of them worked out a life for themselves here or just got used to the conditions and did not want to go back. This included the commandant, the NKWD, the doctor, and even the clinic nurse.

One of the prisoners took the nurse's place. The Soviets told him that all complainers were to be treated with iodine and then chased back to work. Patients had the right to go to the doctor, but not a second time with the same problem. Because the iodine could not be washed off, it was proof that the patient had already been seen at the clinic. Sometimes, a committee was called in to assess a patient's complaint, but the iodine stain was proof this patient had already been seen at the clinic.

And the truth was, there was neither doctor nor medicine at this camp. Many people died from sheer exhaustion, and others committed suicide. One of the friends I made was a fellow prisoner named Anne. She confided to me that she could no longer handle the hunger pains. She said she no longer had the strength to bear the constant feeling of hunger and the inhuman working conditions as a lumberjack. She could never keep up the standard work load to earn enough for even a piece of bread. Her parents were angry with her, each other, and the world. She said she had enough and just wanted to die.

I looked at her and saw that she had once been a beautiful and cheerful girl. But now, she was only a skinny creature with gray, tired skin hanging from a bag of bones. I wanted to help her somehow, but I had nothing myself. I tried to keep her spirits up and improve her mood, but nothing helped. One night, as we said goodbye to each other, she was in an even gloomier mood. I thought about her all the next day, wanting to help her somehow. The following night, after the usual head count at the end of our work day, I heard that she had been killed by a falling tree.

I talked about her quite often, especially since I did not know whether it would be better to share her fate. My bones were frozen; my brain and heart felt anesthetized, without feeling, since my friend died. I was no longer able to think rationally. We could only pray regularly, because this was our only hope. We prayed for a miracle, to suddenly wake up one morning and find ourselves in a different world, where there was no camp, no slave labor, and no more never-ending hunger.

The guards did not like our prayers; they said we should pray to Stalin. "He is your bread giver," they claimed.

One evening, while walking with Chester near the barracks where the guards are eating, we saw two *chaziajeki* (women helpers) covering two rows of huge tables with tablecloths. It looked to us as if they were preparing for a feast. We decided to get inside and try to get some food. I got an idea to hide under one of the tables, since the cloths hung almost to the floor, and they might hide us. Taking advantage of the two women being preoccupied for a moment, we slipped inside and scurried under a table. The long white tablecloths hid us perfectly. Chester and I could feel the warmth from the burning stove. How warm and cozy it was in this barrack.

Soon, the revellers arrived; a group of military officers and NKWD came in, along with our commandant. They took off their huge fur coats and sat down at the banquet tables. We saw their shiny polished boots under the table and were careful that none of them kicked us. The chaziajeki brought in huge dishes full of food. There was no end of abundance here; these men lacked for nothing. The tables bent under the weight of the meat, and we waited like a couple of dogs for a scrap of food to fall on the floor.

For the next hour, the revellers ate nonstop and drank without restraints. Because of the alcohol, their voices got louder and louder, and they started to sing. Sometimes, pieces of food and crumbs of bread dropped to the floor under the table. Chester and I grabbed them immediately and swallowed them. Then Chester grabbed a big piece of bread, about two centimeters thick. I motioned for him to eat it, but he divided it in half and gave part of it to me.

Well fed and drunk, the company was in a happy mood. When the banquet was over, they put their heavy fur coats back on and staggered out, singing "*Rosija maja*" (My Russia). We stayed quietly under the table. Tired, lying on the floor, and feeling such a pleasant warmth around us, we fell asleep. We woke up when we heard the clanging of the plates being collected by two women who were cleaning up after the party. I shook Chester, whispering we had to leave. Then one of the chaziajeki spotted us.

I thought, *This is it; now we are dead for sure.*

But the good woman asked us where we were from and how we got there. She gave us a piece of bread and told us to disappear in a hurry. We left without being seen by the officers and were so happy to return to our parents with this delicious booty in hand.

I talked with Tony about figuring out a way to get more food. We knew we had to exceed existing quantities of production at work. We learned that if we were more productive, we could buy *fufajki* (warm jackets) made from dense quilted cotton. We could also purchase padded pants and *walonki* (warm felt boots), also manufactured from the same cotton. And that was not all; there were gloves and *uszanki* (hats with earflaps) in the warehouses for those who were willing to work hard enough to earn them.

We could not believe such luxuries were almost at our fingertips. We decided to really get to work. The temperature remained around forty degrees below zero. During the night, it was even worse, dropping to sixty degrees below zero. We worked like fools, dreaming about our wardrobe while we worked, but it was still beyond our reach.

Grandfather Frank's health deteriorated. Initially, he started with a cough, then a fever, and he was so pale. As the days went by, he grew weaker and weaker. We took him to the clinic, where the doctor recommended he stay the night. In the morning, we learned that he was probably suffering from pneumonia. They did not have the medication to help him, and he died soon after, on April 12. He desperately wanted to live to see the spring, but he only lasted a month in the conditions of Siberia.

Father, Tony, and Uncle Tom asked the commandant for a day off to bury my grandfather. The commandant gave them permission, provided a few boards for the coffin, and showed them a pine tree under which they could dig the grave. The earth was frozen solid, hard as a rock. It took the three of them the whole day to break through the ice and frozen ground to dig a shallow grave.

Before we buried Grandfather, we quietly prayed for his soul. We formed a small mound of snow, and Father stuck a small branch into it, on which he hung a rosary and a cross. Immediately after we buried Grandfather, the callous guards chased us back to work. We were grieving the loss of our dear grandfather and could not come to terms with his parting.

The next day, we got another blow: The rosary that Father left hanging on Grandfather's grave disappeared. We knew we were not allowed to leave anything on the grave, a cross, any images, or even a rosary, but we still felt terribly heartbroken. After work, we often went to the grave to pray; Sally, my two-year-old niece, said that when she died, she wanted to be buried here with her grandfather.

I had a very difficult time with all I was going through. I became very depressed and was completely exhausted. I dreamed of having just one day off from work. I could not sleep. I tossed and turned all night long and finally decided that enough was enough. I was not going to work. In the morning, I informed my mother that I was staying in bed. She looked at me sadly and said that I tried it once before, reminding me how it ended. She suggested I go to the doctor, but I refused, saying he would not give me a note for a day off and would only put some iodine on me. I stayed in the barracks, and Mother again rubbed me with garlic and covered me with rags, hoping that I would get a fever.

Shortly after the morning head count, the commandant and the head of the NKWD came bursting through the door of the barracks, asking why I had not reported to work. Mother explained to them that I was very sick. She showed them I was still in bed. I no longer cared what happened to me. I showed them my frostbitten legs and also my frozen back. But they didn't care at all. The commandant just shouted at me that if I didn't get to work, I would go to jail. He then told the NKWD to put me in jail now.

They grabbed me from the bunk, stood me on my feet, took me outside, and made me walk to the other end of the camp. The NKWD informed me that tomorrow, I would be brought before a judge and tried in a court of law. Then he opened a caged door, threw me inside, and locked the door with a key.

I didn't care, saying to myself, *Whatever you want to do to me, just do it.* I looked around and noticed there were other girls huddled here. I asked them why they were in here. They said they also refused to work and were waiting to go to court.

Slowly, I realized I had put myself in quite a mess. As Mother used to say, I went from the frying pan straight into the fire. Immediately on being thrown into the cell, I got covered with giant fleas and lice with black crosses on their white backs. Throughout the day, I was tortured by thoughts of whether I did the right thing by refusing to go to work. At the end of the day, they brought me a cup of water and two hundred grams of bread. I could not sleep that night. I was afraid of the judge and the trial. What would my family do? How would they cope without me?

In the morning, I heard the key unlocking the door, and some guards grabbed hold of me and dragged me into the courtroom. The room was spacious, and a woman was sitting at a table, surrounded by armed guards. Behind the judge were several people, likely some advisors. On the opposite wall of the entrance was a huge portrait of Stalin. The judge's unpleasant face looked cold as steel and very severe, with no emotion in her eyes. In an unfriendly, gruff voice, she asked if I understood Russian.

I answered in a shaky, barely audible whisper, "Yes, I understand."

"*Gryżdanka* (girl), why didn't you go to work?"

"I'm sick," I explained.

"*Wresz* (Liar)," she shouted. "*Mankierant!*" (Lazy). "In our camp, there is no room for laziness."

She asked if I knew about the *bile midwidy* (the white polar bears). I knew what they were; more than once, these monsters had threatened me.

If I refused to work again, the judge said, they would throw me to the bears. "*Ponimajesz?*" (Understand?) she asked. I breathed a sigh of relief and started crying because I knew the judge would not sentence me to a harsh punishment this time. My prayer had been answered, and I was sent back to work in the forest immediately.

For a long time now, Father had been losing strength and moving slower as he neared the age of fifty. The poor feeding and the murderous work were ruining his health. I saw that he could not keep up this daily pace; he was suffering and slowing down.

One evening, as we returned to the barracks after another gruelling day, Father said he had lost his sight. It reminded me of when Josephine couldn't see, either. But with my father, it was much worse, because he must work every day. Terrified, we went to the infirmary. The doctor examined him and kept him overnight. In the morning, Father was diagnosed with night blindness, a condition caused by being exposed to the bright white snow for too long. During the day, he could see a little bit, but he was totally blind at dusk.

For our family, this meant Father could no longer work as a lumberjack, cutting down trees, because he could not see the falling trees, and they could fall on him, crush him, and kill him. He stopped going with us to the forest and was given other duties, like cleaning the barracks, collecting branches, sweeping: anything to avoid embarrassing our family.

Some of the young strong men were given the title of labor leaders. Because they worked harder and more efficiently, they earned extra rations of bread. However, they were not able to keep up the fast pace and the long hours, and they soon died from exhaustion.

Tony and I were the only two in our brigade now. We had to feed all eight people in our family. We had no choice but to become *stachanowcy* (the fastest workers). We set ourselves a murderous pace, hustling like mad, not caring about our health or even our lives. We developed a whole new system of work. First, the two of us cut the trees down, pine after pine. The Russian guards loved to see these "angels" fall. Then I cut the branches off and burned them. Tony cut the logs into smaller pieces. I then attached the logs with a chain to the horse and continued through the woods, to the edge of the frozen river.

When the horse moved too slowly, I cracked the whip in the air and yelled, *"Bystriej!"* (Hurry up, go, go). I needed him to move faster so he would not slow us down. In time, we got into this hellish rhythm. As a result, we earned *fufajki* (warm

57

pants and warm cotton boots). Next, I wanted to earn enough
to buy a pair of gloves and a hat.

Since we were always above the normal work load, we got
a much larger loaf of bread for our family. It was not enough
to fill us, and we were still hungry, but maybe a little less than
before, and we were somewhat satisfied.

I looked at the horses with a kind of jealousy. The stables
were built right next to the camp. Their stalls were never
empty. For us, there was never enough food, but for the Russian
horses, there was always enough food and water.

In this hurried pace, Tony and I often forgot about our
safety. I collected the branches and ran, not even looking
around at all. I worried that such carelessness could bring about
a tearful outcome. But we knew that bread was our most
important concern.

One day, I heard Tony scream, "Watch out! Get out of the way; a tree is coming down."

I tried to move but didn't have enough time. I felt the branches hit me and fell into the snow. It got dark, and I lost consciousness. When I opened my eyes, Tony and several guards were digging me out of the snow. Was this a dream? They stood me on my feet, and I tried a few awkward moves. I was okay. Nothing had happened to me; I was fine. The guards said that I was very lucky; if it were not for the branches pushing me into the snow, the weight of the trunk would have killed me and left a bloody mess.

After only a few minutes of rest, it was back to the battle again. After a few weeks of this effort, we welcomed our turn chopping and stacking the logs into piles at the barracks. It was much lighter work than the felling operation.

Soon, it was spring. We had survived our first winter in Siberia.

Not Always a Happy Spring

Day by day, it was getting warmer. The world around us began to turn a pleasant green, showing new growth, and out of the ground appeared small but unfamiliar flowers. At last, spring was here. The snows were melting, but the nighttime frost froze everything. The mud was back during the day, as we tried to truck through it. All the streams were rushing and flowing rapidly because this gigantic volume of Siberian snow had to find an outlet as it melted. As the one-meter-thick ice melted, the river flooded more and more, making the water much wider, with dangerous currents. We walk between wooden pyramids and carefully knocked out the wedges as the flood waters reached the logs we laboriously collected throughout the winter. Then we guided them toward the rushing river.

As I watched this happening, I felt a lot of respect for the power of nature. The crashing logs sounded like thunder as we drove the wedges out, and they tumbled and splashed into the water. The huge part of the forest that had been logged out and cut into three-meter logs was now rushing northward in the river to the sawmills in Archangielsk.

Walonki (cotton boots) were good for the freezing cold, but now with the springtime sun, they become wet and soggy.

But at night, the temperatures were still cold enough to freeze my boots. Putting my already frostbitten legs into these boots caused me terrible pain and suffering. In addition, as the felt boots thawed out during the day, they got too hot on my feet, causing blisters that turned into bleeding wounds. Eventually, the boots disintegrated completely, so I was stuck without shoes again.

I had had enough. In desperation, I learned how to braid slippers out of young branches from a linden tree. Even these makeshift shoes were better than nothing. I continued working at a murderous pace, hustling like mad, not caring about my health, knowing that in the end, I would earn enough to get another pair of boots.

Spring arrived in Siberia in June. The trees and shrubs that lost their leaves in the winter grew quickly and were soon covered with new growth. Out on the farms and in the fields, the farmers sowed and planted everything in a hurry. They had to, since the growing season in Siberia was very short.

Along with the slightly warmer spring temperatures came the spring rains. Our barracks were leaking, and everything was getting soaked. Since we were still cutting the trees down, I decided to build myself a blind in the forest, using branches to protect myself from the downpours. One day, I called to Tony as soon as it started to rain. We were happy to go inside the blind, but it only helped a little, and after a few minutes, we ended up getting soaked because it also leaked badly. Anyway, the guards chased us out to work as soon as the rains let up, telling us that the day was for working, and we could rest at night. Soaked to the skin and biting my lips, I did not want to show them the bitterness and anger that were gripping me.

As the birch tree sap started to flow, I saw people collecting the sap and drinking the juice, getting some nourishment for themselves. I was somewhat hesitant and afraid to drink this juice, thinking it might be poisonous. But I took a small sip and found that it tasted pretty good. I shared some with Tony, and we both enjoyed it. We made a habit of drinking it every day. Tony and I would cut into the trunk of a birch tree and put a piece of bark into the slot. The juice flowed in a slow trickle, collecting into a cup below the cut. As soon as we got a chance, we ran to the tree and drank it. In time, I took a larger pot with me into the woods and filled it with this birch juice. We shared it with our family in the evenings.

Birch turned out to be a very useful tree for both the sap and the bark. I learned to make many things from its bark. If I cut it very thinly, I could write on it like on paper. I wanted to make a notebook, but I knew the Russians would suspect that I was hiding secrets. This could get me and my whole family in trouble. The bark could also be made into bags. I cut and prepared sheets of bark, and using young twigs, I sewed them together and attached braided handles. On my days off, I made whatever I could out of the birch bark and sold it in the camp for a piece of bread or some clothing. Tony showed me how to make a container to collect berries by using a sharpened spoon to cut the bark around the branch. He carefully removed the bark and slowly turned it in such a way that it created a kind of pot. He tied birch twigs around my waist to carry an aluminum pot. We filled this pot with delicious berries from the forest.

Alex was always waiting for us to return from work and always asked if I brought him a piece of resin or something else to eat. He often asked for the bread Mother used to bake in Poland. He begged for just a tiny little bit of the bread. Mother tried to explain to him that she could not bake bread here. He listened, but judging by his expression, we could tell he did not understand.

One day a week, we got off from work (wychadnoj). We could finally go outside the camp. Sometimes, my mother asked me to go with her to a nearby village in search of something to eat. We left early in the morning for the twelve-kilometer walk. We were like a couple of beggars. We went from door to door, but generally no one answered. Knock, knock, we tried again. Finally, at one house, we heard the creaking hinges as a door slowly opened. In the doorway stood a young girl with a kind look on her face. She asked us what we wanted. We explained we would like to buy something to eat or exchange some of the few things we had for food. She invited us inside.

She lived in a poor house and had almost no furniture. The house belonged to her Russian mother, who was blind; she was her only daughter. Her name was Olga, and she was about two years older than me. Her mother was extremely thin and frail. She said she was slowly dying, and they needed help. Apparently, we had come to a house with very poor people.

Mother explained we would help them, but we had nothing ourselves, and we also had the same needs. The Russian woman begged us to take Olga with us because she did not want her daughter to be left alone after her death. Olga asked if she could be my older sister and guardian. Mother explained we could not bring her into our family because we were not even able to support ourselves; we did not have a place in the barracks for an additional person. We didn't even have a bunk for her to sleep on.

Olga promised she would help to get food for our family. We left the house, and she came along with us. As we went from house to house, Olga knocked on the doors and tried to negotiate, but it was always in vain. Finally, a Russian woman opened the door and invited the three of us inside. After lengthy negotiations, we came to an agreement that my mother would give her a full-length slip she still had from Poland, and in return, we would get a sack full of potato peels. However, for this exchange, we had to come in secret, after dark, so no one saw us. Otherwise, the four of us would be thrown into jail for illegal trading. We eagerly agreed to return later that night.

Mother returned to the barracks, while Olga and I went to pick cranberries. In the evening, we returned to Olga's house with bunches of fragrant fruit and waited for my mother, who returned just before nightfall. It was already late when the Russian woman with the potato peels came running out to meet us as we got near her house. She was nervous and out of breath. We reached into the sack and looked at the potato peelings; we could not believe how thin these peels were. They were almost transparent. We finalized the deal quickly; the Russian woman hid the slip under her dress and disappeared into the darkness.

The three of us headed back to camp, but Mother suddenly took a gold necklace from her bra and gave it to Olga, asking her to return to her house. Mother explained that Olga was a Russian, and this was her homeland; we were just prisoners. Olga sadly went away after promising that we would visit each other. In fact, she came to visit me on many evenings or on my days off. We become true friends.

It was almost midnight when Mother and I got back to the barracks. The whole family checked out the contents of the sack of potato peels. We were ready to eat them raw, but we knew it was risky, so Mother boiled two handfuls for us. She put a pot of water on the stove, and we waited impatiently for the water to boil to cook the peels. We all stood around, watching the water slowly come to a boil, salivating all the while. Finally, the water started to boil, and two handfuls of peels went into the pot. I was so happy because now I thought I would be able to go to sleep with something in my stomach.

Finally, the peels were ready. Mother divided them into eight equal parts and gave some to each of us. They were so sour and acidic that they burned our mouths, making all of us pucker. I swallowed my portion quickly. I looked over at my siblings, Chester, Fred, Alex, and Josephine, and watched them enjoy the peels. Even with their twisted faces, it gave me great pleasure to see them finally eat something other than bread. Seconds later, everything had disappeared. All that was left was to lick our fingers after this meager meal. We went to bed, but we were still hungry.

I really liked going into the forest with Olga. She knew where the most delicious foods grew: mushrooms, strawberries, blackberries, blueberries, and farther away, cranberries. Olga said that my eyes nearly popped out of my head when she told me about the foods. She said the bushes and trees were so loaded with fruit that the branches bent to the ground under the weight. I stared at her, felt my hungry stomach cramping, and announced that we should leave immediately to get some of them.

The adults from our camp often sent their children to look for cranberries, which grew in wetlands and swamps. An adult would sink in the wetland, while the small children would not; they could quickly and nimbly move about in the bogs.

In spite of the fear of wolves and bears, Olga and I ventured into the forest. We came to a cranberry field with a huge amount of fruit growing. I knew that I needed to collect the berries for my family, but I was tempted so much that I took one for them and one for myself. It was absolutely delicious and heavenly. I liked how it felt when it dissolved in my mouth and its wonderful taste delightfully fell down into my empty stomach.

I put a few berries into the basket and took one for myself. Again, a few into the basket and another in my mouth. We continued picking from the bushes, going deeper and deeper into the woods. Then we found ourselves in a deeper and wider swamp. Olga said we should return to the camp. But I did not want to leave all this wonderful fruit behind, especially since I had a wolf's appetite for these berries. We wandered farther in the quagmire, up to our knees, then up to our thighs, then to our waist. It seemed like I was under a spell, thinking only of these berries and my hunger.

All at once, I was overcome with fear. I could no longer feel the ground under my feet. The swamp was starting to swallow me. In a panic, I cried out to Olga; carefully and slowly, I tried to retreat, grabbing the nearby plants one by one, using them as life buoys, trying to save myself. I finally got back on solid ground: wet, dirty, but deliriously happy. We triumphantly returned to the camp, overjoyed with our feast of berries and mushrooms, which Mother pickled. I had almost forgotten how good they tasted.

That spring, the day we had all waited for finally came. This was a very happy time for our family: My aunt gave birth to a baby girl. Aunt Mary had been pregnant in Poland before we were forced out of our homeland. We were all very concerned about the health of this newborn baby because of the constant hunger, poor nutrition, and the many dangers we faced along the way to Siberia. We even wondered if the baby would be born alive. But thank God, the baby was strong and well developed.

Auntie Mary breastfed her. They called her Teddy. We wanted the priest to baptize her immediately. The ceremony had to take place at night, in the dark and in silence; otherwise, if the Russians found out, we would all be shot. It was a very quiet and humble ceremony, but for us, it was very solemn.

The weather was getting warmer every day. The black flies and mosquitoes attacked us constantly. The wild animals and snakes were also a constant threat. Everything in this once-frozen land was now flourishing.

Tony and I were still cutting the pine trees down and cutting them into logs on the shore of the Jakodym River. Next, the Russians asked for volunteers to float these logs (bałanów) to the sawmills in Archangielsk. They would not pay much, but they promised to pay double in real Russian rubles, which up to this time we had not seen. Tony and I went to the office to register to float the logs; we knew if we came back with this money, our family's living conditions would improve greatly. We did not realize the risk involved in this undertaking. We were young, brave, and perhaps foolish to take this on. We had no idea what lay ahead. And even if we did know the dangerous conditions we were getting ourselves into, our families depended on our return from this experience.

Tony and I were accepted for this job, and so we prepared for the journey. The Russians told us we must build the rafts we would use; we also collected firewood. We stacked the firewood on the rafts in huge piles. We were given food to last for the entire journey. Early in the morning, we said goodbye to our family and set off into the unknown. Together with a group of other rafters, we used gaffs to push ourselves away from the shore and were immediately caught in the rapid current. We had been instructed to sail north on the Jakodym River to the Waga River, which flowed into the Dwina River. It was five hundred kilometers to Archangielsk.

It took us no time at all to master the art of jumping from

one log to another and direct the log traffic so that everything flowed freely. Very soon, we got onto the Waga River, which was wider and had a much stronger current. We passed many villages and small towns along the way. The water never stopped, day and night. It waited for no one. The current pulled us in its own direction, as though we had no choice in its route. We passed another city, Senkursk. When I got a chance to steal a look, I found I liked some of the nice buildings we passed.

There were NKWD and armed guards on the rafts with us. They said that if we tried to escape, they would shoot us. But now, as we approached the Dwina River, they warned us about the currents, whirlpools, and eddies. In addition, we were told that more logs floating from other rivers would be joining us. They said because of the widespread flooding, we might have a problem recognizing the correct direction of the floating logs. We had to watch ourselves and keep an eye out for the leader, who was guiding us along the center of the river. I kept an eye on the floating logs, jumping from log to log and steering them so they floated straight along the river. Occasionally, we jumped onto our raft to grab a bite of bread or have a drink of kipiotek. This gave us a chance to catch our breath. We had many containers to make kipiotek and plenty of cubes of sugar. They fed us a little bit better now because this job took a lot more effort and energy than chopping down trees.

Although it was warm, we spent our nights on the raft in front of a hot fire. The fires kept the wild animals away from us. There were bears and wolves and other dangerous animals along the shore that could swim out, hop onto the logs, and have a human feast. The fires also helped us to follow our leader. We slept under a plethora of stars, with lots of bright moonlight. We still had to be cautious when we slept because the logs pushed one on top of the other, whether it was day or night.

Finally, we saw the Dwina River on the horizon. The current was getting stronger now, and there was chaos among the logs. All of a sudden, the current made everything speed out of control. The logs groaned and creaked, as if they were in a pot of boiling water. The deafening roar scared me. I'd never heard such a roar. It was like someone had fired a thousand cannons all at the same time. I was so scared and terrified that I completely lost control of my nerves as I rode on the logs. I called to Tony for help, but he could not hear me over the noise. My legs got tangled on the rolling logs, and suddenly, I fell straight into the wild surf.

I tried to scream, but my mouth was full of water, and I could not utter a sound. No one would have heard me in this pandemonium, anyway. I could not stay on top of the wild water. I lost my breath and started to sink. I felt that this was my end. This was what I was afraid of: I could not swim. I could not see; it was so dark. I was under the water, beneath a layer of tumbling logs. In my panic, I prayed, "Lord God, help me, save me, please. I went through so much, suffered so much, and this is to be my end?"

Just then, I could feel something hitting me in the back and tugging at me, but I broke free. In a split-second, I felt something grab me by the neck and pull me to the surface. I gasped for air and opened my eyes. Tony pulled me out of the water, like a drowned rat. He saw me in the boiling, raging water, grabbed the gaff, and used it to pull me from what would have been my death. I thanked God for saving me and for my brother's alertness and quick action. The Russian guards said it was a miracle, as they had never seen anyone survive such an ordeal.

My threadbare clothes dried quickly in the sun. I rested for a short time to regain my strength and warm up. I had a little bit of bread to eat and kipiotek with a cube of sugar to help warm me.

Once I was rested, I had to get back to work. While I was under the water, the logs jammed up into a huge obstruction. They seemed to have a mind of their own and wanted to fly in every direction. We needed every pair of hands to do this work. We had many hours of practice by then, but it still required a lot of skill and effort to relieve the blockage. This time, I was careful. I was sure God would not give me a second chance. I had developed a great respect for the logs and the water. I slowed my pace and worked more cautiously.

The river grew wider and deeper. I thanked the Lord now that at least everything was flowing smoothly down the center of the river, but the current was still very strong. On the left, I saw a large city. I hoped this would be our destination. I yelled to the leader and asked if it was, but he hollered back that it was the city of Bereźnik; there were still three hundred kilometers to Archangielsk. We passed a few more towns. I admired them because of their architecture. The buildings seemed to be large and attractive. And I thought that only dangerous animals like wolves and bears lived here in the Siberian forests.

The Russians said we would soon reach the capital of the region, Archangielsk, the end of our journey. They proudly told us it was a great city full of culture, with a booming economy and a huge port on the White Sea. Eventually, Archangielsk slowly emerged in the distance. To the left, smoke rose from the chimneys of major sawmills and other mills, and on the right were residential buildings. The river got even wider now. In my estimation, the first sawmill was about three kilometers away. I saw tugboats leaving the harbor, moving in our direction. The guards said these tugs would lead us to the sawmills. Within minutes, the tugs surrounded us, releasing long steel cables that captured the flowing logs. Then slowly and calmly, they pulled us safely to the mill and the end of this risky, dangerous journey.

Before returning to the camp, we were given a brief time to rest and restore our strength and energy. Then we were told to gather supplies of food and bread for the trip back. Arrangements had been made to return to the camp by land in two huge trucks. When the trucks arrived for us, they were so huge that I could not see into the cab. To my surprise, the trucks were driven by women. They said we had to climb into the back of the trucks using a ladder. We climbed up the ladder to get inside and were soon on our return journey. These trucks were truly gigantic. Their wheels were much taller than me. Besides, they were strange. I'd never seen any vehicles that looked like these. So I asked the Russians for some details about these trucks.

They apparently took a liking to such a curious girl who asked them automotive questions. They explained these mysterious vehicles used two huge tanks filled with water, much like a kind of steam locomotive, to power the engines. But they did not move on rails, only on roads. Steam was what drove the engines, not gasoline. They burned logs as they traveled to make the water hot enough to turn into steam to power the engines. They said this required a constant supply of firewood. They further explained why the wheels were so large, saying it made it easier for the trucks to traverse the roads where fallen trees or stumps or logs were in the way.

The Russians said we had about four hundred and fifty kilometers to our camp and would have to cross several rivers flowing into the Northern Dwina. The road, if you could call it a road, was only a mud trail through the wilderness of the forests. As the drivers changed gears and the engine roared, great clouds of smoke gushed from the exhaust pipes. We heard the gears grind with each change and were tossed about in the back of the truck. At midday, we stopped for a short break in a small village. It consisted of small, old-fashioned houses. There was also a small church, surrounded by a cemetery. I doubted they would allow me to go and look inside the church, but I asked anyhow.

They growled a reply: *"Niet!"*

After lunch, I asked a different guard, and he asked me if I wanted to stay there forever, in the cemetery. Looking through the open door, I realized that the church was no longer used as a house of God. I could see tractors, plows, and other farm machinery parked inside the church.

We set out to travel again after our short stop. It was wet

and very muddy, but there was still a hint of daylight. But as night came, the women refused to continue driving. They said it would be madness. So we at stopped at dusk, not looking for any special place to spend the night. We got out of the truck, and the night was so dark, it was as if someone gave a signal to turn off the daylight. It got totally black, completely encompassing us.

That darkness was really a swarm of mosquitoes, millions of big, hungry mosquitoes, trying to drain us of our blood. We quickly wrapped ourselves in a cocoon of clothes, leaving only our eyes uncovered. We lit a fire and threw in a handful of green leaves to cause smoke to chase these bloodsuckers away. However, it didn't help us much. They gave us a piece of wet, heavy bread for supper that tasted like mud. I had to swallow it quickly because mosquitoes were getting into my eyes and my mouth. I drank the usual kipiotek to wash the bread down and got a mouth full of mosquitoes, as well. I tried to get rid of the mosquitoes from my mouth, but it was almost impossible. I wrapped myself all the tighter, lay down on the ground, and tried to go to sleep. I was dead tired, especially after nearly drowning earlier in the day.

In the morning, after our usual quick and humble breakfast, we continued our journey back to the camp. Again, we passed by a village similar to the one we saw yesterday. There was a little church there, but it looked lonely and abandoned. I saw that the cross was torn down and statues of the saints had been discarded. Stalin's decree was that former places of worship now had to serve as barns or warehouses for farm machinery. Tony noticed that I was curious and wanted to look inside. He told me the Russians would shoot me like a dog and warned me not to ask any questions.

We stopped again to spend the night, only this time in

an open glade. I hoped I would get a better night's sleep than the previous night. I could not sleep a wink due to the attacking monster mosquitoes and the howling of wolves, which approached closer and closer to us. As dusk approached, we hurried to collect wood for a big fire to keep the hungry animals away. Out of the corner of my eye, I saw a beautiful raspberry color on the edge of the clearing. Could it be? I went to check it out. My curiosity was confirmed: We were surrounded by huge shrubs full of big, ripe fruit. I shoved handfuls of raspberries into my mouth. What sweet, juicy, fragrant fruit. I ate as many of them as possible before the guard chased me back with the firewood I was supposed to collect. Raspberries along with the bread (which still tasted like mud) made my stomach feel a bit fuller than usual.

The ride was monotonous. Every day was the same as the day before: poor food and roads that were more or less muddy. Nonetheless, we were moving forward. We were traveling alongside a river now. There was a sharp turn, and suddenly, a large hill appeared in front of us. We climbed slowly but steadily, and then all at once, the engine stalled. The truck stopped, and what's worse, it started to roll backward: faster, faster, faster. We were locked inside the back of the truck. I felt terror engulf me. But I didn't have much time to think about my fear, for in mere seconds, we landed in the water. The guards yelled at us to get out. We didn't know what happened, but the engine was quiet. When we got out of the truck, we saw that it was half-submerged in the river. It could not get out of the water under its own power. We attached several ropes to the other truck and were able to pull the truck from the river.

Once it was out of the water, the Russians examined the truck and came to the conclusion that the engine and brakes had failed. The truck needed new parts. Of course, in the wilderness, there were no mechanical workshops, so some of the guards must go to the camp to get the needed parts. I had no idea how far it was, but they told us they would leave us there for several days at least before they returned to repair the truck and take us back to our camp.

We were almost at the camp but couldn't get there yet. I was very angry because I missed my family. I pleaded with the guards to let me continue on foot, and to my surprise, they agreed to let me go. I set off the next morning alone, leaving Tony behind, as they would not allow him to come with me. I hid a piece of bread in my bosom and left. I headed south, knowing that moss grows on the north side of trees. I watched the trees and was not afraid of getting lost.

Walking among the beautiful ferns and smelling the pleasant birch resin, I came across a whole meadow of mushrooms. I picked out the largest mushrooms and hid them in my clothing. I imagined how delighted my mother would be when she cooked them. It was deathly quiet there. I felt like I was the only human being among all these pines, spruces, and white birches.

Suddenly, out of the bushes jumped four young Russians. They did not appear to have any weapons, except for one, who was brandishing a nightstick. They asked me where I was from, where I was going, and what I was doing all alone in the middle of the forest. And, of course, did I have any bread? I answered them in a trembling voice that I was from Posiolek Jakodym, and I had only a few mushrooms that I collected along the way. The one with the club grew more aggressive. He hopped around and threatened me with this club. The he asked if I had a husband. My fear made me break out in a cold sweat. What should I do? I told him I did have a husband.

"Where is he?" they demanded to know.

I lied and said he was in jail. Then they asked me if I had children. I told more lies and said I had two children. After more questions, they were no longer interested in my family. They did not appear to want the mushrooms.

The one with the club still wanted to beat me up. His companion, however, stopped him and told him not to touch me. The club holder shouted that they had to deal with me; otherwise, I would squeal on them. I came to the conclusion that they were escapees from prison. I started to wonder if it was better to simply make a run for it, but I was sure they would catch me, so I just waited, counting on the one sympathetic young Russian. They let me go after I promised I would not say a word to anyone about this encounter.

I started walking briskly toward our camp, gathering armfuls of mushrooms along the way. Finally, when I reached the camp, the NKWD men stopped me at the gate and asked if I had seen a group of prison escapees. I gave my solemn assurances I had not seen or met anyone in the woods, and they released me.

My siblings jumped up and down with joy at the sight of me. My parents were also happy to see me back safe with them. But they said they had suffered terribly with hunger. Tony and I were the main breadwinners for our whole family. When we were not there, the food ration dropped drastically. I took the mushrooms from the hiding place under my clothing and put them on the table, along with the piece of bread I managed to save from the eyes of the escaped prisoners. Mother immediately prepared and cooked the mushrooms, and we all ate them, together with the bread. This was the first meal we shared together since Tony and I left to float the logs to Archangielsk.

In the morning, I was allowed to leave the camp to go back

to the truck buried in the mud. This time, I got there without any unpleasant encounters or adventures. Once I reached the site, the parts for the truck had also arrived, and after a quick repair job, we got back into the truck and returned to the camp. There was much joy on our triumphant return. Many families did not know if their sons and brothers would return from the risky rafting journey. Mother, even though she had just seen me, hugged me tightly and cried happily that we were together again.

Then came the moment for our pay. All the participants in the rafting were brought into the commandant's office for their payment. For the first time in many months, I had real money in my hands: Russian rubles and even a handful of Russian *kopiejki* (pennies). We got more food, but not as much as we had expected. Sadly, however, it turned out no one in the camp wanted the Russian money. It was a poor trading item. The ruble was not suitable to buy food or clothing. In fact, it was worthless.

I went to the village, hoping I could buy something there with my hard-earned money, but even in the village, the situation was similar. Even the Russians did not want to trade the rubles for goods, only if by chance you happened to meet someone who was willing to take the rubles in trade for a bag of flour or a sack of potato peels. All our dreams of full stomachs had gone into oblivion.

It was summer, and we needed new shoes and lighter clothing. The higher temperatures also brought new problems: different bugs and insects. At work in the forest, we were attacked by swarms of big, hungry black flies. We could not free ourselves from them. The Russians only laughed at us when we waved our arms to try to chase these pests away. They reminded us of our work quota. In the evening, when we returned from the forest, we were attacked by swarms of mosquitoes and small flies that bit us mercilessly. I covered myself as best as I could, but it didn't help. At night, not only did we have the bloodsucker bugs attacking us, but other forest creepy-crawlers showed up from nowhere and attacked us too.

One morning, when I woke up, I felt so weak that I didn't know if the insects that fed on my blood had injected some poison or disease into me, or perhaps I didn't have enough blood left in my body. I didn't have the strength to get up for work. I told Tony that I could not get up and had to stay in bed.

Tony reminded me of the previous episode and repeated what the female judge told me. I remembered it well, but it did not give me the strength to get up. He said no matter what happened, he promised to figure something out for me and helped me to my feet. He went to the commandant and came back shortly, declaring that because we were model leaders, the commandant gave us permission to sleep not in the barracks but on piles of branches and thus avoid the damned vermin. It was not very comfortable sleeping on these branches. My bones ached a little, but at least I was not as badly bitten. I regained some strength and returned to my old self again.

Life and the rhythm of work in Siberia was dictated by the seasons. The winter was very long, lasting at least eight months. During this time, we cut the trees. The short spring was interlaced with the thick melting ice of the rivers and the gigantic amounts of melting snow that caused the rivers to flood. In this short time span, the logs and timber were floated down the rivers to the mills of Archangielsk. The summer had duties of its own.

The commandant kept his word, and in June, as soon as the weather was better, he organized brigades to start construction of the new barracks. The Russians made sure the tools we used to cut down the trees were sharpened regularly. We needed these tools to be in excellent condition to cut the branches off and to fit the logs together. These sharp tools made it easier to work and allowed for precise fitting of each log to form the walls of the new barracks. They fit so tightly, there was no need to fill the gaps with moss. Now, hopefully, we would not be bothered with the different bugs and insects we had in the old barracks.

The interior of the new barracks was divided into smaller partitioned rooms. Each family had its own room. The rooms were all the same size regardless of the size of the family. "*Vsio rawno*" (Everyone is equal). There was a hallway down the center of the barracks. The inner walls were only one meter in height, allowing for minimal privacy. There were no inner doors in these new barracks, so if the commandant came inside, he was able to see immediately what everyone was doing.

In the clearings of the forest, water gathered in the lowlands, creating marshy ground in the spring. When June arrived, grass started to grow in these areas. As the grass dried out, it grew to almost a meter tall, becoming a hay field. As the warmer weather continued toward the end of June, the Russians announced we must cut down the hay fields using scythes and sickles. We were told to cut it down within a centimeter of the ground. At first, they asked for volunteers for this chore, but when there were not enough volunteers, they chose workers by force. Tony and I volunteered, thinking we would benefit from this task (either getting more money or more food). The hay we cut down would be used to feed the horses.

Tony and I, along with the other volunteers, were led to a clearing in the woods a few hours away. We came upon a beautiful meadow that was covered with tall grass, reaching in places to my waist. After watching a short demonstration, we were handed a scythe and a whetstone (to sharpen the blade) and told to cut the grasses very carefully, almost to the ground, and to make certain that every centimeter counted. We had to work quickly and carefully, taking great care to cut every centimeter of hay.

As I wielded the scythe, it felt as though my arms would fall off. I was using muscles I had not used before. I tried to stay near the edge of the clearing, knowing from previous experience there were raspberries growing there. In the distance, I could see the red color of the berries, and when I got close to them, I quickly filled my hands with fruit. I needed to watch out for the guards and the wild animals that sometimes prowled around the bushes. We were told that we would be cutting this grass for two or three weeks. They brought us our food every two or three days, as we were not allowed to return to our barracks. We slept under the stars, with fires burning to keep the wolves and bears away. The food here was slightly better than just the bread we were given at the camp. We were given cabbage soup with noodles or meat. We might get one noodle, and if we were really lucky, we'd get two noodles in the whole pot of soup. With the meat, it was the same situation. I searched the soup to the bottom of the pot, and if I was lucky, I'd find a tiny little piece of what reminded me of meat. This pot of soup was supposed to last us two or three days. When I ate a little bit of this soup, I smacked my lips at the delicious taste.

The grass-cutting agreement guaranteed that while Tony and I were cutting the hay, Mother got a fuller portion of bread for the whole family, according to the stachanowcy standards. It was a consolation to me that my family was not suffering, as they did when we floated the logs on the rafts, especially since we could not return to camp for the night. At the end of our day, just before it got dark, we collected firewood and stacked it in piles. The fires burned all night, and we were careful so as not to set the dried grass on fire.

Tony and I sat around the fire, and they gave us a piece of bread and a scoop of soup. At dinner, hardly anyone spoke; everyone was fatigued and ready for sleep. The night was cool, but the heat radiating from the fire was so soothing that we fell asleep almost immediately. From time to time, I woke up, hearing the roar of the nearby bears and howling wolves. I was scared. This was the only time I thanked God for the presence of the Soviet armed guards. The guards threw huge logs into the fires to keep them burning; the animals could be seen from a long distance away. The fire was to keep the wild animals away from us, but as I looked into the forest, I saw dozens of shining eyes reflecting the glow from the fire. I tried to sleep until morning, but when it was time to get up, I was still half-asleep but relieved that there were no incidents during the night.

After a quick breakfast, we left the cut hay to dry and marched on to the next clearing to continue cutting. After a few days, we returned to the first clearing to turn the hay over so it could dry completely. When all the hay was cut and dried, other teams came with carts to load it and take it to the camp for storage. One day, the guards said this was the last day of hay cutting. Although I longed to see my family and wondered what was going on in the camp, I was sorry to be going back. I had taken a liking to this farm life. Even though we were still prisoners and slept in the open air, we had a bit more freedom there than in the camp.

Upon our return to the camp, we were immediately organized into a new brigade. We were told we had to build a *woszobojka* (a two-room steam bath to kill fleas). We had no idea what this word meant. The floors were sheet metal, under which we were told to dig trenches and fill these trenches with firewood. On top of the trenches and firewood, we covered the sheet metal with a layer of stones; after several days, our job of building the woszobojka was done.

Our next job was to set fire to the wood in the trenches under the floor. The sheet metal and stones warmed up quickly. We asked the guards what this was for. The Russian guards laughed and told us we were a primitive people with no culture and therefore did not know what we had built. We carried buckets of water and poured it on the hot stones. This made clouds of steam. The bellowing and hissing steam was frightening to many people. Then the guards chose a few people and told them to strip naked in the first chamber. Their clothing stayed in the first chamber until all the bugs were dead from the steam. The prisoners went into the second chamber as naked as God created them. The only item they held was a birch rod. There, in the hot steam, the chosen people entered the second chamber and start hitting each other with the birch rods. The lice and fleas fell off and died from the hot steam, while the thick layers of dirt and pine resin fell off in patches like scales, leaving the underlying skin clean.

I could hardly wait for my turn. I was eager and excited to step into the steam chamber so I could bask in the warmth, clean myself, and get rid of these parasites. Our clothes were also subjected to the hot steam treatment. Now, we understood: We had built a delousing steam chamber. However, we did not have anywhere to dry our clothes. Whether I wanted to or not, I had to put my wet, bugfree clothes back on because I did not have a change of clothes. I had to walk around and wait for them to dry while I wore them. So I went outside in the warmth, and the sun dried them. Well, it was nice outside, but what would it be like when winter came?

The commandant and the NKWD chose workers for the harvest. I heard they would be paid with horse meat. So without hesitation, knowing the pay would be good, I ran to volunteer, and they accepted me. Early the next morning, they gathered us together and took us to the commune farms. When we got to the farm, before we even started to work, they warned us that if one of us stole even a few grains of wheat, we would be shot instantly. They showed us a combine and told me to jump up into the driver's seat. I got a short lesson on how to operate the combine. My job, however, was not to drive this machine, but to watch that everything was working as it should. The workers below the combine had to receive the grain. Since we didn't have any silos or barns or sacks to store the grain in, we poured the seed onto the ground, forming them into huge piles.

We worked from five o'clock in the morning until sunset. They paid us every day with the promised pieces of horse meat. At the end of my work day on the farm, I returned to camp and ran into the barracks, giving Mother the meat. My whole family was happy. Mother quickly put the meat into a pot, poured water over it, and put the pot on the stove. We stood around, staring anxiously at the bubbling contents, which had to cook for a long time before it was soft enough to eat. Finally, it was tender enough to chew and eat. Mother divided the meat among all of us and gave each of us a piece of bread with a cup of broth. How delicious it was.

August passed, and it began to get chilly again. The leaves fell; nature took her clothes off the trees and got ready to sleep. I wondered what troubles another Siberian winter would bring. I grew depressed, knowing how hard it would be again. Right at the beginning of September, we got a good frost and a pile of thick snow; everything was freezing up. It was time to start cutting down the trees again, just like we did before.

Tony and I worked as leaders again. On my days off, Olga and I looked for the last of the cranberries, which were now bitter and frostbitten.

Unexpectedly, the Russians announced we would have a day off. It was the biggest holiday of the year, the day of the November Revolution.[1] All young people were ordered to take part in the parade, and for this, we got a double portion of bread. Transport trucks would leave at five o'clock in the morning for Welsk. They woke us early; we got a quick breakfast, and then we were on the road. Once we got there, we were immediately formed into army divisions. There were many crowds of people from the city and many brought in from the villages to be involved in the parade. We marched through the streets, prancing around in front of parade marshals with countless red flags with the hammer and sickle. I saw a huge picture of Stalin. It seemed that we were honoring him. Disgust overwhelmed me, but I tried to keep my thoughts focused on that extra piece of bread we'd get when we returned to the camp from the parade.

1. *On November 7, 1917, Bolshevik leader Vladimir Lenin led his leftist revolutionaries in a revolt against the ineffective provisional government (Russia was still using the Julian calendar at the time, so period references show an October 25 date). The October revolution ended the phase of the revolution instigated in February, replacing Russia's short-lived provisional parliamentary government with government by soviets, local councils elected by bodies of workers and peasants. Liberal and monarchist forces, loosely organized into the White Army, immediately went to war against the Bolsheviks' Red Army, in a series of battles that would become known as the Russian Civil War.*

I thought we would always be prisoners. I saw no hope for the future. Everyone was already so resigned to this life that no one even mentioned freedom anymore. People were dying, and in their place, the Russians brought new prisoners. I tried to remember my old life in Poland, but now it seemed so distant and unreal that I didn't know if it really happened or if it was only a dream.

Freedom

At the end of October, we heard rumors of amnesty for the Poles. I was afraid to believe it. The Ukrainian and Russian prisoners in the camp who were more familiar with this system said it was impossible, that the many thousands of Poles who were taken from their country and deported here to Siberia would never be allowed to leave; impossible. Even we didn't believe it; it could never happen. This was our fate: convicts, laborers, deprived of any dignity or the right to own anything. Surely, it just could not be true. Then suddenly, the rumors stopped; all was quiet, and we returned to logging.

Then just as quickly as they stopped, there was whispering in the corners; the same rumors of freedom started again. One evening, the commandant told us to gather under the speakers where he often spoke to us about Stalinist propaganda. This time, however, the message was quite different. The commandant informed us that Stalin, Churchill, and General Sikorski signed an amnesty for the Poles. This caused immense surprise. Young men could be released from the camps and make their own way to the Middle East to join the Polish army that General Walter Anders was forming. Families of those who joined the army would be granted freedom. We could hardly believe these words. Did we hear correctly? Some Poles were so emotional and overjoyed that they started to cry; others laughed and danced.

"My children, listen up!" the commandant said. "You don't know what you will be up against. You have no idea where to go or how to get to the Middle East. This is a huge country, and you will face many diseases and plagues. You could die quickly," he continued, trying to warn us about this new freedom.

But no one listened to him anymore. I was so stunned that my head was spinning round and round. I felt as though I was drunk and about to collapse. I asked my parents to repeat what the commandant had just announced. They explained everything to me because I feared that I did not hear exactly what he said. Mother confirmed exactly what I heard. She began to hug me so tightly that I felt she was strangling me. I could not get enough air into my lungs. This was the greatest day of my life. In my wildest dreams, I never thought this would ever happen.

The commandant did not discuss when we could leave, what transport we could take, or how it would be organized. Tony was drawn to the idea of joining the Polish army, but because of the scarcity of accurate information about the Middle East, we did not know how this could come about. The Russians said it would be quite some time before anyone was allowed to leave the camp. They continued to drive us into the forest to cut down more trees. In fact, there was no change in their attitude toward us because of the amnesty. We were still treated like prisoners.

My father said the commandant did not want to let us go free because he had a duty to meet production quotas. Some men tried to escape, but it was madness; there was no place to run, and after only a few days, the soldiers brought the prisoners back. Now they were even more emaciated. Because these men tried to escape, the soldiers showed no mercy toward them.

Frank, our neighbor and companion in our barracks, talked quite often about escaping and going back to Poland to visit his sick mother. He said she was waiting for his return. One day, he disappeared. I prayed for him, but I had bad feelings about his escape. After a few days, the NKWD brought Frank back to the camp, surrounded by angry, violent dogs. As a warning, the Russians allowed the dogs to tear Frank apart in front of our eyes. I grew more and more disgusted with the Russian Bolsheviks. Along with these feelings, my joy at the news of amnesty disappeared, for where was the freedom we were told would be ours?

Since the commandant's announcement of amnesty in the camp, things got worse instead of better. We had to wake up earlier to start our march of almost ten kilometers to where we were cutting the trees down. We had to start work on time. The horses also had a greater distance to pull the logs from the forest to the river banks. More importantly, to earn our normal wage, we had to work much faster and harder. We all complained as we returned from our day's work, tired and having walked the extra distance back to the camp. If anyone rebelled at the extra workload, the Russians reacted with even more brutal treatment. They admitted there was now amnesty but would not tell us where the Polish army was forming.

One day, Tony called me aside to talk. He said he had enough. He hoped that the commandant would give him and several of his friends permission to leave the camp to join the army. He was worried, however; would we be able to manage without him? He asked if I would be able to keep up the workload to feed the whole family. I doubted it, but I didn't tell him this. I solemnly assured my brother we would manage somehow. We would probably be lacking, but maybe Father could help. Our parents were not enthusiastic about the idea. I heard their conversation; they felt I would not be able to earn enough bread to feed our whole family without Tony's help. They openly opposed his leaving, but he insisted; nothing would change his decision. He would go with a group of his friends to join the army and fight for his country. Besides, he saw no future in Siberia, but he might have a future with the army.

Tony, along with a group of his friends, went to the commandant, asking for a letter to be assigned to the army. The commandant told Tony he had instructions from the Kremlin to direct the young Polish youth into the Red Army.

He used all means to get them to sign up temporarily into the Russian army, but all the boys replied, "All you are trying to do is cheat us. Why should we join your Red Army when we can join the Polish army and fight for our country? We know what your 'temporary' means. You want to draw us in, and that's it; we will be taken advantage of. We will not fight in the Soviet army; we have suffered enough."

The commandant finally promised they would get letters soon and would be released from the camp to join the Polish army. Tony told us about the commandant's lies and said he would not believe him until he actually had the letter in his hand. But if it was true, then we as a family should also get a letter (*spišská*) to leave the camp.

Early in November, the much-anticipated letters arrived for Tony and eleven of his friends to join the Polish army. Now they had every right to leave the camp and go to the Middle East to join Anders's army. Tony was nervous; the Russians were not only not helping, they were actually hampering the young men. They gave each of the young men a bag of black bread and said that if they wanted to join the Polish army, they would have to find their own way to the Middle East. The young men received no information of any kind, not even a map. No one knew where to go or how to get there. They only knew they were going somewhere in the Middle East.

Before my brother left, he gave me his beautiful officer's boots and told me to sell them if I was unable to feed our family. Sadly, we tearfully said goodbye to Tony and his eleven friends. Mother was crying, and Father was even more depressed. It was very difficult for me to part with him. We worked side by side for so many months, day after day. We had lived through so much together. And I knew it would be even more difficult without my brother, but I also felt somewhere in my heart that I would surely see him again someday, somewhere. Early the next morning, I went to work with my father, while Tony and his friends walked to the train station in Welsk.

My family and I went through some difficult, cold, and hungry days. Some people tried to outwit the Russians. They received the spišská and the bag of bread, but they did not leave. After they ate all the bread, they found out that the Bolshevik system would not allow them anymore food to go on the journey to join the army. For them, it was over. They felt great despair and cursed their fate. Now all they faced was starvation, and eventually, most resorted to suicide. They had no other way out except to die.

News came to us of those who left the camp, and it was not good. Almost every day, we heard of their sickness or disease, and many of them died from starvation. But some who left were never heard of again; it was as if they disappeared from the face of the earth. The commandant's warnings were not unfounded; everything he predicted had come true. Even though those who remained had the opportunity to go, they were afraid of this freedom and preferred to stay in Siberia. They talked about being hungry and freezing cold, but basically, they were at home; they were accustomed to this life.

I listened to them assess the survival chances of a starving person living in freezing temperatures of minus forty degrees Celsius and suddenly finding themselves in thirty degrees heat. They said the survival chances were slim. Add to this the uncertain transportation and the many thousands of kilometers to travel; who could live through this? The people were in doubt. However, my family and I were increasingly considering taking this opportunity to leave and break ties with this camp, since we were free to leave because of Tony joining the army.

I worked every day with my father now, from dawn to dusk. We were not doing well for food rations. We barely made the basic norms expected of us. The supplies we managed to gather and store up disappeared all too soon. Poverty was screaming at us. I missed my brother so much; I could not forgive myself for not stopping him from leaving. More and more, I looked at his boots he left for us. He hid them on his person when we left Poland. He never even wore them. He kept them hidden and saved for a special occasion. Finally, before leaving the camp, he said goodbye to them. I looked at his boots, which were beautifully polished, with tall leather uppers that glistened in the sun. Initially, his boots were our reminder, our memory of Tony, but I started counting the portions of black bread that we could receive for trading his boots. We finally decided to part with this memory of Tony.

On one of my free days, Mother sent me to the nearby village with the task of bartering Tony's boots for food. I wrapped them in an old scruffy shawl, so no one knew what precious cargo I was carrying. I tied them up into a bundle and attached it to my back, and off I went along the road to the nearest village. I walked twelve kilometers through the forest until I reached the village of Stunima. I wondered whether I was doing the right thing by getting rid of my brother's boots. I knew I must, so I started my traditional pilgrimage, going from door to door. Nobody wanted these beautiful officer's boots, or maybe they were afraid because we were not allowed to go door to door, bartering or trying to sell things.

I knocked at the front door of the one of the houses; the door opened, and there stood a man. Seeing him made me freeze completely. I could have just died of fright: It was our commandant. I didn't know what to do. Should I run? No, it was too late. I held Tony's boots in my hands and knew that I could be sent to prison for attempted illegal trade. If someone reported me, I would be thrown in jail.

I backed up slowly, ready to run, but the commandant saw that I was troubled; he grabbed me by the arm and pulled me inside with a strong, powerful tug. He saw my anxiety and asked what I was hiding in my arms. I hesitated but realized I had no choice but to unravel my headscarf and show him the precious officer's boots. The commandant looked at them, first in silence and then with unconcealed admiration. He then asked his wife to give me something to eat. He grabbed the boots and disappeared with them into another room. I thought he went to try them on. He soon came back empty-handed and declared he would take the boots. He asked what I wanted for them.

I could not hear him; I was not even listening to him. My eyes were on what his wife was preparing for me to eat. I could not focus on anything but her movements. She carefully arranged a plate with a few potatoes. Then she opened a wooden barrel and ladled out a few marinated mushrooms and poured some sauce onto the potatoes (*kartoszki z ryżkami*). She smiled as she gave me this amazing dish.

As I was eating, I could feel my ears shake and tremble. What a delightful dish this was. I could not remember how long it had been since I ate such delicacies. As I cleaned off my plate, a sense of guilt encompassed me; I felt like I had cheated my family. The commandant looked at my face and could see that something was wrong. He asked me what was on my mind. Instead of answering, I cleaned the last of the crumbs from my plate. He asked again, now in a stern tone of voice.

I looked at his wrinkled and demanding face and slowly and shyly explained what was tormenting me. I told him of my feeling of remorse and said that I felt like a criminal with a guilty conscience, who had deceived her family. I felt tears coming to my eyes. He looked at me and kindly explained that I deserved to eat a meal, especially after the long, tiresome journey, and before I went back, he added, I had to eat more. He asked his wife to prepare a package for me. She took a few kilograms of potatoes, put them in my old shawl, and wrapped a large portion of meat separately. I did not know what kind of meat it was or which animal it came from, but I did not care. My eyes were smiling as I saw all this food. I had an excellent meal and had a tummy full of food. I happily hid the package of meat in my bosom and put the scarf with the potatoes on my back. Then the commandant's wife poured a litre of milk into a metal can and pushed this container into my hand. I did not know how to thank them. I was so touched with their hospitality and thankful for the food that in appreciation, I bowed to my waist, almost kissing their hands. They wished me a hearty farewell as I left to make my way back to the camp.

As I walked, I felt elated. Then it dawned on me that I should be very concerned; I grew terribly afraid that someone might rob me. But I finally reached our camp without any incidents, and when I stepped into our barracks, I proudly showed my parents what I brought. Their faces showed their excitement. They were happy and rejoicing. I was ashamed and confessed to Mother that I ate a wonderful meal at the commandant's house. I asked her not to prepare any dinner for me. She told me not to be foolish, that I worked very hard, and I had to eat whenever I got a chance. Mother peeled some of the potatoes and put them into a pot of water and cut off a nice portion of meat. The aroma of the cooking meat floated around the barracks.

She heated up the milk and gave the children each a cup. Alex, being the curious one, asked Mother what this white liquid was. Mother explained to him that he used to drink it every day after the cows were milked in Poland. As soon as Alex tasted it, he remembered. It was as if he woke up all of a sudden. He remembered the taste and drained the milk to the bottom of the cup, without taking a breath. The white liquid disappeared in a blink of an eye, not even leaving a drop in the cup. Our dinner included the usual piece of bread and kipiotek and was absolutely delicious and wonderful. I ate some of this meal but a very small portion.

We had to take turns all night long, guarding the leftover meat so it would not get stolen. Unfortunately, the meat was all eaten by dinner time the following day. But the potatoes were vigilantly guarded day and night and lasted for a few more weeks. When they were gone, we went back to our usual hunger.

Hunger was constantly with us in Siberia. It was a feeling stronger than suffering the loss of a loved one. Everyone here suffered the misery, degradation, and physical pain from the cold and fatigue. The hunger we felt was totally inhumane.

We were always hungry and looking around nervously for something to put in our mouths to eat.

Many young girls were jailed for stealing *kartoszki*, potatoes they found half-frozen in the snow somewhere in an empty field. One of them was my friend Hania from our barracks. On one of her days off, while walking through the wasteland far from a Russian farming village, she spotted the remains of some frozen potatoes. Hania dug some of them up with her hands from the snow and brought them to her parents, but apparently someone saw her and reported her to the NKWD. Without wasting any time, the NKWD came, arrested her, and threw her into a jail cell. As she was waiting for her trial at the camp court, she was given two hundred grams of bread and a cup of water per day. Normally, a hearing would take place immediately or at least on the following day. But they held Hania for several days, probably as an example to others.

When she was finally taken to court, the judge asked her whether these kartoszki or the field they were in belonged to her. The judge then asked who gave her permission to dig them up and take them home. What was a poor girl to answer? The judge harshly told her that the potatoes belonged to the government.

"Everything here is government property; even if it rots, you must not touch it," the judge lectured her. He sentenced Hania to three months in jail, with a stern warning that if it happened again, she would be sent into the claws of the white bears.

After serving her three-month sentence, Hania returned to our barracks. No one recognized her. She looked like a starving skeleton with dry, gray, and ulcerated skin. Since my brother Tony left, we suffered from hunger so much that we also looked like starving skeletons, but she looked even worse than us.

Christmas Is Approaching

The Russians not only did not allow us to slow down, they maliciously and purposely chased us, forcing us to work even harder. *"Poskarej, dziewuszka, rabotaj!"* (Hurry up, girl, work), they yelled, driving me mercilessly, knowing full well I was using the last ounce of my strength. I was also very concerned and worried about Father. I saw how poorly he looked, just skin and bones, a mere shadow of a man, wobbly on his feet, barely able to walk. He must somehow regain some strength or he would be finished completely and die.

To barter for any more food, my last hope was the Krakow costume I hid in my bosom when we were forced from our home in Poland that morning long, long ago. No one knew I had it. I looked at it with fondness and had a difficult time remembering the old, bygone happy days. It vaguely reminded me of the dancing and fun I used to have. I had forgotten about those fun evenings. As I allowed myself to go back in time, I realized it was not so long ago. I had great difficulty remembering those days now, though. *Batko* (Father) Stalin took those good old days from us. That time would never come back; Stalin would never allow me to wear my adored costume again.

The next day, I was off from work, so I showed my secret treasure to Mother. Looking at it with love, she spread out the costume with the matching skirt on her bed to admire it. She asked me what I wanted to do with it. I could not answer her question. She asked if I wanted to sell it. I told her that I was so sorry to get rid of this costume, but all I could think of was the shortage of food. So I admitted I had already made that sad decision.

The next day, I left early in the morning for Kiszermy, another farming village about fifteen kilometers from Jakodym Posiolek. As usual, I went from door to door and knocked, but few people answered the door. I came to a house that looked very poor, but I decided to knock on the door anyway. When the door opened, I saw a woman standing on the threshold, with a friendly smile on her face. She saw me as a bag of bones, nervously holding a small bundle in my hands. We understood each other without words. I could see she too was afraid, looking nervously around to see if anyone nearby was watching. There were spies everywhere, but since she saw no one around, she pulled me inside, slamming the door shut behind us.

I proudly showed her my great outfit. She could not believe her eyes as she stared at the costume, saying she had never seen anything so beautiful in her life. She really liked my costume and wanted to buy it from me. She told me she did not have much money, but perhaps we could swap or exchange some goods. She invited me to sit down at the table.

She asked my name, and in response, I told her the Russian version: Katyusha. She asked me where I lived and what I did. I answered her that I lived as a prisoner in Jakodym Posiolek camp and was a lumberjack. She seemed to be moved and started singing a familiar song, using my name: "*Wychadziła na byrek, Katyusha,"* and then continued humming the rest of it. She said I look starved and neglected. She put a bowl of potatoes with mushrooms in front of me, and I swallow them in a minute. She offered to give me a sack of flour, a large loaf of bread, a piece of meat, and some potatoes. Without any discussion, I agreed to her proposal. To my surprise, she asked me if I would go with her to the cellar. We went down, using a kerosene lamp; I could hardly breathe. The cellar was dark as night and very stuffy. She opened a large trunk, apparently searching for something. After removing several coats and many articles of clothing, we finally reach the bottom of the trunk. Then she pulled out a great beautiful frame and an old image of the Virgin Mary. As I held it up in my hands, I asked her if she was afraid to have something like this in her home.

Her answer astonished me: She was mostly afraid of her own son, who was in the NKWD. If he knew of the existence of this image, he would report her immediately to his supervisor, and she would be arrested and put in jail. She said she had two sons. The NKWD lives with her, and the other was conscripted into the army and sent to the front. She was afraid for him, since he might be killed. She gave me her hand and asked me to tell her fortune. She said she was sure I could foretell her future.

I tried to explain to her that I was not a fortune-teller or even a Gypsy, but she was bound and determined that I would tell her future. I had no choice. I took her hand, and as I opened it, I could tell it was a hard-working hand. I studied her hand and said that the day would come when her son returned from the war and that even the image of the Virgin Mary would be safely hanging there on her wall. She was delighted and said she would wait for the day of liberation. She thanked me warmly and confessed that she liked me very much. I also felt fondness and sympathy for her. She made me promise to visit her again to get the rest of the payment for my costume. I told her I would definitely return.

I hid the food carefully. She added a few more potatoes into my scruffy shawl and tearfully hugged me goodbye. As I headed back, I was so happy; it promised to be a wonderful Christmas Eve, and we would have some decent food, not just this black clay the Russians called bread and a cup of boiling water.

Christmas Eve

When Father and I returned to the barracks in darkness after our workday ended, he announced that today was December 24, Christmas Eve. We had to celebrate this vigil. I was so preoccupied at work, I could not believe I forgot one of our most celebrated days of the year. I remembered when we were at home, we used to look up into the sky for the first star of the evening. I told my siblings about the tradition that we did not eat all day until the first star appeared in the sky, then we would eat. I took them outside so they could look for the first star. We did not have to wait long. The young children quickly spotted the first bright star and ran back inside the barracks, with me following close behind. They happily informed Mother that the star was shining and it was time for the vigil, time for us to eat. Mother hustled and bustled between the stove and our makeshift table, trying to make this a festive meal. Father quietly whispered a prayer, remembering Grandfather. We were so sad he was no longer with us. Grandmother reminded us that our custom dictated that we forgive each other and come to terms with all those we were angry with. We did not have any wafers to break as communion bread, so in its place, we shared a piece of the black muddy Russian bread. We prayed to hear good news from Tony, that he safely reached the Polish army. We also prayed we would soon be released from captivity and return to our home, where the pantries were always full and we never felt hunger. As we ended our collective prayers and wishes, we threw ourselves into each other's arms, with tears in our eyes.

After eating, we felt the urge to sing some Christmas carols. However, it was forbidden. We looked through the dirty windows at a much stronger-than-usual group of guards. We waited impatiently for the guards to wander away. Time passed; they seemed to be socializing right in front of our barracks door. Finally, someone said they thought the guards had left. We began to hum softly, almost in a whisper, but slowly, as our voices rose, the whole barracks joined in singing Christmas carols; we were singing from the bottom of our hearts.

Suddenly, the commandant and a group of NKWD plainclothesmen and some Russian guards burst into our barracks. The commandant asked what the singing was about. We knew he was only pretending. Only a fool did not know it was Christmas Eve and we were singing Christmas carols. Apparently, however, he did not want to bully us today. He prohibited any further celebrations, did an about-face, and left.

The Siberian winter days passed slowly. We worked hard and desperately waited to hear some news from Tony. It had been four months since his departure, and we had not heard a thing about him or his eleven friends who left with him to join the army. The commandant continued to make it as difficult to leave as he could, by discouraging those who were strongest and most efficient at clearing the forest. The most vulnerable were single women with children and widows. The Russians gradually took the children and sent them to orphanages and trained them as Komsomols. However, different families began leaving the camp because their sons had gone to join the army. Apparently, no more Poles were to be taken out to Siberia.

Friends of ours, a married couple with two children, received a spišská (letter permitting them to leave) and were preparing to move out. They were so happy they were leaving this place of hell. Sadly, the woman was suffering from typhoid and died. The NKWD came, arrested her husband, and shot him immediately on the pretext of a threatening plague. They burned all their meager belongings; their neighbors took the children into their care, but not for long. As soon as the Russians found out these children were orphaned, they took the little ones and sent them to an orphanage to train them as Komsomols.

Uncle Tom's three-year-old daughter Josie was dying. But before she left us, she asked to be buried under the pine tree next to Grandfather. It was so difficult to say goodbye to such a small baby. As the whole family gathered under the pine tree at her grave site, the ruthless guards immediately dispersed us and chased us back to work, not even allowing us time to say goodbye to this dear baby.

Somehow, Father found out we could get a spišská without receiving a letter from Tony. It turned out the need for a letter confirming that Tony joined the army was just an excuse to hold us in the camp. We came to a family agreement that we would not wait any longer. Somehow, we had to get out of this place of constant hunger and certain death. Grandmother told us firmly that she was not going anywhere. We tried to convince her otherwise, but she was so stubborn, she would not change her mind. She said she would not leave Grandfather and wanted to be buried next to him and Josie when she died.

I accompanied Father to talk to the commandant about giving us permission to leave the camp. He questioned us, pretending not to remember about Tony and his eleven friends leaving to join the army. He looked Father up and down with his cold eyes. He advised us not to leave, giving us all kinds of excuses we heard him say to other people. We insisted on leaving, even against his wishes. Father said he had enough of his lies, that his son Tony had left and that we were entitled to a spišská. Finally, the commandant softened and said he would attempt to free us, but he could not promise anything. In the meantime, we must continue working.

After a few days, the commandant informed us that the spišská was ready. But he would not give it to us until we arranged some kind of transport to the Welsk train station. He recommended the names of several Russians who could take us there in their sleighs. We found a Russian sleigh driver who agreed to take us to the station. We then went to the commandant for our documents. The commandant dragged his feet again and said we would get the documents and a bag of bread the day before we left. But right now, we must prepare ourselves for our journey.

This really irritated Father. He told the commandant to stop preventing us from leaving, as we had nothing to prepare; all we had was what was on our backs and a few battered pots. Finally, the commandant gave us permission and then said to take one blanket for adults and one blanket for the children. He promised to give us the documents and a bag of bread for each person the next day. We were overwhelmed with joy. Finally, we are going to leave this Communist "paradise." We were as happy as young children. We did not realize this was just the beginning of our wanderings around the world.

Farewell to Siberia

We left the next day, which was almost the end of March. We were heading into the unknown but bursting with happiness for our freedom. It was hard to say goodbye to Grandmother and my married aunts and uncles, along with their children. Grandmother would be looked after by her daughter Josephine; Auntie Sally was also staying behind with her two sons. It was really difficult to part with them. We didn't realize that we would never see them or receive information about them ever again. Grandmother probably lived in Siberia to the end of her days, and she likely got her wish to be buried next to Grandfather.

I also had to say goodbye to Olga, my best friend from the village. We hugged each other, weeping together. She said her mother was so sick, she would probably not live long. Olga would be left all alone. We both knew we would never meet again this side of heaven. I thanked God that he gave me the strength to endure this horrible Siberian prison and that I was able to survive these times until our final day at this camp.

We learned later that Posiolek Jakodym was to be closed permanently. The commandant, the NKWD, and the Russian soldiers left. The current regime fell apart. The barracks were abandoned. People did whatever they wanted. No one knew whether this freedom and lawlessness would last or what to do about it. The Russian, Ukrainian, and Latvian prisoners were transported to a different camp. Posiolek Jakodym closed. Still later, we found out that it was reopened. They gathered small groups of Polish prisoners from the other camps and brought them to Posiolek Jakodym. They also brought in the Russian troops who survived the nightmare of defending Moscow; many of them lost their minds. These soldiers were brought in to continue the work of logging. A new commandant and new NKWD were brought in, and the camp functioned again.

Finally, the Russian sleigh driver came to pick us up. We hastily got into it and covered ourselves with the blankets.

"*Dawaj, pojechali!*" (Come on, let's go), the driver shouted, cracking the whip. The horse moved into a gallop, leaving our prison behind. As I looked back, I was reminded of the two terrible years of horrendous hunger and suffering we endured. I clearly remembered the moment they brought us here. My thoughts now were just to get out of here, even though it was only to the train station in Welsk.

We didn't have much with us, just a few bags of this miserable Bolshevik bread, old, worn-out clothes, and a few damaged pots: not enough to pack into a suitcase, if we had one. We arrived at the train station, and the sleigh driver asked to be paid. Father gave him a vest instead of Russian rubles. We had a lot of Russian rubles saved from when Tony and I floated the logs to the mill. We tried to buy different things with these rubles, but no one wanted them. People told us the money was worthless. It would be useful, however, to buy train tickets.

We walked up to the cashier, and Father said we wanted to travel to Swerdlowsk, which he heard was the best way to the Middle East. The cashier asked where we ultimately wanted to go. We tried to explain that we didn't really know, except that we wanted to go where the Polish army was being formed. The woman looked at us very carefully, eyeing us up and down. She saw such a ragged and poor family that she kindly advised us to ride in a freight train, not the normal passenger train, because it would be much cheaper for us. Perhaps we would be an embarrassment to the other passengers.

She asked if we had permission to leave this area and if we had money to pay for the tickets. Father showed her the documents and put the money on the counter. The cashier counted the rubles and said that we had enough money for tickets to the town of Saraj. But before we got there, we would have to change trains in Wologda. We didn't have much choice, so Father bought the tickets and assured us that we would find a job to earn enough money to continue our journey onward from Saraj.

Our train was due to arrive the following day. We searched for a corner where we could spend the night. We must have looked very suspicious because the local NKWD asked to see our documents. He looked carefully at the spišská, the letter issued by our commandant from the camp, and asked to see our train tickets. We showed them to him, and he warned us that free-riding would result in being arrested and thrown into prison. Finally, he left us alone.

We had no place to sleep. As the darkness fell, we clung to each other under the blankets, trying to get a bit of warmth from each other. Father shared out a piece of bread, and I gathered some snow into one of our pots and tried to melt it so we could have something to drink with this humble meal. It was so cold. Now, even the *kojki* (wooden beds) at the camp would be a luxury. Finally, somehow, we managed to fall asleep, dreaming of freedom.

In the morning, the cashier gave us some work for the railroad. This allowed us to earn enough for a few cups of hot water and some kopiejki (Russian money smaller than rubles). The freight train we were waiting for finally rolled into the station, with a clanging and banging. As our shivering family climbed into the wagon, I experienced this horrible sickening reminder that this was the same kind of wagon we were deported in. Only this time, the door was open; it was not locked behind us, and no one was guarding the door. This brought me some relief. So we sat on the floor and waited. All day. The freezing cold was unbearable as we waited. As dusk approached, Father said he would partially close the door, and this would help to keep us a little warmer. Although I did not like this idea, I kept silent. I did not want to arouse panic. I thought about my grandmother and other relatives that we left behind in the camp. I tried to dismiss these last memories, memories of reliving life in camp. I tried to convince myself I needed to think about the future, a new life. But I did not know what to expect, and it scared me. But I finally managed to fall asleep.

The morning was sunny, and the frozen snow sparkled with an icy glow. We still waited throughout the day. And then, another whole day of waiting. They explained to us that this was wartime, and there was no permanent train schedule. However, on the evening of the third day, the train finally left the station. I felt strange, but in the depth of my heart, I was overjoyed.

It was hard to believe it, but it was true: We were free, at long last. I didn't even know how to smile; it was as if I'd forgotten how. We were finally on our way out of there. The train wheels clickety-clacked on the rails, leaving behind memories that would haunt our family for the rest of our lives. As we traveled slowly through the frozen white Siberian countryside, the train made frequent stops. Father tried to comfort us by saying that spring was coming and soon it would be warm, nice and warm.

Nearing Wologda, I heard a rumble in the distance. Father explained that it was the sound of war. The train stopped at the station, and we jumped out of the wagon. Here was where we changed trains. I ran around the station in search of our next train, only to find that not only was it not here, no one knew when it would even arrive. This was war, after all. Everyone repeated the same words. I asked about the banging, and it turned out Father was right. The Germans had surrounded Moscow. For three days, we waited, grabbing any job we could just to earn a little bit of cash to continue our journey. Finally, our train arrived. After our tickets were checked, the train left almost immediately. The sounds of war were left behind, and there were no obstacles on the way to Saraj.

Money was something we did not have, so we had no choice but to look for work when we arrived in Saraj. We were given jobs unloading the railway wagons. I walked from one wagon car to another, looking for food. It was very cold, and the wages were miserable. After two weeks, we had enough money to buy tickets that would take us as far as Swerdlowsk.

Again, we were happy because we were traveling farther toward freedom and a better life. By now, the bread given to us by the commandant at the camp was gone. We stopped at the railroad station in Kirow, and I jumped out to look for some food for us to eat. Father warned me to be on guard because our train could leave at any time, and if I missed it, I would be left behind and all alone. I took note of the wagon number and its location and set off on my search. Father decided to come with me. We happily returned to the train with a piece of bread and some boiling water. We enjoyed our meager meal while the train was still at the station.

We wanted to continue our journey, but each time we asked someone when we would be leaving, the answer was always, "We don't know." We had already traveled about seven hundred kilometers and were approximately halfway to Swerdlowsk. But this part of the trip, this waiting, made time pass at a snail's pace. Again, I went in search of food. We must watch ourselves; we did not want to fall asleep while we were hungry, for there was the danger we may not wake up. I lost track of time and didn't know how long we were standing in this railroad station. But eventually, the train started moving, gliding slowly through a beautiful, snowy landscape. We stopped occasionally, and at dawn, we arrived at a large city. The white snow had disappeared and was replaced by black tarry buildings. As far as my eyes could see, there were only smoking chimneys and factories. The train slowed down and stopped at this huge station. It was big, dark, and gloomy. It reminded me of Moscow. We got off the train and realized that we had arrived at Swerdlowsk.

We looked around to see where we could spend the night, but we did not have much of a selection; there were others like us, leading this nomadic life. So we slept wherever we found a little space to lie down. We thanked God at least we were free. The good thing was it was a huge station, and we would have no difficulty finding a job. We did not see any young people because they had been drafted into the forces to fight against Hitler's troops, defending the capital city of Moscow. Several families of those too old to work or to fight in the war and children too young to fight and those who had not been drafted into the army stood or sat around the station. We all looked like tramps, bags of bones in dirty and torn clothes.

An NKWD officer approached us. He interrogated Father, asking to see our documents and wanting to know where we came from. He asked how long we intended to stay and where we were going. He seemed to be genuinely sympathetic as he looked at our sickly, emaciated faces and our hands that were blistered and scarred from hard work. He helped us to find a job at the railroad yard, loading wagons. He told us that all the young men had been drafted into the war, so only women worked here now. He promised he would try to take care of us because he was often on duty here.

I set out for a walk between the cars in search of food. I came upon a wagon filled with sacks of rice. I quickly tore a small hole in one of the bags and collected the rice in my tattered scarf. Happily, I ran to Mother with this valuable booty so she could boil it for a meal. Father rushed to get water from one of our battered pots, while I took the children with me to look for dry firewood. Our friendly local NKWD helped by telling us where to find dry logs and firewood. He even gave us a few matches to light the fire. Mother put the pot on the burning logs, brought the water to a boil, and threw the beautiful white beads into the pot. What a tasty meal we had that night. I did not remember the last time I ate rice. As soon as we finished eating the tasty white morsels, we fell asleep, with our hunger assuaged at last.

In order to work, we needed to get up early. Regular duties filled our time. We now had a permanent place to stay at the station, but someone always had to stay in our spot to guard against someone else moving in on us.

We tried to find a map to plan our route onward, but there were none to be found. We would have to continue our journey, guessing at our direction. We asked some men if they knew which way we should go to join the Polish army in the Middle East. But it was always the same dry answer: "*Nie znaju*" (We don't know). No one knew, or no one wanted to tell us. Could this be a war secret?

While we were waiting for the train, the food was a little better than at the camp. In addition, I came upon a wagon full of sugar. We ate bread, sugar, rice, and hot water. Without realizing the passing of time, we spent two months waiting at this station for our next train. The friendly, helpful NKWD officer who took a liking to us told us his name was Yuri. He came to check up on us to see that we were all okay. He advised us to go to southern Kazakhstan and Uzbekistan, which was in central Asia. He said that many Poles had left to go to this area. When I heard about traveling as far as Asia, I was stunned. This was unbelievable to me. I could not imagine that we could go such a far distance. But Father declared that we had already earned the money for the fare to continue the onward journey, and soon we would be leaving.

We learned the trains ran infrequently in the direction we wanted to go, only once every two or three weeks. And the journey would take at least ten days. When we said goodbye to Yuri, he surprised me by suggesting that I stay behind with him. Despite his insistence, I assured him that I would not part with my family.

Finally, our journey was planned. First, we were going to Orsk, which was about seven hundred kilometers to the border of Kazakhstan. Then further still, over sixteen hundred kilometers to Tashkent, the capital of Uzbekistan. Father bought the tickets, and we collected our meager belongings and supplies of bread, rice, and sugar. The train finally arrived, and we loaded ourselves into a wagon: certainly not the comfort of a passenger car, but our only means of transportation to continue this next course of our southward trek.

We traveled south to Aktubińsk through Chelyabinsk. Time seemed to drag as the train continued between the endless snow-covered forests and beautiful mountains and tunnels. The train seemed to struggle as it labored to reach the mountain peaks. It wound its way slowly between the many hills. It made many stops to pick up other groups of ragged Poles with sad and dejected faces, who had managed to gather enough money to purchase tickets to freedom. They piled into the mostly empty wagons. When we talked to them, they said we would pass the Ural Mountains. The train stopped many times for several hours, but we had no idea why. Finally, we approached Novotrick and Orsk. Our food was running out, almost gone, as a matter of fact. But we were almost at the border of Kazakhstan and soon we would be at Aktubińsk. This thought gave us some hope.

At Aktubińsk, we stopped to change trains. Everyone had to leave the wagons and wait for another train, which was expected in a few days. There was no information about the next train. A few hours or a few days, what did it matter? We were used to the unpredictability of our situation. After all, we lived in a time of war. From the wagons came loud sobs of our countrymen, grieving the loss of their loved ones, for whom the journey turned out to be too difficult. Survivors in the train did not want to get out of the wagons, leaving their dead loved ones inside. However, the local NKWD were ruthless and showed no sympathy for the dead people or their relatives. They checked each wagon and pushed the survivors out of the way, dragging the emaciated corpses of their loved ones out of the wagons. The relatives of the dead clung tightly to their loved ones, sobbing desperately, not wanting to let them go, not wanting to leave them behind to the brutality of this cruel regime.

The scene taking place around me shook me to my core and would be burned in my memory until I die. I saw three tiny children, holding tightly to their dead mother, crying, screaming desperately for their mother to wake up. The NKWD shouted at the children to let go of their mother. The woman was dead, and her body was already quite stiff. Nowhere did I see the father of these little children, which probably meant he had been taken to Siberia or was already dead. The friends and relatives of the mother were trying to keep the children, but the officers would not allow this. Instead, they took the children, likely with the intention of sending them to an orphanage.

When the train finally arrived, we boarded again and found that as we traveled, the temperatures were starting to get warmer. The snow and frost were finally gone, left behind us. We were happier now because of the warmer climate. We would be able to survive easier, since we did not have a roof over our heads. The train stations were our home wherever we stopped. As we waited for the next train, we worked as the occasion arose in the different stations. Whenever we waited for our next train, I searched for food, looking through the wagons and trying to avoid the police. Sometimes, I managed to steal something. This time, I came across some sugar, a bit of rice, and some poppy seeds. I learned later that the rice and sugar were for the army, and the poppy seed was likely feed for the horses. The poppy seed was compressed into dense, round, very hard rings. Although the seeds were food for the animals, we managed to slowly suck and munch it. Mother noticed the poppy seed was destroying the enamel of our teeth. She asked me to eat only the cooked seeds, but how could I, when I was constantly hungry?

We encountered other Poles who were also waiting for the same train. They talked about their time spent in the Siberian work camps. They were in other camps, but their experiences were very similar to ours. They were extremely poor and starving because of their forced labor and enslavement. We asked them about the Polish army, but always in vain; they listened, but no one seemed to know. They had heard rumors there were soldiers around Tashkent, but they were not certain, saying the rumors could not be confirmed. Father decided this was where we would go next.

Some cargo trains came through this station. We watched many starving Poles getting off these trains. Suddenly, we heard one of the trains at our station was leaving for Tashkent. We rushed to gather our belongings and boarded the train before it left. Now at least I had some hope and felt excited at the thought of seeing my brother again. I could not wait to see Tony; it had been over six months since I last saw him.

This journey seemed to drag on and on, as usual, and was filled with frequent, unexplained stops. Every day, passengers died of typhoid, typhus, or dysentery. We tried to use these stops to bury their bodies, as the ground was no longer frozen. We helped those we could, but we had so little strength or energy ourselves. We did not have any tools, so we dug shallow graves with our hands and covered the dead with a thin layer of dirt, sand, turf, or stones.

We traveled at a snail's pace, passing small towns, villages, and settlements, and noticed more and more of these small hand-dug mounds along the railroad tracks. This proved to us that other trains had passed this way before us, carrying the same commodity: our people from Siberia. Some graves were ransacked by jackals, hyenas, or other animals. Sometimes, these animals emerged from the shallow graves with torn fragments of bodies. Always flocks of vultures and buzzards circled overhead. There were times when the train slowed down so that dead bodies could be thrown from the cars; the train did not even stop for them to be buried. This sight terrified me, as I knew we could be next. It disgusted me as well, as I realized how much the Russians had dehumanized us.

Our food was gone. We had absolutely nothing left to eat. For several days, we did not have even a crumb to put in our mouths. When we finally stopped, it was at a siding, not a station. I immediately flew around the trains in search of food, but alas, my search yielded us nothing. I must be careful in my search, not only to avoid the police and guards but also to be ready to jump onto the train, as it gave no warning when it left, and I could be left behind, with nowhere to go, alone, without my family. I memorized the train number and our wagon number so I would not get on the wrong train or the wrong wagon.

In time, we crossed the border into Uzbekistan. The railway signs told us we were going into the city of Sasdy. This journey took three times longer than Father had expected. They said that in a few hours, we would arrive in the capital city of Tashkent. The weather was getting warmer and warmer. We took off some of the rags we had worn every day since our long trek began. I was sick and tired of living under the Soviet regime.

Stolen Freedom in Uzbekistan

We arrived in Tashkent. It was midday, and the overhead sun was scorching. I was sure it was more than thirty-five degrees Celsius inside this wagon. The only relief from this oppressive heat was the shade from the wagon and the cross breeze coming in through the doors. Looking around, I saw desert, flat and sandy, with mountains far away on the horizon. The train slowed down and stopped. Someone yelled, "Tashkent!" We had traveled fifteen hundred kilometers from Aktubińsk and were finally at the end of our journey.

Tashkent was an old Arab city. The buildings were completely different, something I had never seen before in my life. They looked as though they were molded from clay and had little windows and doors. Above some of the roofs were soaring spires called minarets. Father explained that Muslim mosques called the faithful men to prayer five times a day. When the signal sounded, the men threw everything aside and rushed to the mosque, leaving their sandals outside and going inside to kneel on their prayer mats. They bowed their foreheads to the ground to give reverence to their God, Allah. They bobbed up and down, sometimes bruising their foreheads. I was told women were not allowed inside the mosques because of male-dominated segregation. Father said this was a Muslim tradition in the Arab culture.

When we tried to get off the train, we were met by a committee and some Polish troops who held us back, not allowing us to get off the train. They forced those who managed to get off the train to get back on. They told us we must continue to travel another two hundred kilometers to Kokanda. Supposedly, there was a special committee waiting to greet us that would organize our stay. Father was very upset and angry; he said he'd had enough. This wandering had reached the limit of his patience. He shouted that after so many thousands of kilometers toward our freedom, there was still no end in sight. Our journey was not over yet. People in the wagons were angry and rebelled. They shouted to their countrymen, calling them Communists and Bolsheviks. Some cried, others cursed viciously, but all to no avail.

After a few hours, the train set off on yet another leg of this journey, in the direction of Kokanda. As we left Tashkent, the landscape changed from sandy desert to rocky and mountainous terrain. We crossed over bridges and rivers. I had a feeling our long journey was finally about to end. As we approached Kokanda, still in the distance, we noticed the Russians had built buildings with new architecture, creating a huge, cosmopolitan city. As we traveled through the suburbs, the train went slowly because of the crowds of people milling around, many of them traders. We saw large crowds of people gathered in marketplaces, bargaining and haggling with the merchants, who were shouting out their goods and prices. All of them were well fed and well dressed, while we were starving and in rags. We were almost destroyed by the hunger we had to endure.

At long last, we were allowed to get out of the wagons in

the metropolitan area of Kokanda. I looked at all the people milling around and could tell they came from different countries, as some were yellow-skinned Mongols, others were tanned Uzbeks, as well as some Poles and other Europeans. The Polish soldiers who were waiting for us directed us to where we had to register. We were so hungry, we could not survive much longer. We went to the indicated place, and Father constantly asked the different soldiers if they had any information about Tony: whether he reached the army or, worse, if he was dead. They said they did not know him but explained that the Polish army headquarters was located in Buzuluk; perhaps there, we could get more information about him.

Looking at these soldiers, I could not believe my eyes; they appeared to be emaciated, like us. Their uniforms were hanging on them, as if they were skeletons. We were not the only ones who were hungry; clearly, they did not have easy lives, either.

After we registered, they gave us food vouchers and led us to a *kibitki*, a house prepared for us. It was a miserable Uzbeki clay hut, but we were grateful because at least it was a house, and without a doubt, it was better than anything we had had since leaving our homeland.

I noticed as we were being led inside our kibitki that there were no doors, only a hole in the wall for a doorway. I saw four bare walls made out of mud. There was a small window with a small shelf under it. The floor was also made of packed mud. The roof was flat and also made of mud, with a hole in it for the smoke from cooking to escape.

We put our little bundle of possessions on the floor and looked at the humble cottage. Mother took out the pictures she had hidden for so long of Our Lady and Jesus; she asked Father to hang them on the wall. "Let them watch over our destiny now that we are free," she said.

Our main concern now was to take care of this unrelenting hunger. The soldiers showed us where to go to line up to get our food at the main storage building, where all the meals were issued. We hurried in that direction and saw that there was a long line of people already waiting for food. I promised myself and my family that since we had survived Siberia and traveled the many thousands of kilometers to get here, I would not die. I would not die of hunger or starvation. I might claw for food, but I would not die.

After arriving at the building, we got into the long line of people waiting for food under the scorching heat of the sun. There was no shade anywhere to hide from this burning hot sun. Right behind me was a young girl about my age. I introduced myself to her and asked her name. She said her name was Helen, and she became my first friend in Kokanda. We were very happy to meet each other, and as we got closer and closer to the door where the food was issued, I could see that they gave each person a small bag. When it was finally my turn, I was handed a small bag too. I looked inside the bag and saw that it was flour. I thanked God and prayed it was enough for all of us. I ran quickly to our kibitki to give it to Mother so she could turn it into something we could eat. Father brought some water in a bucket (I don't know where he got the water or the bucket). Now we learned that there was no firewood available here. I would have given anything to get just a few pieces of firewood like we burned in Siberia. We learned that to make a fire here, we needed to gather some brown rings, which we learned later were donkey and sheep dung, animal waste. So we started looking for dried-out pieces of animal waste. If we did not gather enough, we would have nothing to make a fire to cook. We finally gathered enough to make a fire, and soon the water was boiling. Mother sprinkled the flour into the hot water and said it would be *poliwka* (porridge). There was enough to last us the whole day. We sat down on the bare mud floor, leaned against the wall, and ate a few spoonfuls of this nutritious and incredibly good-tasting meal.

The sun went down, and it got dark. It was very dark inside our mud hut, and we didn't have a single candle. We did not even have a bunk on which to lie down. We were so very tired that we lay down directly on the ground. We were dirty and ragged, had no strength, and were still hungry, but we quickly fell asleep.

In the morning, Mother went to get another bag of flour. She sent the children to search for fuel for the fire.

After we returned from gathering dung, my younger sister Josephine suddenly started screaming, saying that a giant spider bit her. We asked her where she was bit, and she showed us her left arm. We asked her what the spider looked like. She said through tears that it was very large, black, and hairy. Father said it was probably a black widow spider. Nearby, people gathered quickly around Josephine, who was crying, wondering what happened to her. We did not know what to do about this bite. So we wrapped her arm in a very tight scarf, using it a tourniquet. Josephine's arm was tied so tightly with the scarf that it cut off the blood circulation. Her arm swelled up and turned blue.

People gathered around us, attracted by my sister's screams, and showed us where the local doctor lived. We ran with her to the Uzbeki doctor. Father spoke to her in Russian, explaining what had happened. The doctor examined Josephine's arm and asked her questions about the spider, finally concluding that the spider was harmless. Her hand and arm were swollen because of the tight scarf tied around her arm. Father was greatly relieved and returned to our kibitki to find the spider and kill it. Josephine now forgot about the bite and remembered that she had not had anything to eat, and she was hungry. Hunger replaces all other feelings.

We soon realized that the Uzbeks did not like the Russians and even more so their godless communism. They looked down on the Russians. However, the Russians were still treating us like slaves. The Uzbekis resented us because the Polish army was being formed in Uzbekistan to fight the Germans. It made no difference to the Uzbekis that we would be fighting the Germans. They believed we were helping the Soviets and their allies, that we were their enemy. We tried to explain to them how we were displaced from our homeland and taken to Siberia as prisoners by the Russians, that we lost everything and were forced into slavery. They did not want to listen to us; they only said it was an excuse. They tormented us, as though we were Russians. The freedom we had been dreaming of was not here. The freedom we were promised was a lie. I felt cheated.

Uzbeks were a proud people who bragged about their history. They said that hundreds of years ago, God gave dominion over all the earth to their leader, Genghis Khan, who was the head of the Mongolian nation. All Russian lands were under his rule. The Mongols ruled the Russians with an iron fist and traded them as objects in their markets. Now the Russians destroyed all traces of the ancient power of Genghis Khan and mercilessly persecuted the Uzbeks.

There in Uzbekistan, we were in a crisis situation, as our starvation continued. We were certainly not used to this heat, and we were not able to work. Without food, life was not easy for us. Here, we did not even have drinking water. At least in Siberia, we could melt some snow to satisfy our thirst, but here, there was absolutely no water to drink. Mother and I searched for water and found some in a ditch flowing from a dirty stream, which was a common sewer. Further upstream, we saw an Uzbek washing himself in this stream, and next to him, we saw a woman doing her laundry. I asked Mother what she thought about this water. She said not to drink it.

We returned to our hut, and I begged her, "Please, if I can only moisten my lips. I am so thirsty."

Mother refused to listen to me. But she grabbed a pot, and we returned to the ditch. She looked at the sewer, then at me, and asked if I could see the dirt. But I was beyond caring; I needed a drink. Mother threw up her arms in frustration. She put some of the water in a pot, grabbed the hem of my ragged dress, and started to strain the water through my dress. My dress was not clean, but it was a little bit cleaner than the water. We returned home and put the pot of water on the fire that was always smoldering, and soon, the water came to a boil. I could not even wait for it to cool. Mother poured some of the boiling water into a container and blew on it to cool it so I could have a drink. I immediately drained the container, right to the last drop. My thirst was finally quenched, at least temporarily. Although we did not have any soap, Mother helped me rinse the rest of the water from the container. I used this water to wash some of the dirt off myself.

A Feast

In the evening, we were all gathered together in our mud hut. The entrance did not have a door, only a piece of cloth to cover the opening. Suddenly, the cloth moved, and in walked a sad-looking, skinny dog. The dog just stood and looked at us, waiting for a friendly gesture. Our eyes nearly popped out of our heads at the sight of it. We looked at the little dog and envisioned swallowing him alive. No one spoke, but I was certain you could hear the noisy rumblings of our empty stomachs. Finally, I broke the silence, telling Father the dog came to feed us. I was sure the poor thing would be glad if it no longer had to wander around, suffering from starvation.

My siblings agreed by nodding their heads quietly. They whispered they were hungry and needed to eat a piece of real meat. Father got up and looked at all of us intently, and I could see tears in his eyes. He could not believe that our family had stooped to the level of having to eat a dog in order for us to survive. His heart broke as he looked at the dog, with tears rolling down his cheeks. Father looked at the family, then at the dog who was to become a means of food for us. The need to survive was stronger than his compassion for this bony dog.

Father looked again at the dog with pity while the whole family anxiously awaited his decision.

We made a unanimous family decision: we would eat the dog. Father picked up the dog so skillfully it was barely aware of being handled; it hardly budged as he ended its life. Father quickly removed the skin from the dog and cleaned the meat. Mother put a bucket of water on the fire and threw the skin into the fire; the meat went into the boiling water. We were all waiting eagerly, salivating over the boiling dog. When Mother announced that supper was ready, Father divided the dog meat among the whole family. The dog was so thin, there was little meat on his bones, not much meat at all, really. I had almost forgotten the taste of meat. And it was so fresh, well cooked, and tasty. After we ate, we drank some of the broth. After dark, Father and I went to bury the bones in the sand.

In the morning, Mother went for the flour while I went with my new friend, Helen, to see if we could get any information about the Polish army. Maybe I would even find out something about Tony. We asked different people along the way but were told that it was all Bolshevik lies. They told us they knew nothing about it. So all our asking and searching was useless.

Work on Cotton Plantations

We came to another small group of people. We overheard their discussion about working for some Uzbeks who were recruiting people to harvest cotton in the fields. We learned that *Babaje* was what they called the Uzbeks. We could earn money to buy food. We hurried to look for this place but could not find it. We asked everyone we met.

On the streets, the women wore long dresses and covered their faces in veils, so only their eyes were visible, while the men dressed in long robes. The men had overgrown beards and wore cotton turbans or caps on their heads. Finally, someone gave us the directions to where we could work. We walked into a field overgrown with chest-high bushes covered with white flowers as far as our eyes could see. Women were working in the field, collecting these white flowers. We did not know what they were doing because we had never seen these flowers before.

We headed to the edge of this field and realized these white flowers were clumps of cotton. We told the Uzbek farmer we needed a job, and he asked us if we had done this work before. He asked to see our hands and saw that they were used to hard work. Our hands were as hard as stones from cutting down the trees in Siberia. He said the work started at sunrise and continued to sunset. He asked where we lived and told us a transport would pick us up in the morning and bring us home at sunset. He said our pay would be one pita bread, something like a small, flat cake of bread, for a kilo of picked cotton.

We were issued aprons, and he showed us how to collect the cotton. He said to use only three fingers to pluck the beautiful white cotton from the bushes. Then he gave us a huge bag that was attached to our aprons and said the cotton we picked must be pure white (*biela krasivaja*). When our bag was filled, we brought it to the farmer, who weighed it.

Never in my life did I ever think I would be doing this kind of work. The one thing I found strange now was that there were no armed guards behind us to make sure that the work was done properly. It was burned into my brain what the guards would say to us in Siberia: "You don't work, you don't eat!"

When I look around, I saw only women working to collect the cotton. I recognized the Uzbeki women because their faces were covered; the Polish women didn't have their faces covered at all.

Helen and I put on our aprons and walked to the row of bushes the boss indicated. We eagerly started to work, but with the first pinch, I got a nasty surprise: my fingers started to bleed as they got hooked on the dry, spiny spikes. It dawned on me now that because this cotton was so light, it would take a long time, maybe forever, to accumulate a kilo of the fluffy cotton. As noon approached, I felt as though the sky was raining fire; the sun was burning my skin. I tried to protect my head and shoulders, but I had nothing to cover myself with.

In no time, I learned how to pluck the cotton off the bushes without pricking my fingers, choosing the most beautiful and largest cotton tufts and putting them into the bag. At sunset, the

Uzbek announced that the work day had ended. We brought him our collections to be weighed. To my surprise, my bag weighed a kilogram, so in return for my work, I got a pita bread.

Two-wheeled donkey carts arrived to bring us home. All the workers climbed onto the carts, and the driver took us to our mud huts. All the way to our hut, I was so tempted to take a bite of this pita bread; I hadn't eaten anything all day. But I fought this urge because I knew I had to share it with my younger siblings and my parents. It was dark when I arrived at our hut. My parents were a little worried about me. I explained how I had spent the day and surprised them with my wages, the pita bread. With delight, we all shared dinner consisting of my pita bread and the boiled flour Mother made. Soon after, we spread out on the floor and fell asleep. Early the next morning, the Uzbek's carts arrived to take me and the other Uzbek women to the cotton field.

After a few days of working in the fields, I was able to double my rate of pay, collecting two kilograms of cotton. My family was very happy because of my raise in pay, but unfortunately, it did not last long. It ended too soon because the first harvest of cotton had been picked, and then we had to pick the poorer quality. We started picking again at the rows where we first began. This job was much worse than I thought. It was more dangerous for me because I hurt my fingers with each pluck of the dirty cotton. Although I had hardworking hands and my skin was tough, these dirty buds had small black seeds that were barbed and thorny. Each time I plucked one, I got blood on my fingers because the buds were full of spikes. But I didn't care about my bloody fingers; all I cared about was filling my sack so I could get bread for my family. My legs hurt me terribly, and my back felt like it was breaking, but I didn't complain. I protected my head from the scorching sun by covering it with a piece of tattered fabric so it did not burn me. After a busy day, all I earned was one pita bread. I felt strongly grieved, as though I was being punished, but what could I do? These wages were better than nothing.

One evening, after I returned from the field, I told my mother about the black cotton seeds, and she told Father we should bring some of these seeds back to Poland so we could plant them and start our own cotton plantation. Mother told me to collect a handful of seeds to take back with us to our homeland. I liked this idea, so I collected some of the seeds and put them in my bosom. The Uzbek was vigilantly watching me and finally asked what I was doing. I answered him truthfully, saying my mother wanted to take the seeds and plant them in Poland when we get home.

He burst out laughing. He showed me his hand and asked if I ever saw anyone with hair growing on their palms. He said this meant that these seeds would not grow in Poland. He laughed and made fun of me.

When I returned to our hut at sunset, I gave Mother the pita bread and a handful of cotton seeds. She sensed something was wrong and asked why I had such a sour face. So I repeated to her what the Uzbek said. Father got angry about Mother's plan and said we were talking nonsense. We spent the rest of the evening reminiscing about Poland and our plans for when we would finally return home.

The cotton harvest soon ended and with it, our only regular supply of pita bread. Our hunger returned. I looked for a job every day. And every day, I looked for food. I was always hungry.

Goat's Cheese

One evening, as I walked back to our hut after looking for work all day, I felt disheartened. I noticed a neighboring Uzbeki woman making cheese. I quietly spied on her and watched her tie the cheese bag onto a mulberry tree between our huts. My stomach overruled my head, and I just knew that this cheese would be mine.

Mother had the boiled flour ready for dinner when I got home. She said that there was a little extra that day, because she added more water to the pot. We ate what we had, although it was not enough, but I thanked God for what we had. That night, all I could think of was the bag of cheese dangling from the mulberry tree; I could see it right before my eyes. After dinner, we lay down to sleep, but my thoughts were focused on that white bag of cheese. I could not sleep. I decided right then we would eat it for breakfast, and then I dozed off to sleep.

I woke up early, before the sun came up. I went outside in the dark and looked around to make certain no one could see me. I was safe; no one was around. I walked behind our hut to complete my mission. I climbed quietly onto the back of our roof, praying only that the mud and straw roof would not collapse. I was only a bag of bones, not heavy at all, so the roof held my weight. I moved nimbly along the edge of the roof in the direction of my prey: the mulberry tree with the cheese bag. There it was; I could clearly see my treasure, the white bag still hanging from a string tied to the branch. I inched gently along the edge of the roof, taking care not to break even the smallest twig or make any noise to waken the neighbors. I was aware of the dangers if I was caught. Everyone here suffered from hunger, and food was considered to be a most precious treasure; its theft was punished severely.

I reached the tree and stretched myself out on a limb, snaking along to reach the bag, but it was still too far away. I could not reach it. I cautiously moved farther, stretching my fingers until I got a grip on the bag and broke the string. I held the precious booty with my teeth, and as quickly and quietly as possible, I hurried back out of the mulberry tree and then climbed onto the roof and down to the ground. I ran into the house, with my heart racing and pounding in my chest. I ripped open the bag and threw it directly into the blazing fire; the evidence of my theft disappeared. I gave the cheese to Mother, who was already awake.

She was shocked but asked no questions about how I got this treasure. She happily divided the cheese into pieces and gave some to all the family. What a delicious breakfast we had. I was afraid of being caught with this cheese, but we all swallowed it quickly. After the cheese was gone, there was no sign of our having eaten it. The bag burned away and turned to ashes. Only then did Mother ask where I got this delicacy, sternly reminding me that I should not steal.

We waited in suspense to see if anything would happen because of my theft, but there was only silence. Then all of a sudden, we heard someone screaming, "*Karapczuk! Karapczuk!*" (Thief, thief). The neighbor woman was screaming to the high heavens.

Mother looked at me straight in the eye and asked if this pertained to me. "Are you the thief the neighbor is screaming about?" she asked.

I did not deny it and explained that the neighbors were much better off than we were; they were not as poor and destitute as us. At that moment, a woman burst through the doorway into our hut. She demanded to know who stole her cheese. We all tried to look innocent and said we didn't know. She said her husband had already gone to the NKWD. She continued to yell at us.

Mother turned to me and said in Polish that she would rather die of hunger than steal from our neighbors. I answered emphatically that I did not agree with her. The Babaje did not suffer from hunger as we did, and they treated us as though we were slaves; they were worse than the Russians in Siberia.

All at once, two Russian officers came into our hut with a dog and asked about the goat cheese. We insisted we knew nothing about it. But they were very suspicious of us. It seemed clear that we were major suspects, if not the only suspects. The police dog ran around all over our hut, sniffing everything, including our bellies. I was scared to death; who knew what the dog might smell in our stomachs?

The officers could see that I was jittery and asked me a series of sharp questions. I answered in a strong voice, emphatically denying the theft, but knowing that I was guilty of this crime. I recalled now what had happened to me in Siberia, which was not as terrible a crime as I committed that morning. I knew thieves were punished severely. We sat quietly on the floor and maintained our innocence. They searched through the fire's ashes, but in vain. They found no evidence of a crime. Finally, they left, and the fear was over temporarily, but would they return to take me away?

Delicious Poppy Seeds

Helen and I often looked around the camp for something to eat. We were always hungry, and this thought was always on our minds, from dawn to dusk: getting something to eat, even a piece of bread. We got to know the city of Kokanda rather quickly. We learned where we could beg or steal. I felt like we were the dirt of the earth, the worst paupers in the world, having to beg and steal for even a tiny bit of food. This was our fate.

One morning, Helen and I went with Chester to the train station to look for food inside the train wagons. We looked through the wagons for food, while watching for the guards. We searched wagon after wagon, finding all kinds of goods, but we were only interested in finding something to put in our mouths to fill our stomachs; nothing else interested us. Finally, we came to a wagon that had large round lumps; they looked like poppy seeds that were compressed into round cakes.

Chester tried to bite a piece of it, but it was very hard, and he had to suck on it to make it soft enough to bite. He crunched a small piece and found that it tasted good. He said it reminded him of the delicious poppy seed cakes that Mother used to bake. I bit into a piece, and it was very tasty. It did remind me of the cakes and rolls Mother used to bake at home in Poland. We sat there, remembering our former life, when suddenly we heard voices. They were getting closer and closer to where we were hiding in the wagon, eating the poppy seeds. We looked out and saw two armed guards, who had spotted us. We grabbed some of the poppy seed rounds and jumped out of the wagon. We started running as fast as our legs would carry us because we knew what the consequences would be if we got caught. After running awhile, I looked over my shoulder and saw they were falling behind. They finally gave up and stopped chasing us.

We returned to our hut and showed Mother the poppy seeds. Her eyes lit up with delight, and she began talking about the different delicious baked goods that she could make with the black, fragrant, and tasty seeds. She said she would fry cakes with the flour and use some of the poppy seeds.

Father took some of the seeds into his hands and checked them. He said the rounds were made for feed for animals like cows and horses. But it didn't matter to us; we just wanted something to eat. So he took the rounds outside and tried to break them up with a stone. He put a round onto a rock and then hit it with another stone to break it apart. We were delighted to have a meal that consisted of some of Mother's treats, like pancakes, and for dessert, she made some round balls from the poppy seeds. They were so delicious. We had enough left over for more pancakes the next day.

The Marketplace

The next morning after breakfast, I asked Chester if he would like to come with me to the marketplace. I told him we might find something to eat there. He was reluctant at first, saying it was too far, but then changed his mind and agreed to come with me. We set off together. We walked over some sand dunes and rocks behind our settlement and encountered a bearded man in a turban. I knew he was a native, and we were interested in what he was doing: He was catching wandering turtles. He set them on their side and split their shells, hitting them with a rock and throwing the meat into a bag. He said when it was cooked, the meat was delicious, and the shell could be used for dishes. I wondered if Chester and I could do this and asked him if we could try to catch some turtles too. He said we should.

We started searching among the rocks. Finally, Chester spotted a turtle with its head sticking out of the sand and yelled to me that we could catch it. He dug it out with his hands; the turtle had no chance to escape. We noticed how pretty it was. As I looked into its sad eyes, it bothered me; I wasn't sure I had the heart to kill it. I asked my brother what he thought, and we concluded that we had to let this pretty turtle live. We released it and continued on our way to the marketplace.

When we arrived at the market, there was a huge traffic jam. It was very noisy and crowded with people. Women wore long blue robes with their faces covered completely with veils, except for their eyes. They were busy selling cotton and rolls of fabric. The men were sitting on the ground in circles, sipping chai or eating yogurt. Some were eating lamb prepared with fragrant, local Uzbeki herbs. Everywhere we looked, we saw the Uzbeks eating and drinking while we suffered from hunger, terrible hunger. I felt as if I would go crazy because there were so many delicious aromas and so much food for the Uzbeks, while my stomach ached from the constant hunger.

We heard everyone talking and shouting at the same time and in many different languages. I understood Russian and a little Uzbek but no other languages. I thought they were speaking Chinese or Mongolian. Someone had told my father there were people here from Tajikistan, Kazakhstan, and Turkey, and there were Persians from Iran. I saw that the Uzbek lifestyle had not changed. They lived as they did hundreds of years ago when they ruled Europe and Russia. They didn't care what happened in other parts of the world. Few changes had been introduced; they felt they did not need them.

The market was operating in full swing. Merchants were selling milk, goat's cheese, onions, vegetables, and many fruits unknown to me. We saw large mounds of spices and even dried animal dung (to be burned as fuel). Everyone was selling something. Chester and I wandered through the bazaar, looking for any scraps of food, even something that had been tossed out because it was slightly rotten, but we found nothing.

I came up with what I thought was a clever idea. We approached a man who was selling cheese and asked him if it was tasty. We told him we wanted to try it before we decided to buy it. He gave me a little piece that I divided in half and shared with Chester. It was delicious, but I told him, "Thank you, but it has too sharp of a flavor."

We went to the next stall and did the same thing, asking for a sample. We walked from stall to stall in the market and ate little by little of the cheese samples; it helped with our hunger, but only slightly.

In the afternoon, we were tired from the heat, the surrounding crowds, and the noise of people yelling out the goods they were selling and bartering over the prices. We left the market and looked for a place to escape the hustle and bustle. We wanted to sit and rest under the shade of a tree, but we could not find any trees. I told my brother that it was time to go back to our hut, but Chester rebelled, telling me that he was still hungry. I explained that we must return before it got dark, or we could lose our way and get lost. But Chester did not want to listen to me. Trying to persuade him, I mentioned the turtles, and he agreed to return home with me.

Turtle Soup

We went back using the same route by which we came to the market. We intended to capture at least one turtle and take it home for dinner so we could all have a feast. We knew how the turtles dug their bodies into the sand, leaving only their heads visible, but we did not see even one. Chester remembered the place where he previously found the turtle and saw it again. It was basking in the afternoon sun on the warm sand. I caught it without any qualms this time, as my hunger was stronger than pity for this soon-to-be meal. We put it on its side on a rock and banged it with another stone, just as we saw the Uzbek man do, and sure enough, the shell split. I pulled up my dress and put the turtle meat inside. Chester and I hurried back to our hut, happy that we had something for our family to eat today.

Father cleaned the turtle meat, while Mother prepared a bucket of water for cooking it. This would be a delicious soup. And, in fact, it was extraordinary. We ate the turtle meat soup with gusto.

The Fleas with Crosses

After dinner, I went to see Helen and arranged to meet her in the morning so we could go together to look for the Polish army again. I awakened early and made my way to my friend's house. I met Helen, and we went to where the trains stopped on the siding. We hid behind a huge rock, trying not to be seen, and waited. In a few moments, we heard an approaching locomotive. Our wish came true as the locomotive slowed and stopped. We jumped into a wagon and impatiently waited for it to start. We heard the whistle blow, and the train jolted to a start. At the next village, the train came to a stop, and we looked outside to see where we were. Then we noticed the police checking all the wagons. We tried to hide, but the guards were very thorough in their search. We were spotted, even though we were hiding in a dark corner of the wagon. We were caught. The guards chased us out of the wagon and threatened us, saying we could be thrown in prison for being stowaways and not paying the fare. But they let us go, and we thanked them for their kindness and continued on our way to find the Polish army.

We had no choice but to walk along the tracks. We hid ourselves in a hole we found near the tracks and waited for another train. We had no idea when it would come; we only knew the trains ran without a timetable. After a few hours, we finally heard the clacking of train wheels in the distance. The train slowed down and came to a stop. I shouted to Helen that we must run and jump inside the last wagon. We managed to make it inside the last wagon. When the train stopped again, we saw many Polish soldiers congregating. So we got out of the wagon and asked one of the Poles if this was the military headquarters. He said yes, it was here, but we had to queue up, because there were many people like us here. Meanwhile, the sun was going down, and we heard that the office of the Polish army headquarters was closing for the day. We were told they were not taking any more inquiries and to return in the morning.

So Helen and I looked for a place to spend the night. We looked around and saw a small animal stall. We went over, and it looked as if it would suit us just fine, it could be quite comfortable. When we went inside, a goat was staring at us. We didn't know what to do but decided to stay there for the night. We lay down on the ground. The goat remained standing and wouldn't take her eyes off us. We began stroking her lovingly and talking to her, and she slowly accepted our presence.

Helen whispered that the goat had a large udder, and this meant that she had milk. She told me to slide under the animal and open my mouth, and she would milk the goat. I did as she said, opened my mouth wide, and waited for the milk. Helen started to milk the goat's udder, but it did not cooperate. Not a drop of milk. We wondered why, because we felt the udder, and it was firm and swollen. We stroked the goat and tried again. This time, the milk flowed, and it squirted all over my face.

I asked Helen to slow the flow down and let me get closer

139

to the udder so I could fill my mouth with the milk. It tasted wonderful. We took turns drinking our meal of goat's milk. We had more milk than we expected, and for the first time in a very long time, we actually had full stomachs. We were able to lie down, cuddling each other, and the goat even joined us. We fell asleep contentedly.

In the morning, we woke up early. Neither Helen nor I felt well; we were both sick and had fevers. When I looked at Helen, I saw that she was covered with bugs. So I looked at myself and found that I was also. These bugs were lice, larger than the ones I knew in Siberia. I had never seen bugs like this. They had nasty-looking black crosses on their backs. Helen tried to joke, saying we should call them Racial Crusaders.

We decided to go back home as soon as possible. So we walked slowly to the area where the trains stopped and were blessed to find a train going in the direction of our settlement. We quickly got inside a wagon. I told Helen that we must try to stay awake on the train and not fall asleep, or we might miss our village. We just wanted to go home and nowhere else. We were both really ill; we were tired and did not learn anything about the military, but I consoled myself that at least we had more than our fill of goat milk. We got off the train in the vicinity of our settlement and slowly shuffled our way home.

Hospital Buajda

When I entered our hut, my parents looked at me and asked what had happened; they knew something was wrong with me. Just then, my eyes got dark, and I lost consciousness and fainted. Father immediately found an Uzbek with a camel and hired him to take me to the hospital. I briefly regained consciousness as they led me to the waiting camel, but I had no idea what was happening. The camel knelt down, and they put me between its humps and secured me so that I couldn't fall off. The Uzbek took up the leather reins and removed a leather water pouch. He gave me some water to drink, and I took a few sips. The camel got up, and we set off on the road to the hospital. I was dizzy, the whole world was spinning, and I lost consciousness again.

When I woke up this time, I found myself lying in a bathtub. I felt terrible. Above me were two nurses. One scrubbed me with soap and a brush, while the other cut my hair as close as possible to my scalp. The nurse who was cutting my hair laughed and said that if I were an Uzbek, no one would know how old I was after my haircut. I asked why. They explained that Uzbeks determined your age by weaving braids in your hair: one year for each braid.

They asked where I had been, so I told them I was in a stable, and that was why I was covered with lice. They commented that I was so dirty, they could plant turnips on me. They managed to scrape the dirt off of me, but with great difficulty. They gave me a clean hospital gown to wear and put me in a clean bed. I didn't remember the last time I had this luxury of lying in a bed between sheets and with a pillow under my head. Oh, how comfortable I felt. I could not believe how wonderful I was being treated, as I drifted off to sleep again.

A doctor came into the room to examine me. He said I had the symptoms of typhus and said there were many people there with the same symptoms. Before he left, he said he'd be back to talk to me again in a few days when I felt a little better. And in a few days, he did come to see me again and asked if we could talk. He asked me if he could ask some personal questions about my family being taken out of Poland. I explained to him how it was done. He sympathized with me and said he felt sorry about our situation. My story really moved him. He then told me about himself and his family. His father was a doctor in Poland, and several years ago, the Russians deported his family too. In the end, they settled here; his father founded the hospital and taught him to be a doctor.

Every morning, he brought me a sugar cube and a pita bread for my breakfast. The nurse gave me a bit of boiling water, and I even got soup for lunch. In the evening, I was given a few dry biscuits and kipiotek. Once, I had been so hungry, I only thought about food, but now, I just didn't care. I was sick, had a high fever, and was weak, and I didn't even want to eat. The doctor visited me and the other patients every day. He was tall and slim and looked at me carefully. I asked him to please bend down close to me so I could tell him something because I did not have the strength to sit up. He bent down close to me, and I thanked him most warmly for the wonderful care that he and the nurses were giving me. He said that many people were dying of typhus in the hospital but that I must recover. He brought me a bag of food every day and hid it under my pillow. This showed me I was one of his favorite patients.

There was another female patient in my room who was strong enough to walk around. She noticed the bag of food that the doctor placed under my pillow every morning. One morning, after the doctor left, she came over to my bed and grabbed my food. She knew that I saw her take my food, and I began to cry, as I was too sick to resist her and get it back. She was stronger than me and had no qualms about taking my sugar and pita bread; she ran away to eat it herself.

Time passed, and I slowly began to feel better and regain some strength. I could even take a few steps on my own, but only in my room The other patients on the same ward started calling me names because I had no hair, had sunken cheeks, and was as skinny as a rake, like a bag of bones. My skin was just hanging on me. They said I looked like a ghost. Eventually, I was strong enough to visit with other patients in the ward. I saw that they were distributing food to these patients. I saw one lady who was getting a pita bread. I was still so hungry; my appetite was returning, and I thought about stealing it from her. I walked up to her and could see that she was in such poor health. Then the memory of the woman who stole my food came flooding back to me. I looked at this woman's face, smiled at her, and stroked her head. I felt so sorry for her that even though I was starving, I could not bring myself to steal her food. I just didn't have the heart to do that to her. I told her that she had to try to get well. As I walked away from her, she looked at me with gratitude and smiled weakly, for she likely sensed that my intention was to steal her food.

The doctor still visited me and asked me to promise him that I would not leave the hospital without his permission. I didn't understand why he said this, but I promised him. On my last day in the hospital, he came to sign my release. Finally, I was free to leave. The doctor handed me a bag and told me to bring it home and share it with my family. I looked inside the bag and couldn't believe my eyes. It was filled with bread and sugar cubes. I thanked the doctor with tears in my eyes. I had no words to tell him that I was grateful for his care in bringing me back to life. We said goodbye to each other.

The rags I was wearing when I came to the hospital had been taken from me and laundered. I dressed in my rags and prepared to leave the hospital. I hid the bag of food inside my top so it wouldn't get stolen on my way home. Before I left the hospital, I asked the nurses how to get to my home. They told me that I must follow the train tracks and walk toward the sunrise to reach my settlement.

It felt strange leaving the hospital. My hair was starting to grow back, but it was still very short. It was so short, it looked like a man's crew cut. As I walked out of the hospital, my stomach told me I was hungry. I noticed a queue of people with basins and cups waiting for something, probably for some kind of food. For hungry people, bread is always on their mind. I saw an open door and wondered if someone was giving food to these people. I approached this door and saw that it was a small kitchen that belonged to the hospital. I saw them washing the pots that were used to prepare the lunch served to the patients, and they were giving out the liquid swill from washing these pots to the people in the queue. I was hungry too, so why not get into this lineup? I found an old tin can and grabbed it and lined up in the queue, along with the other starving people. I was hungry and so impatient that I could not wait to get some of this food. I had the bag of food from the doctor, but I had to be very careful not drop it. And I was extra careful not to draw attention to myself because I was afraid of theft. We moved at a snail's pace toward the kitchen. Finally, it was my turn. They rinsed out my can and poured a ladle full of swill into it. For a hungry person, even this was a luxury, and I was grateful to get it.

After drinking the swill, I started to make my way home. I was happy that I had a gift to bring to my family. I had not seen them for a long time; I hoped they were healthy. I didn't know how long it had been since I was brought to the hospital. When I got to the tracks, I started walking in an easterly direction, toward the sunrise, as I was told. But I became tired quickly, as I was not completely recovered. I walked for many hours, and my strength and energy were fading. The sun began to set, and I knew that before long, it would be dark. I walked slower now and knew that I would not be able to reach my family that evening. I had to find a place to stop and rest my head for the night, under the starry, moonlit sky.

I was surrounded by the darkness of night and did not know where I was. I saw a cemetery and decided to spend the night between some tombstones. I was not afraid because it was a rather bright night with a full moon, and I could see my shadow. I found a comfortable place between two family vaults and checked to see if there were any scorpions around. I lay down on the ground and said my prayers before I went to sleep. I also prayed for the dead people who were lying below me in the coffins. Then I felt tormented by thoughts of jackals and different beasts that could attack me. I didn't know how I could defend myself. I put this idea out of my head and instead thought about meeting my family again after such a long time. Eventually, I fell asleep.

I woke up as soon as it was daylight. I did not eat breakfast because I wanted to save this food for my family, especially for my younger siblings. I set off for home again, with different thoughts roaming around my head. I wondered what condition my family would be in when I arrived. I wanted to get there before the sun was above my head, at the greatest heat of the day. I walked along the tracks, and they seemed to never end. From time to time, I saw some huts, but mostly I saw sand dunes and lots of rocks. In the distance, I saw soaring peaks covered with white hats reaching for the sky. I was worried that I missed my settlement or maybe I was lost. Strange thoughts went through my mind. The sun was very hot and burned my skin painfully. My mouth was so dry I could not even make saliva. I was very thirsty.

Suddenly, an image appeared in front of me, something I never expected. In the distance, I saw a beautiful, tall tree, densely covered with leaves. It looked like a tall girl wearing a long, dark dress. Was it an illusion, a mirage, or did the tree actually exist? I found new strength and started running toward this mirage. As I got closer to this pleasant view, it appeared larger. As I approached the tree, I saw some animals under it. Getting even closer, I saw the animals were donkeys, and with them was an Uzbek man, sitting next to the trunk of the tree. I asked him for some water, and he pointed to the bucket from which the donkeys were drinking. Looking inside the bucket, I saw the water was quite clean and clear. I dipped my hands into the bucket and splashed my face with the pleasant, cool water. Because I was so tired and still weak from my illness, the water dripped onto my chest and breast, but I was careful not to get my hidden package wet.

The water was wonderfully wet and soothing. I drank a little and then splashed some onto my neck and face again. I looked at the Uzbek, and he burst out laughing. With a hint of a smile on my face, I asked him what was so funny. He replied that the desert climate would kill me because I was not used to it. I splashed my face and neck a little longer and sipped more of the water, and then I sat down in the shade to take a little break, to rest, and to get out of the constant blistering sun that was burning me. I asked him what kind of tree this was, and he said it was an acacia tree. After our brief conversation, I thanked the Uzbek for the water and for quenching my thirst and for regaining my strength, and then I continued my journey toward home.

When I looked back at the tree, I couldn't believe how a tree could grow like that in the middle of the desert. I walked for the rest of the day. The sun was getting lower and lower and losing its power. From a distance, I recognized our settlement and thanked God that he gave me the strength to return to my home safely.

Father Is Ill

As usual, there was no door to our hut, only a piece of cloth waving in the breeze. When I walked through the open doorway, the first thing I saw was Mother and my four small brothers, kneeling over my father. He was lying on the floor, and his body was swollen like a balloon. This sight frightened me terribly; it looked as though he was dying. They turned to look at me, and their expression was one of surprise, like they were looking at a ghost. After a brief exchange with Mother, I learned what I saw at first sight was true: Father was seriously ill. I was grateful that they were all alive because I did not know what I would find when I returned home. I was prepared for the worst, for anything and everything. After a brief conversation, I took the gift from the doctor from under my ragged blouse: the few biscuits, some dried-out bread, some pita bread, a few lumps of sugar, and even some candy. I said it was a gift from the doctor who saved my life. I gave it all to Mother and asked her to divide it among all of the family. Watching them made me happy, especially the reaction of the little ones; they were smiling with big grins on their faces, especially at the sight of candy.

The next day, we got up before sunrise, and I hurried to

the Uzbek with the camel and asked him to take my father to the hospital. He agreed to take him, and we slowly put Father onto the camel between the humps. Mother said she would not leave Father; she would accompany him. Her last words to me before she left with Father was that she would stay at the hospital to look after him until he recovered. She asked me to care for the little ones while she was away.

I fed the remains of yesterday's dinner to my younger siblings. I asked Josephine to go to get the flour while I went to look for work. We were still starving; I must help provide for our family with a little bit of extra food. We could not go around and beg for food or water because the locals didn't have anything themselves. I walked around, looking for work anywhere I could find it. Finally, an Uzbek hired me to help with his goats. I worked from sunrise to sunset, and my pay was one pita bread per day.

When I returned at sunset after working all day, my siblings demanded to visit our parents in the hospital. I explained to them that I would like that very much also, but it was not possible. We would have to go after my work at sunset, and the hospital was too far away. We could not afford for me to take any time off from my job.

My friend Helen brought me information about my father. She said he was in a very poor state and would probably die. Mother was very worried and was also experiencing the same health decline; she could not cope with Father's stay in the hospital. I did not tell the little ones about this situation, but it worried me. Different thoughts came into my mind about how we might cope with our lives here, especially if all I could earn was one pita bread a day. Even with only one pita bread a day and the flour we got from the office, we would survive. I knew I had to work all the time, as I was the only source of our food other than the flour. I just could not let us die.

Thief

After I came home from work, I cooked the usual flour with water. The little ones were so hungry, they were even crying. I gave them a little boiling water and sugar, saying they must wait for supper to cook. They wanted me to divide the pita bread that I brought from work. However, I put it on the shelf under the window and said we would divide it between ourselves for breakfast. I opened the window to ventilate the hut because it was so stuffy and smoky from cooking the flour and water. When the poliwka (flour with water) was ready, I divided it equally for the family. Because our parents weren't home, they all got a little bit more. We sat down quietly on the dirt floor, and after a quick prayer of thanksgiving, we started eating. (My father was going to become a priest until he met my mother and was very strict about praying before meals, even in Siberia, when the Russians were not around to witness our prayers.) The only sound was that of the scraping of the spoons on our metal plates and the loud slurping and smacking of lips as we devoured our meager meal.

Later that evening, I shared the sad news with my siblings about Mother and Father, trying to prepare them for the worst outcome. I told them people here were always getting sick and picking up many different diseases. Death was always all around us, and people were dying like flies. I shared my thoughts about how we would manage without our parents if they happened to die. They listened to me in silence, with horror on their faces. I tried to get them to share their feelings with me.

Suddenly, we heard a noise at the window. We looked over and saw someone's hand coming in through the window, stealing our pita bread. We started to shout and scream, and we jumped up and raced outside. I looked around, and even though it was dark, I saw the silhouette of a man running away with our pita bread. We ran after him, and I started shouting, "Karapczuk! Karapczuk!"

People came outside, curious about all the noise and commotion. I continued chasing him, knowing that if I did not catch up with the thief, we would be without food for breakfast. I saw the shadow of another person in front me, who was joining in the pursuit of the thief. It was the neighborhood NKWD. He yelled for the man to stop, pulled something from his belt, and started to swing it over his head. I recognized the object in his hand; it was a large knife called a *kitmen*. The little ones were left far behind while I continued the chase with the local NKWD.

He screamed that this was his last warning. The thief kept running. The officer threw the knife and hit the thief between his shoulder blades. The thief fell facedown; the chase was ended. The officer leaned over the man, pulled out the knife from between his shoulder blades, and turned the thief over onto his back. The captured Uzbek groaned in pain and cursed his fate. The officer shouted for someone to get a camel to take the wounded man to the hospital.

A curious crowd had gathered around us. The NKWD pulled the pita bread out of the thief's hand and gave it to me, asking how the thief stole the bread. I told him the whole story and said I was not angry at the thief. My siblings and I were just happy that we recovered the pita, for now we would have something to eat for breakfast, even if it was only one pita. Someone arrived with a camel, and the wounded thief was put on it and set off in the direction of the hospital. My siblings and I were relieved; we returned to our kibitki, and I tried to settle them down so they could go to sleep for the night.

Happy Day

Mother sent a message to us through Helen that she was recovering but would remain in the hospital to take care of my father. Even his condition was improving, but very slowly. Unfortunately, I now had a new problem: One after the other, the little ones had started to get sick. Helen came to visit us and said she must take them all to hospital or they would die. Now the whole family was in the hospital, except for me. I was alone in our hut.

I waited impatiently, counting the days until the little ones returned home again. Slowly, one by one, they all came back.

One night, I came home from work, and my siblings rushed toward me, shouting with joy that both our parents had returned from the hospital. I ran to our hut, threw back the curtain, and almost cried with joy at the sight of both my parents. Both Mother and Father, now in better health, were happy that after nearly a month of separation, we were together again. I was so ecstatic that for a long time, I could hardly take my eyes off them, just hugging and kissing them. I could not get enough of both my beloved parents.

The Lizards

As usual, we were going through terrible times of hunger; we were almost insanely hungry. I looked for work, but none was available. I decided to go hunt for turtles, as I did before with Chester. The place was easy to find, so off I went to get us some food. As I approached the area, I saw an Uzbek chase and catch an animal that was quite long. I watched with fascination as he grabbed it and quickly hit it on the head with a stone. I approached him and asked what kind of animal it was and what it tasted like. He explained that the animal was a lizard and told me the meat was delicious. The lizard was huge, about five feet long, and would be enough food for many meals.

I looked around and noticed a lot of lizard tracks all over the sand. It was as if someone had drawn patterns in the sand with a stick. I followed the footprints but lost the trail because of the rocks and boulders. There were plenty of nests for deadly scorpions, which I carefully avoided, knowing how dangerous and poisonous they were. When I looked up, there stretched out on a rock was a very long beast. Stunned, I stared at this handsome lizard basking in the sun, not paying any attention to me. I was afraid because it was so huge. But I was brave enough to approach it because of what I endured in Siberia. The lizard was so high up on the rock that if I fell, I would surely break my neck. But my stomach had been empty for so long that it drove out the fear.

Climbing slowly, I creeped toward the slumbering beast, quietly, almost imperceptibly, like a snake getting closer to its victim. I moved slowly on my belly. One more meter, and it would be mine. I accidently pushed a stone off the rock, whereupon the lizard heard the noise, leaped up, and ran away. I tried to chase it on top of these rocks but was not able to catch it. I had no shoes, and my legs hurt terribly. I was disgusted and discouraged, so I stopped for a rest.

The Uzbek laughed at me, saying I would never catch a lizard. When I asked him why, he said I needed to hunt it down like a wild animal. He told me I should be like a wild animal myself, looking for its prey; if I forced the lizard to go onto the sand, it would be virtually defenceless. He encouraged me to try again and to focus my attention on one lizard.

I looked for another and spotted one that was not too high up on the rocks. As I got closer to it, I tried to block its escape. I managed to get it to jump off the rocks onto the sand, where it waddled awkwardly, almost blindly. I could tell it was not capable of escaping from me in the sand. Adrenaline began running through me, and I raced over to the lizard, without even feeling my legs. I didn't see anything in front of me except for this huge lizard. I caught up with it and threw myself on top of it. I grabbed it, slid it underneath my body, and held its snout. Next, I looked for a stone to kill it. To my amazement, I saw a stone that the lizard uncovered with its thrashing tail. I used the stone to bang its head until it stopped moving. I actually killed it.

I looked at the lifeless lizard and was speechless, not believing that I was able to catch such a prize. My heartbeat slowly subsided. I caught my breath and heard someone behind me clapping. I looked up and saw the Uzbek, who was congratulating me on my successful hunt. He asked if I would like to work for him for a pay of one pita bread a day. I thought to myself that he was joking. Of course, I needed a job, but I preferred to catch these lizards for myself. I thanked him kindly for his offer, but I didn't accept this job.

My lizard was not that big, only about a meter long. I proudly carried my prey into our settlement while the neighbors looked at us with curiosity, asking where I got it. I walked into my hut, and Mother panicked; she was afraid of my bounty. My younger siblings watched as Father and I removed the skin and cleaned the insides. We put the meat into a bucket of water to clean it. Mother said we would have a delicious soup, but it would take a long time to cook. Finally, we got to eat our supper; the soup was absolutely delicious. We got a few pieces of meat with our meal.

Over supper, Mother started talking to Father about a man who died from a family of eight people and left five children behind. Then his children also died, quickly, one after the other. Father said this was nothing to be surprised about because there was so much dirt and so much hunger and so many diseases here.

After a few days, I went looking for another job, but as usual, there was no work available; no one was hiring. We were starving again. Finally, I decided to try to catch something for us to eat, perhaps a turtle or maybe even another lizard. The young ones were listening and asked if I would take them with me. They promised to behave themselves and be good and obey me so they wouldn't get hurt.

So we all set out together on a food hunt. We went to the same place where I caught the lizard; the little ones played and behaved well while I started hunting. After a while, they called me because they wanted to show me something. I asked them not to bother me, but they said they found something. So I walked with them, thinking they would show me a turtle. Instead, they took me to a place where something was buried in the sand, covered with stones. What I saw was a hoof sticking out of the sand. This really intrigued me, so we used our hands to uncover it. It was a freshly buried animal. I sent Chester and Fred to go get Father while I guarded the dead animal.

Father returned quickly with the children, almost running. When they reached us, they found we already uncovered the animal, which turned out to be a mule, a very large mule. After trying to pull it out of the hole, Father said that he could not do it alone and would go get two men to help him. In exchange for helping us, Father said he would give them some of the meat. When the men arrived, they look at the mule and said whoever buried it knew what they were doing because they didn't want wild dogs or coyotes to pull the mule out and tear it apart.

Father and the two men pulled the mule out and carried it to our settlement. They noticed the meat did not smell very nice, and in some places, it was even covered with foam. We attracted quite a few people in the settlement. They followed us like a procession, eyeing our mule, hoping they would be able to get a piece of the meat if it fell on the ground. When we reached our kibitka, the men got to work, tearing off the hide from the animal and dividing the meat among themselves. The poor people who followed us wanted to get even a small piece of the meat because they were starving, just as we were. Mother waited with a bucket of boiling water and declared that the meat was already rancid and would have to cook a very long time. We were so happy that we would get a piece of meat that we could hardly wait for it to cook. I was so impatient that I didn't care if it was raw. I turned around to see if anyone was looking and snuck a little tiny piece and swallowed it. It was quite tasty. Finally, the meat was cooked, and Mother divided it among us. We ate this mule meat and were so happy. We talked about how lucky we were to find this mule. When we finished eating, we fell asleep easily with full bellies.

In the middle of the night, I woke up with stomach pains so severe that I doubled over in pain. Mother tried to help me, but there was nothing she could do; she was helpless. The pain increased all during the night, and I didn't know if I would live to see morning. At dawn, I was still suffering, and I also had a high fever. Mother looked for a doctor and found a *wracza*, Uzbek for doctor. The woman doctor was reluctant to see me, but Mother begged her to come to save her daughter from death. Finally, the doctor agreed to look at me. She examined me and asked what I ate. I confessed that I secretly swallowed a piece of raw mule meat.

When Mother heard this, she started sorrowfully lamenting and asked me how I could do that. The doctor gave her some medicine for me, saying that the meat had poisoned me and it would take some time for me to recover. She also gave Mother some pieces of soap and some disinfectant. For many days, Mother did not leave my side, not even at night. She slowly helped me get back to health.

Sugar Beet

When I regained some of my strength back, I wandered around looking for work, but food was always on my mind. I wanted to eat so badly. The kids were also terribly hungry. I felt so sorry for my younger brothers and sister. I was interested in my family's well-being, so I even went outside the settlement through the desert sand and the rocks. As I looked in the distance, I saw something that was strange. There was a green color in this desert landscape, and this green was calling to me. Walking toward it with interest, I saw that I had come upon a field of sugar beets. I could not believe it: a whole field of sugar beets. They were wonderful and ready to be picked. I looked around, guessing that someone had to be keeping an eye on them. I considered coming back at night, but since I didn't see anyone around, I decided to bend down and try to pull one of them out, just a little one, at least one of the smallest. The earth was as hard as a rock, and I was still quite weak. I could not manage to pull out even a small beet. But I didn't give up. I began to wrestle with the beet, slowly loosening it from its grip in the soil. After it loosened up, I tore it out of the ground and flew backward, landing on my behind but holding the trophy in my hands. I looked at this sugar beet with astonishment; I couldn't believe that I had this prize in my hand. I raised myself up from the ground and got to my feet, with the sugar beet tucked under my arm.

Suddenly, I heard someone's voice yelling, "Karapczuk! Karapczuk!" Turning around quickly, I saw an Uzbek running in my direction. I knew what this meant, what this threat could mean to me. What to do? I had to make a decision right then. Should I throw the sugar beet away, flee empty-handed, and run for my life? Thoughts flashed through my mind, and I saw the NKWD throwing a knife into the back of the man who stole our pita bread. In a split-second, I decided to keep the sugar beet and started running. I ran as fast as my legs would carry me, with my trophy under my arm. I refused to give up.

I could hear his voice coming closer, still yelling, "Thief." I could tell he was catching up to me. With a surge of adrenaline, I ran even faster. I ran so fast that my heels were hitting my buttocks, but still he was getting closer and closer. Out of the corner of my eye, to my horror, I saw that he had a gleaming knife, a kitmen. I turned around and looked at him and saw that he was getting still closer. I broke out in a cold sweat from fear, but I had to keep running, even though he was still getting closer. I knew that stealing was punishable by death, and I remembered again the thief who stole our pita bread, who was stabbed with a kitmen by the NKWD.

Still, I did not want to give up. I used all my strength and continued running for my life. I was certain he would kill me, but I refused to give up. My heart was thundering in my chest. The Uzbek was on my heels. What to do? Where to run? I was sure he would kill me. I prayed to God and asked him to give me enough strength to get home. Only my father could save me, but could I reach our kibitka before my pursuer killed me?

I could see our kibitka. What gave me hope was that there

was no door, only a rag covering the entrance. I tore the rag away from the doorway as I ran inside and threw the sugar beet in the corner. I fell to the ground with my heart pounding wildly. My chest felt as though it had needles in it. My lungs felt like they would explode. I could not get any air into my lungs. I was gasping for air. I tried to shout for Father to save me but could not utter a single word; no sounds came from me.

The Uzbek came flying inside our kibitka right behind me, and Father realized in a moment what was happening. He began to beg the Uzbek to forgive his daughter. Mother picked up the sugar beet and handed it back to him. But he did not want to hear any of this. He demanded justice and said the penalty for theft was death. He was swinging the kitmen in the air and shouting, "Karapczuk."

Mother was crying, trying to defend me. Father spoke to the Uzbek in Polish and in Russian, asking for forgiveness for me. They could not communicate with each other. The Uzbek continued to jump up and down, screaming, "Thief," and waving the big knife around, demanding justice. He wanted to hurt me. Father finally got down on the ground, kneeling before the Uzbek, and begged for my life. The Uzbek cooled off a little and looked around, demanding that Father give him his hat. Father was bald; he did not like this proposition because without his hat, he could get sunstroke. The Uzbek got mad again and started screaming, "Karapczuk." Father took his hat from his head and gave it to him without a word. Mother handed him the sugar beet. The Uzbek took Father's hat and the sugar beet and left. Mother, talking through her tears, helped me up and said she would rather die of starvation than go through this kind of experience again.

In the evening, Mother called us to supper. We were more than starving. She divided the poliwki between us, giving us larger portions, saying that she received a larger portion of flour. We eat without complaining, for this was our fate.

As darkness approached, we went to sleep, but we were still hungry. We lay on the bare ground next to one another. I could not sleep. Mother and Father got up; apparently they could not sleep, either. They started to discuss something; I tried to listen but could not hear what they were talking about. Maybe they were praying, but as I tried to listen to them, I realized it was a normal conversation. They walked up to us children and looked at us. I got a different idea. Maybe they were deciding what they were going to do with us. Or maybe they are talking about our future. Or possibly they were talking about our food.

Since I was the oldest and the largest, even though I was just a bag of bones, I still had the most meat on me. Perhaps I should talk to Father about preparing me as he did that dog who wandered into our kibitka. They would be able to have some food, if even for a few days. Thus they could manage to live a little longer, and maybe in the meantime, some help would come. In the end, I fell asleep.

Hungry, Starving Vultures

From day to day, we were barely alive. We didn't know if we would be alive tomorrow. I woke up in the morning starving and told my younger brother Fred that I was going to the market. He asked if he could come with me, and I said okay. So we left together. It was still very early, barely dawn and cold. We walk along, always looking for something to eat, some weeds or roots growing. But in the desert, there was only sand and rocks. There was nothing growing in this desert.

We got to the marketplace, and it was hustling and bustling. Many people were moving around, looking for goods The crowds of customers and merchants made it very loud. The merchants spoke in many languages, trying to outshout one another. I understood some of the Russian and Uzbeki language, but other languages were completely foreign to me. We smelled the aroma of roasted lamb and other tasty dishes. I told Fred that he should breathe in these scents, so we could fill our stomachs with the smells. We passed by sellers who were sitting on the ground with large, colorful mounds of fruit, vegetables, spices, salt, and animal dung rounds. We saw some people drinking chai and eating meals of fruit, bread, vegetables, and lamb. We hoped maybe one of them would throw away a rotting piece of meat, vegetable, or fruit, but no.

As Fred and I walked along the rows of stalls, we saw that they were full of carpets, bolts and bales of material, and a variety of pots, pans, and dishes. The merchants encouraged us to buy their goods as we passed them by. We got to the area of milk and goat cheese. Now our mouths watered as we looked at the food. We saw other people sampling the cheese and milk, and we hoped to get a taste of some of it too. However, we were dressed so shabbily that we were chased away many times. But we were so hungry that we persisted, praying for just a morsel of food to put in our empty stomachs.

I decided to pretend that before I bought some cheese, I must sample it. We found a merchant who gave us a piece of cheese, and I shared it with Fred; he winced cleverly and claimed that it was too sour. We tried another piece, and Fred said it was too dry. We asked for a little bit of water to drink to swallow the sample. We kept trying this as we move onward, asking for more samples until we reached the end of the dairy stalls. But every moment, we were ready to make a run for it because we may be chased away.

As the delicious stalls ended, we come to the bolts of fabrics and materials. The Muslim women, with veils covering their faces, tried to tempt me with their pretty fabrics to buy some to make a dress for myself because they saw I was dressed in ragged clothes. We returned to the dairy stalls, but in a different lane this time, and asked for samples again. We spent the whole day at the market and still didn't have enough samples to fill our stomachs. On top of that, we were fatigued by the overwhelming noise, the crowds that were pushing and shoving, and the heat. I told Fred that it was time to go back home, and he agreed.

We walked through the sand and rocks, with the sun slowly setting. We dragged our feet as we walked slowly. We were so tired and numb from this hunger that I didn't even care what was happening with us. Fred looked up at the sky and pointed out some birds circling overhead. I lifted my head and saw that the birds circling above us were vultures. I explained to Fred we had to be careful, because they were also hungry and probably wanted us for supper. Fred told me not to make jokes like that.

We walked bravely ahead, glancing occasionally at the sky and seeing that the birds were still following us. And not only following us, but they were circling lower and lower. That was now starting to worry me. I knew that we were very weak, and they were voracious and determined. I did not want them to attack us because we could not defend ourselves; they would tear us apart. I didn't want to show Fred how worried I was. I told him he should be prepared to try to catch one of them by its legs; it could be our supper.

We walked farther and farther along through the sand and rocks. Once in a while, we passed some small, dry, and prickly trees without any leaves. As many times as I had walked along here, I couldn't believe I had never noticed these trees. Fred asked if we could stop and rest for a little while. We came up to a tree, and I checked it for scorpions, which like to nest in such places. We slid under the thorny branches, hoping that they would protect us from the hungry vultures. Fred immediately fell asleep. I lay still and watched the sky with the circling birds. I realized if one of the vultures dared to come after us, we could not defend ourselves; we were exhausted, starved, and dying from hunger. We were deprived of energy and strength and could not defend ourselves. I determined to stay awake and watch these birds and asked God for protection and mercy. But in no time, my eyes grew heavy, and I fell asleep too.

All of a sudden, I woke up and found it was dark and cold. I didn't know how long we were sleeping. I woke Fred up, and he immediately asked about the vultures. I told him they left us and probably went off to sleep. We slid out from under the little tree and went on our way, traveling as fast as we could in the moonlight. It was so bright on these sands that it reminded me of white Siberian snows during our enslavement there. I wanted freedom, but I was reminded of what my grandmother used to say: "We have jumped from the frying pan into the fire." At least there, I could earn some extra food and some clothing, but here? We were so poor that starvation and poverty screamed at us. Finally, Fred and I reached our settlement and entered our kibitka. Mother was so worried; she was crying and asked us where we had been all day, thinking we could have been harmed.

Protect Your Children

One evening, as the sun went down, my mother was visited by one of her girlfriends. She was carrying a bundle wrapped with a tattered piece of cloth. They stood in a corner, whispering to each other. I tried to listen to them but didn't understand what they were saying. She was showing Mother some beautiful meat. Food! Now, I understood what this was all about. I could not take my eyes off them. To my surprise, Mother began to shy away, but her friend stubbornly pushed the bundle into her hands, forcing her to accept her gift. Mother did not want anything to do with it, but her friend raised her voice, trying to force her to take it.

The woman started to cry; with tears running down her face, she shouted, "Save your children." As I listened, the woman told my mother this meat would have to be buried in the ground, and certainly it was better to help someone with it. The two of them were distraught. I listened to them with bated breath; finally, in the end, Mother accepted the bundle, and the woman and Mother hugged each other. Soon, her friend left.

I asked Mother what that was about, but she did not answer me. As she opened the bundle, she looked so sad. I went over to her and looked at the beautiful, beautiful meat. I asked Mother again what it was about, but she still did not answer me. She loaded the fire pit, put a bucket of water on it, and placed the meat into the bucket to boil. In the meantime, she gave our family a ladle of poliwka to fill our stomachs.

As we waited for the rest of the supper, Mother regained her composure enough to start telling us a story about a tragedy that had happened to our neighbors. I asked which neighbor. She reminded us of the man who had a swollen stomach that looked like a balloon because he was starving from hunger. I remembered the man. Father tried to help him and his family, but we were starving as well and had no food for ourselves. We did help them, but only on rare occasions. The man's wife died a month ago, the son went into the army, and he was left with a five-year-old daughter named Christine.

Father shared a story about when he visited a friend and was told that his wife had died and now his last child had also died. He was left all alone and told Father he did not want to live anymore. He was so overwhelmed with grief at his loss and this way of existing, he felt his life was over without his family and the constant starvation.

Finally, the supper was ready, and Mother divided the meat between us. But I was very suspicious about the meat. I had a difficult time biting and chewing it. Everyone except for Mother was eating this meat that was so delicious. Mother was hungry, and yet we had to get through these times. We were all afraid to ask about the source of this meat.

After supper one night, Mother was talking with another one of her friends when they heard a shrill cry from Christine. They went to see what was happening and found the tear-stained girl, kneeling by the body of her dead father. They tried to calm her down, but they ended up calling the commissary. The commissary came and took her dead father away to the mortuary. She was so heartbroken that they had a difficult time trying to separate her from her father. I asked Mother if we could take the poor girl with us, but she explained that the Uzbeks had already taken her and would raise her. I felt so sorry and sad for Christine because I knew that she would always stay here and never leave this country.

Grinding the Wheat

I usually woke up early in the morning and left in search of work. I walked from one Uzbek farm to another. Eventually, I came upon a farm, where I saw piles of grain. Something told me this would be my job. And I was right. The Uzbek needed help to grind and mill the grain. He asked me if I had ever done this kind of work. With full confidence, I lied and said yes, but I did not know quite what this job was. He showed me how the seed grain must be spread on the ground, and a donkey was harnessed to a post in the center of a circle, making him go round and round, grinding the grain with its hoofs. The donkey had to be beat with a whip to keep it going round and round because it was hungry too. From time to time, it stopped and tried to eat the grain, then I had to stop him and use the whip to force him to keep going. It was difficult because the donkey wanted to eat the grain and was stubborn. I worked from sunrise to sunset. I tried to put a few grains in my bosom, but fear overwhelmed me, because I knew that if anyone saw me, the NKWD would be called, and I would be in big trouble.

My pay for working with the Uzbek was one pita bread per day. I was as hungry as a starving dog. I would have liked just a tiny little bite of this pita bread, but I would not be tempted. I had to share it with my family. As I walked home at sunset, I was on a different pathway, not my usual route. I came upon a field of dark bushes. It was a clear moonlit night, and I could see clearly. When I walked, I looked closer. I could not believe my eyes. I saw vines literally laden with big clusters of fruit. I plucked a few and put them into my mouth. They were grapes. But the acid was so strong that it made me pucker up and twist my mouth out of shape. I took it as a good sign because they were not ripe. This made me think no one was watching them. I quickly plucked a bunch, hid them under my clothes, and rushed home.

I managed to get home without anyone chasing me. I gave Mother the pita bread and the bunch of grapes and the few grains that I stole. We were very happy, rejoicing because we had some food now. Mother divided the bread and grapes among the family and then threw the grains into the poliwki. We ate the supper with much enjoyment. I watched the little ones shake and shudder as they ate the sour grapes. Mother and I agreed that we would go to gather more of the sour grapes after supper. We started walking on this clear moonlit night and easily found the grapevines. Mother could not believe how many of the goodies were hanging on the branches. Mother filled her scarf, and I threw a few bunches in my bosom and put some in my mouth. Mother saw me doing this and said I might be eating some bugs on the dirty grapes. We had all the grapes we could carry, so we happily returned to our impatiently waiting father and little ones, without anyone seeing us.

The next day, early in the morning, I rushed to work and walked the donkey around in the circle to grind the grain. I had to keep whipping the stubborn animal. The only break I got was when I swept and picked up the trampled grain and flour. The owner always checked on me and the donkey. Occasionally, he disappeared for a short while. This gave me an opportunity to hide a few grains in my bosom. At sunset, the Uzbek gave me my one pita bread for my day's work and said that tomorrow, I would begin to grind the rice.

When I looked around at his yard in the back, I saw a round oven where the Uzbek woman baked their bread. She took pieces of dough and threw them so they stuck to the wall or ceiling of the oven. After it baked in the oven for only a few minutes, the woman took browned, fragrant pita breads out and put them aside. She noticed me watching her. She looked at me with compassion and with a good heart handed me one of the breads. I took it and thanked her and hid the bread in my bosom. I wasn't sure what the owner would say about this, but I rushed home happy because we would have extra food for supper, a second pita bread.

When I reached our kibitka, the little ones immediately surrounded me, shouting that Mother was very ill. She was laying on the ground. I asked Father what happened, but he said he didn't know. I could see that the supper had not been prepared yet. I asked what happened to the food. They told me some boy ripped the flour out of Josephine's hands when she went to get it from the office.

Flour Thief

I asked Josephine to tell me what happened. She said that after I left for work, Mother woke up but could not get up. She told Father she was very sick. She gave the flour voucher to Josephine and sent her to get the flour. She warned her several times not to lose the voucher because if she did, we would not have any food that day. She got the bag of flour, and on the way back, she noticed an older boy following her. She kept looking over her shoulder and saw he was still following her. When she started to run home, the boy attacked her. He tore the bag of flour out of her hands, pushed her to the ground, and took off running. When she fell, she hit her head on a rock and fainted. When she came to, there were four women standing next to her, asking if she was in pain. She told them that her head was hurting terribly from falling down on the rock. They took her immediately to Mother; one of the women told Mother she actually saw the whole incident and watched the strange boy run away. Feeling sorry for Josephine, I tried to comfort her and said that we couldn't do much about it. I divided up the pita bread and started to boil some water, tossing in the few grains I had hidden in my bosom.

While eating supper, Father shared a story about a family

who had eight people who all died, except for the mother. But that day, he found out that even the mother died. I asked Father what kind of life this was. We were surrounded with starvation and death. People were dying all around us, dropping like flies. I asked him if he had heard any information about my brother Tony, but he said no. Were we doomed to spend the rest of our lives like this?

Mother slowly recovered. Over the next few days, I worked for the Uzbek, grinding rice into flour. I earned the same pita bread wage per day and regularly snuck a few grains of rice to take home. But what were a few grains in a family as large as ours? Father said he had enough of our living conditions. He said he didn't know what was happening or what the authorities were waiting for. He considered going to the Polish army offices. He decided that we must get out of there, somehow. We went to sleep hungry, and I thought to myself, *This is probably the end of us.* I figured we were probably going to die.

Polish Army Headquarters

In the morning, Father said he was going to look for the Polish military headquarters. He wanted to find out if they could help us. He asked me to go with him because I had been there once before and knew the way. He said that we might find out something about Tony, and perhaps they would give us something to eat. I agreed to go with him, but I reminded him that when I was there with Helen, we went by train. I asked him if he could manage to jump onto a moving train. He said that he was too weak, and we would have to go by foot. We set out toward the railroad tracks; I said the tracks would take us straight to the Polish military headquarters.

As we walked, it felt as though we had been walking for hours, and we were so tired and thirsty, barely able to continue under this hot, hot sun. We met an Uzbek with a camel and asked him for some water. He took off his *miszok* (leather pouch with water) and told us to drink the water very slowly, in small sips. We were so thirsty, if we drank too much, we would get sick. Father then asked the man if he would be kind enough to give us a ride on the camel for a part of our journey. The Uzbek surprisingly agreed; he got the camel to kneel down and helped us to climb between his humps. We set out, and the camel was rocking slowly back and forth, almost rocking us to sleep. It was so relaxing, and the rocking was so pleasant that we were able to rest. We rode the camel for quite a distance, with the sun beating on us and burning our skin. We were thankful for the good rest we had. The camel stopped, and the Uzbek said it was the end of our ride because he was going on in another direction. He was so very kind and did not even want any money. He pointed us in the direction we must go to reach the army headquarters.

Father and I continued to walk, and eventually, we saw the headquarters. As we approached our destination, we saw rows of people lying on the ground, covered with thousands of flies. Clouds of flies hovered above the people; some people were lying in pools of blood. Father said these people were likely suffering with bloody dysentery. We could plainly see they were ill; their lips were parched and cracked from the heat from the sun, and many were delusional with fever. Some begged desperately for help or a few drops of water. Some were so weak and helpless, they didn't even have the strength to utter a word; we were not even sure whether they were dead or alive. Some of them were lying not just in pools of blood but also in human waste. My heart broke for them. As much as I would like to help them, I could not; we did not have any food or water to give them. We were barely alive ourselves. I was struck by fear, my imagination running wild. As I saw my family lying in front of me, right there on ground, tears streamed down my cheeks. Father shook me and asked me what was wrong, why was I crying. I could not answer him.

Father made me take hold of his arm as we walked on. There were Polish soldiers in front of the headquarters, and I was so happy to see them. I listened to them talk and was totally surprised at how some of them complained about their provisions, saying they were very poor and they too were suffering from hunger. We went inside, and they could see that we were poor and ragged. They immediately gave us some water and something to eat.

Father asked about Tony, but they didn't know anything about him. They said that here in Uzbekistan, many soldiers were dying from exhaustion, starvation, and widespread disease. Father talked for a long time with an officer. I heard Father asking them for a departure permit from this country. We were a military family, after all, and we had that right. He showed them the spišská from the commander in Siberia, where it was written that his son, Tony, left for the army. He asked them to check the military documents to see if he registered. Father claimed he must be there somewhere in the army and demanded that we be allowed go anywhere, as long as it was not here; otherwise, we would surely die.

After listening to us, the officer, whose name was Andrew, asked if we saw the people lying on the ground in front of the building. He explained that thousands of people were waiting to leave this country, and everything must be done in secret because this was Russia.

After that, I asked him for help, crying and begging for compassion. He had mercy on us and said he would try to issue the paperwork for our departure. He could not promise us anything. However, he gave us a bag of dried-out bread and a little bit of food and said that we needed to come back in two weeks.

We returned home and told Mother about our experience at the Polish headquarters. She divided the dried bread and rations so we'd have enough for the two weeks we had to wait. A little bit of this bread, along with the usual poliwki, and that was our food for the day. In the morning, I started looking for a job again, hoping that I would not have to work too much longer. Of course, no one wanted to hire me. The days were getting longer, but time just seemed to drag. I could hardly wait for the two weeks to pass.

Finally, the time came for us to return. Father and I walked to the army headquarters, hoping that we would get good news. As we approached the headquarters, we saw that it was exactly the same, no change. People were still lying as they were. We went inside and waited in a huge crowd of people for our turn.

Finally, Officer Andrew called us. He said he remembered us very well, adding that I had enchanted him. He had hopes that we would meet again, after our departure from this place but under more pleasant circumstances. With a friendly smile on his face, he said that everything had been taken care of, and it was now okay to leave the country. He gave Father the papers and some food rations. He explained that our evacuation was not yet organized. When we left, we would search for our way as if we were blind. He quietly gave us mysterious instructions, saying that tonight, we were to go south until we reached the main asphalt road. There, we'd meet some soldiers who would take us to Tashkent. He continued to tell us we must not talk about our departure to anyone and to make sure we left after dark. No one must see us. He explained that if anyone learned of this, it would be a terrible problem for the army because everyone would want to leave.

We thanked him a hundred times and promised to keep this secret. Father and I walked back to our kibitka as fast as we could in the scorching heat to share with the family the good news that we were finally leaving this place. What intrigued me was, where would we go, and what was awaiting us? Once before, we jumped out of the frying pan into the fire. This was supposed to be our freedom. I asked Father what his thoughts were about this, and at first, he didn't answer me. Eventually, he said he didn't have the faintest idea.

Walking Blindly

When we finally reached our kibitka, Father went to Mother and whispered that we had permission and the paperwork to leave immediately, this night. We rejoiced about our freedom, but only in our hearts, not openly, as we had to keep this a secret from our neighbors. We began to prepare for our departure after dark. We packed our bundles. It did not take long, as we had very little: only a few pots, some ragged clothes, leftover food, and the pictures of Mary and Jesus. The little ones didn't understand what was going on, but we were compelled to keep our departure a secret. We didn't tell them anything.

We lay on the ground early to rest and gather some strength before beginning our journey. My heart swelled with joy that we were leaving. Everyone fell asleep, but my thoughts about leaving were scrambled. I could not get these thoughts out of my head, nor could I imagine what would happen to us. I wondered where we would go and what was ahead.

We got up while it was still dark. Mother cooked a little poliwki and divided it among us. This would be our last meal in this kibitka. Father prayed before we ate, giving thanks for the nourishment and asking for God's guidance and intervention; when we left here, we would be free at last. He also asked God to help with our future and prayed that we would no longer suffer the problems we had here. I looked around at our hut, knowing that I went through so much here that I would surely never forget this place.

After we ate, I helped Mother wash the pots and pack them along with the last of our belongings. We left quietly. It was after midnight and quite chilly but bright. A full moon illuminated our path. We left our kibitka in haste, not looking back. The little ones were sleepy and started to complain about having to walk outside in the chilly night; they wanted to lay down and sleep.

We heard the sound of an approaching vehicle. It was a two-wheeled Asiatic cart pulled by a donkey. There was an Uzbek sitting on the cart, and we asked him for a ride. He looked us over, felt pity for us, and, after a short conversation, agreed to give us a ride. We loaded ourselves into the cart, and the gentle swaying and rocking was so soothing, it put the little ones to sleep. I could see that my parents were also starting to get heavy eyes. I tried to be vigilant and keep an eye on the road to make sure we were going in the right direction.

We soon came to a stop, and I wondered if this could be the end of the ride so quickly. I thought I must have fallen asleep too and did not realize it. The Uzbek said we had been traveling for three hours and now he would be changing direction, so we had to get out of his cart. He showed us which direction we were to go and advised us to watch the moon. I got down from the cart and woke up the little ones, while Mother and Father got down and gathered our belongings.

I did not know where we were going, but we did as the Uzbek told us, looking at the moon to get our direction. There was no one in sight, no cars or trucks in any direction. It was beginning to get light, and as I looked around, all I saw was desert: just sand and rocks. Far, far away, I saw a mountain range. Finally, we came to the main road and were filled with hope that our soldiers would soon come and lead us away. So we just settled there in the open air and waited.

Later in the morning, we started to walk again. The sun started to burn us, so we tried to protect ourselves from the scorching heat by covering ourselves with some of our ragged clothing. Even the asphalt was getting hot from the sun and started to melt. Despite this, I felt calm and relaxed. Each of us shared the load of carrying our belongings with our last ounce of strength.

Walking along in this intense heat, we felt we were finished. We had no energy left to continue. Mother fainted, and as we waited for her to revive, the rest of us were falling down or sitting or lying on the ground from sheer exhaustion. We were barely walking as the day came to a close. We carefully put our belongings beside the road, making sure we did not disturb any insects, spiders, or scorpions. We decided to spend the night next to the asphalt road. The air grew cooler, but the sand was still warm, and we slept on this warm sand. Everyone fell asleep. I prayed to God, looking upwards into the sky. It was a clear night, and the moon was bright. I fell asleep before I finished my prayers.

All of a sudden, Mother was in a panic and started to scream. Chester was missing; he was nowhere in sight. We all woke up, and Father asked us to look for him. We started looking and heard Father shout he found him. We ran in the direction of the scream and saw Father calling out to Chester, but Chester walked away as though he didn't hear us calling him. He was sleepwalking.

Father grabbed him and shook him to wake him up. As Chester woke up, he was confused and didn't know what was happening to him or why we were all around him, calling his name. We let out a sigh of relief, returned to our resting spot near the road, and lay down again. Mother and Father discussed Chester's sleepwalking; no one wanted to go back to sleep. It was still dark, but we could tell that it would soon be daybreak. Father asked all of us to get up so that we could have a quick breakfast before we started to follow the road again.

Daybreak was soon upon us, and the sun came up from behind the mountains, casting huge shadows. We were cold and shivering, covering ourselves with the thin blankets that were given to us by the commandant in Siberia. As we walked along, we started complaining because we didn't know what was awaiting us. The sun slowly rose, and we felt its warmth. We finally got warm. We could barely walk, just skeletons, skinny tramps. And the sun, the unrelenting heat from the sun, was burning us without mercy, draining the very last of our strength. Mother was almost crying; she could not walk another step. Father walked to the side of the road and sat down, and the rest of us followed him, happy to get some rest. We had only a little water, and Father said we could only take small sips because we had to save it. We didn't know how long we'd have to wait there.

From a distance, we saw people ahead of us sitting on the side of the road; we thought they were resting. We decided to walk closer to them and saw that they were indeed resting. I counted five of them: three children and two adults. We sat down next to them for a short while to rest. My parents started talking to the adults and learned they were given the same instructions as we were. We all got up and started walking together. After several hours, we met up with a man sitting all alone by the side the road. Being very tired, we all sat down next to him. He explained to Father that his oldest son went into the army, and the rest of his family, his wife and seven of his children, died. He said he did not want to live any longer and did not know what to do. But since he had the same instructions, Father felt compassion for him and asked if he would like to come along with all of us. He agreed to join us.

Some of the little ones were now feeling sick, whining and complaining, and the other little ones played in the sand beside the asphalt road. Suddenly, one of the younger ones started yelling that he could see something in the distance. Everyone got up to their feet, wanting to see what he was looking at. We went out onto the hot asphalt road and saw something in the waves of heat above it. Something large was fluttering and bouncing, traveling toward us. We recognized it as an army truck. Could it be our soldiers?

We jumped up and down, waving our arms and yelling with happiness while both my parents cried. This really was an army truck. It pulled up and stopped beside us, and two Polish soldiers got down from the cab. Everything grew quiet except for Mother, who was crying from happiness and praising God for answered prayer. Father asked if they could take us to the Polish army headquarters in Tashkent. He also asked if they knew Tony. He said that Tony registered with the Polish army, and he was certain he was in Tashkent. They looked at each other as we waited anxiously for them to answer, but they said no, they did not know him and had not heard of him. We were disappointed. They explained to us that Tony could be in Karaganda or in a different city.

They checked the spišská from the Siberian commandant and the documents from Officer Andrew from the Polish army headquarters in Kokanda. They said they would take us to Tashkent; the army was forming there, and many people were gathering there to leave Uzbekistan. They had rescued us. Now we would not get lost or die out there in this desert. They helped us into the back of the tall military truck, and we settled ourselves in and tried to get comfortable for another leg of our journey. We soon arrived at the headquarters in Tashkent.

We saw many poor people dying of starvation and many soldiers milling around. The truck stopped, and the driver came back to warn us that Tashkent was a city of thieves and people who were up to no good. They told us to be very careful and constantly be on guard in every situation and at all times. Father smiled wryly, explaining we did not have anything to steal. We said goodbye to the soldiers and headed to the Polish army headquarters. I was reminded of the same scene I saw before in Kokanda: rows of people lying in the dirt, in puddles of blood, and huge swarms of flies circling above their heads. Many were delirious, begging for help or even a spoonful of water. They were shaking from fever and had no strength to speak above a whisper.

All of us entered the building and were led down a hallway to a large room. Kipiotek was ready, and they invited us to have a cupful and a few pieces of dried bread to strengthen ourselves. Father talked to some of the soldiers, and they said there was a delegation of Polish emigration set up in Tashkent. As Father talked to them, he asked out of curiosity why the Polish soldiers had English uniforms. It turned out that the English army was supplying the Polish army with uniforms.

Leaving for the Port

The soldiers informed us we would be spending the night at this office before being transferred to the port of Krasnovodsk on the Caspian Sea. From there, a ship would sail to Pahlevi in Persia (Iran). They gave us a light supper, which was a cup of soup, a couple pieces of dried bread, and some hot water. We lay down to sleep, and my heart was full of happiness, although my head was all mixed up and full of curiosity about the future. Outside, the sick people were making loud noises and moaning. I could not fall asleep. The night seemed very long to me. We were incredibly excited that tomorrow, we would be free from the clutches of the Soviet nightmare.

The early morning hours brought great confusion. People bustled about, collecting their belongings; the children were hungry and crying. Everyone eagerly waited for transport out of here, causing even more confusion. They gave us breakfast, which was the same as we had last night: soup, dried bread, and hot water. We heard a voice coming from the front doorway, telling us to gather our belongings and line up outside, where our transport was already waiting for us. I didn't have the patience to wait. We rushed to pick up our bundles and leave the building. We waited outside in a long, curving lineup.

Some of the people left in trucks, and other empty trucks pulled up, one after another, to pick us up. We were loaded into the army trucks; the poor and the beggars were being taken away. A convoy was forming, and it was becoming longer and longer. They said we would be leaving in a short time. Our travel was expected to last a week. The trucks were each supplied with two military drivers, one on each side of the truck cab. The trucks stopped only once a day, in the evening, to rest and for supper. They fed us soup and bread, and we slept on the bare ground.

As we traveled, we passed through different villages, towns, and oases. The drivers told us we were getting close to Samarkand, Uzbekistan. They explained that a hundred years ago, it was a huge oasis, and now it was a beautiful city. Traveling farther, we could see the Pamiru Mountains on the border with Turkestan, known as the "roof of the world." These mountains were made of granite and were so huge and stately that they reached above the clouds into the sky. Traveling across the Kara-Kum Desert and getting closer to the Caspian Sea, the landscape changed, and everything looked white, like snow. They said it was white because of the sea salt, which was deposited on the ground from the sea. The air was full of the smell of oil, which became more and more unbearable. It was so saturated with oil that I felt nauseous. The soldiers laughed and called the oily smell the Russian perfume of Krasnovodsk.

From far away, we could see Krasnovodsk was a huge city, a Russian port on the Caspian Sea. Traveling through a part of the city, we headed to the port itself. As far as the eye could see, we saw thousands of Polish people, some in our same condition but many looked even worse than us. We got down out of the trucks.

It was so hot and humid, we could barely breathe. I felt as though I was in the underworld in this crowd of thousands of people. The ghastly stench from wasting human bodies and of filth was overpowering. Many of them were lying on the ground. Here, too, a lot of people were dying from malaria, typhoid, dysentery, and other diseases. Human dirt was everywhere, and swarms of flies spread even more disease. I watched soldiers load corpses into trucks and take them away. I could no longer look at the dying people. What a sad scene when families held onto their loved ones, not wanting to part with their dead. There were lots of tears, and many were praying. Many people told us about their experiences and exchanged memories with new friends they encountered.

Seeking refuge from this scene, I walked toward the water. I wanted to splash around and bathe in the sea, but it was very dirty and full of oil that floated on the surface of the water. I returned to where my family was and asked someone what they thought they would do with us. Father talked to some of the soldiers and found that the war with Germany and Russia caused terrible shortages of food for Uzbeks, the Poles, and the Russians themselves. We looked around and saw thousands of Polish soldiers roaming all over the city. They said they belonged to General Anders's Second Corps, and they were also waiting for a ship. They complained about the poor food. They said many adults, children, and even soldiers already died from hunger and starvation. Death did not choose; it had no favorites. Father explained that because of the war, Russia had such a lack of food, it was not able to feed the Poles in Uzbekistan. The Russians had to agree to allow the Poles and their families to leave the country where we were held captive to go to Pahlevi because of the shortage of food. But most importantly, our promised freedom was waiting for us on the other side of the sea, in Persia.

Soldiers made us stand in queues to register before we

were allowed to board the ship to freedom. They checked our documents to be certain we were on the passenger list. We moved in this lineup at a snail's pace in the direction of the ship. I could see they were carefully checking each person's documents and registration Finally, we got to a table and were very nervous. There were three high-ranking NKWD officers sitting at the table, checking the list of prisoners, deciding whether to let someone board the ship or not. My heart beat like crazy with fear. They could deny us the right to sail. Thankfully, after they checked our documents, a soldier showed us the way to go to board the ship. We headed toward some high, steep stairs. They led to a huge cargo ship flying the Russian Soviet flag. I looked up, and a shiver ran down my back; my hair stood upright, and I didn't know if it was a joke or a trap. Our ship to freedom was called the *Stalin*. We continued climbing the stairs, and when we got to the main deck, we were told to walk to the back of the ship. Here, we were given kipiotek and some dried bread. I watched many soldiers helping and sometimes carrying the weak and sick up the steep stairs. Some of the soldiers themselves climbed aboard and disappeared among the people.

Night fell, but no one slept. There was a lot of sickness and loud complaining, as well as discussions about the future. After being in port for four days, I went out on the deck at sunrise and looked over the side. The lineup of people getting on board was shorter. When Father came to join me, I pointed to the shorter line, and he said we would leave port soon.

I looked at the ship's giant chimneys and saw they were starting to send out black smoke. On the fourth day, at suppertime, we finally left. The ship slowly left the port and sailed into the open Caspian Sea, leaving this horrible, cursed place behind. I hoped I would never, ever see this place again. In front of us, I saw the open sea: our release to freedom at last.

Sickness on the
Beaches of Pahlevi

The old tub, which was a commercial freighter at one time, banged and rattled, and the engines rumbled. Father said he was not sure we would reach our destination and wondered if they wanted to drown us all. The Polish military was stationed under the deck, and the rest of us were on top, burning in the sun by day and shivering under the stars at night. The ship was terribly cramped and dirty, full of human filth. There was hardly any room to move among all the people on deck. The authorities tried to console us, telling us the journey was short, barely five hundred kilometers, and that tomorrow afternoon, we would reach the port of Pahlevi.

We were now on the open sea, traveling in a southerly direction. We were all extremely weak. I looked around and sadly noticed a bunch of people shaking and shivering with malaria, some with dysentery, and some barely alive. The sun went down and turned into a beautiful red ball. As it set, it disappeared into the depths of the sea. Everyone looked for a place to lie down on the deck, to sleep or rest for the night under the stars. It was so crowded that we were squashed, pressed tightly against each other. People continued to moan and groan with pain. Occasionally, there were screams from the dying or from loved ones still alive, mourning those who died. I guessed not many people would sleep that night. As the night went on, I dozed off and on, and dawn soon approached. It was morning, a new day.

All day and night, there was a long queue of people waiting to use the toilet at the back of the ship. While it was labelled a toilet, it was in fact just a board with a hole cut in it hanging over the back end of the ship from ropes. You squatted over the hole, and the waste went directly into the sea. You had to really hold on tight to keep your balance, but many people were too weak and slipped and fell into the water, lost to us forever. What a shame. So many survived the deportation from their homeland and suffered such cruelty in Russian captivity, only to have their lives end in such a humiliating way.

There was no room for the dead on the ship. Soldiers threw the dead overboard into the sea. I saw a distraught mother grieving over her little daughter. The little girl's body was still warm. A priest approached the crying mother and prayed with her for a moment. As soon as the prayers were finished, the soldiers threw the little girl's body overboard into the sea. The mother was so broken up and distraught that she wanted to throw herself into the sea after her daughter. She screamed that without her child, she wanted to die too. My heart broke when I looked at this suffering. It took place all too often.

I had to get away from the sadness, so I pushed my way through the crowd to the back of the ship to look out at the sea, hoping to get the suffering out of my mind. I found an empty spot to rest on the railing and looked into the wake of the ship. I could not believe what I saw: There, right behind the ship, floating on the surface of the water, I saw several bodies following the ship's wake. I felt light-headed, weak, and was about to faint when suddenly someone grabbed my arm, preventing me from falling over the side into the water. Looking at the arm holding me, I saw it was a soldier. He said it was not a pleasant sight; they should put weights on these bodies so they would sink, but they didn't have any weights. They were not prepared for this. He took me to different part of the ship and made me face into the wind so I could get a few breaths of fresh air and a different view. The breeze was pleasant and helped to refresh me. I thanked him for his help, and we start chatting.

He was around thirty years of age and looked quite handsome in his elegant uniform. He asked where I was from, so I told him about our house in Poland and our exile to Siberia. He was sorry about my experiences and my sad memories. He told me the history of the Persian empire, how the language and alphabet came into being. The history of Persia went back to the seventh century BC. Later, Persia became Iran.

After a while, the soldier stopped talking and said he had responsibilities he must see to. But before he left, he removed a chain from around his neck; it was a medal of the Virgin Mary. He put it around my neck. He thanked me for my friendship and asked if we could meet again sometime in the near future.

I returned to my family and found that my youngest brother, Alex, was bent over, feeling sick. He was not as sick as some on the ship, so we hoped that he would regain his health before we reached port. As we continued sailing slowly in this tub of a ship, we were still not sure if it would make it to the port. And we didn't know what would happen to us once we arrived. Everyone had hopes that soon we would have total freedom. Once in a while, we looked southward to see if we could see land on the horizon. We were completely surrounded by the vastness of the water. The sun was getting much hotter and baking us again, without mercy.

All of a sudden, someone shouted they could see land on the horizon. Everyone was curious; what could it be? Some said it was likely Pahlevi. We sailed closer and closer to the ragged outline of land, and it became clearer. I could hardly wait to see the city. We entered the port, and everyone was happy. It was deathly quiet when the engines stopped. All we heard was the sound of people collecting their belongings, eager to get off the ship. We headed for the steep stairs and descended to the dock. Alex was worse, so soldiers helped us get him off the ship, along with other sick people. We made it; we were on solid ground. Some people were so happy that they laughed and danced with joy. Others cried tears of happiness and even kissed the ground.

The climate was terribly hot and muggy. We were exhausted and starving, while others were wasting away from typhus and a host of other diseases. Some people were literally dying as they walked. Death could take anyone; it had no favorites, adults or children. This was the freedom we were waiting for, and this was the freedom we got. We walked in lines to the commissioner's desks, men and boys on one side and women and girls on the opposite side. We were registered in this land of freedom, and once that was done, we were led into huge tents. The people taking us to the tents were dressed in army uniforms or in white. They all had white armbands marked with red crosses. I asked what the armbands meant and was told they belonged to the PCK, the Polish Red Cross. As we walked along, I listened to people talking about their experiences. It turned out all of those who were ousted from their homeland had lost family members to death. From the beginning of our forceful removal from our homeland until today, I saw this was not to be the end for us.

Now that we were segregated, males from females, we were taken to tents and made to strip off all our clothing, leaving us naked. Our filthy, ragged clothes, with the nightmarish lice and other different bugs, were thrown into piles that were immediately doused with gasoline and set on fire. Next, they sheared our hair right down to our bare scalps, packing our hair in bags and throwing the bags into the fire with our clothes. Then they led us into showers, where they scrubbed and disinfected us without any gentleness or mercy. I looked around, and all I saw were skeletons with white, glowing bald heads. Once they were certain we were clean and free of bugs and lice, we were vaccinated to avoid spreading any diseases in this new land. We were happy to be rid of the dirt, but the issue I had was that I no longer had my hair. But I consoled myself that it would grow again; maybe it would be even healthier. We were given a set of clothes and some shoes. What they gave us was not the right size, but they said this was temporary; later, we could choose something more appropriate. I finally felt clean, even if it was without my hair.

The Red Cross took Alex to the hospital as soon as he was showered and had his head shaved. Mother, who was now also sick, said she was going to the hospital to help Alex and would take Josephine with her. Before leaving, she handed me the pictures of Mary and Jesus as well as the bag with the gold spoons. She had them hidden somewhere the whole time we had been wandering. I was amazed they had not been taken from her. We had nothing else left; all our belongings had been taken away from us and destroyed or thrown into the fire. I started searching for the rest of my family, but it was not easy. Father, Fred, and Chester were lost somewhere in this crowd.

We would be living in a camp on the sandy beach near the harbor. It was huge; thousands and thousands of tents had been

194

set up by the Red Cross and the soldiers, tents as far as the eye could see. Everyone was assigned to an army cot with a pillow and blanket. They said it was just a temporary arrangement.

The next day, the officials showed us piles of clothes and shoes, telling us we could choose whatever we wanted. I excitedly picked through the clothes and found some that fit me nicely and were elegant. I had not worn a dress or shoes for so long, I had forgotten how good it felt.

I could hardly walk among the tents because of all the ropes and pegs that were driven into the ground. I looked for my father and brothers but panicked when I couldn't find them. I circulated among the tents, but I only saw hundreds of sick people, lingering in their tents. I could not find my family.

At lunchtime, the Red Cross workers brought food to our tents. Some of the people who were too sick and not able to help themselves were fed by these workers. We were served a meal of cooked mutton soup, dried bread, and coffee. They forced everyone to eat. Two Red Cross nurses came to our tent to deliver the food. There were four of us in this tent. They fed each of us, one by one. They came to me, carrying the food. I said I did not want any mutton soup, explaining that it was too greasy for me. I only wanted to eat the bread and coffee. They said I had no choice; I must eat the soup. I refused. Now the two of them forced me to drink the soup. They tried to pour it down my throat. I spit it out, shouting that the mutton soup stunk, but they patiently ignored my protests and again tried to pour the soup into my mouth. I cried and spit it out again. I grabbed one nurse's hand and bit her. They slapped my face. One of them grabbed my head, and the other tried to pour the soup straight down my throat.

This was too much; it made me vomit. I felt better after I vomited. The nurses finally gave up and left, leaving me the bread and coffee. I did not understand; I was so hungry, but I could not look at this food. I was tired after the struggle with the nurses, so I lay down on the bed and fell asleep. When I woke up, I ate the bread and drank the coffee and fell asleep again. I continued to sleep for the next few days, eating only the bread and drinking coffee. I didn't know what happened to me. I felt as though I was fused to the bed. I lay there all day and slept, not aware of the time or the number of days I slept.

Finally, I was starting to feel a bit better. I knew that several days had likely passed and that I must look for my family somewhere around this camp. I got up and decided that I wanted to see what I looked like after such a long time. I had not seen my face since I left Poland. I borrowed a small mirror, and when I looked at myself, I was shocked and got goose bumps all over me. I had changed beyond recognition. My head of hair did not exist. On my head, I had moss instead of hair. My face was skinny and sunken, covered with patches of dry flaky skin. I looked at my neck and arms and saw that I was covered with scaly patches. I was in shock; what happened to me? I gave the mirror back and looked at the others in the tent and saw they were in the same condition. I asked if they knew what was wrong with us, but they had no idea. They said they asked the nurses, but even they did not know.

Next, I looked for the bag of spoons but could not find them. I asked one of the people in my tent what happened to them, and they said one of the nurses took them when I was sleeping. I tried to find the thief but couldn't; the spoons were gone, after all Mother went through to save them. I was very sad.

I started looking for my father and brothers again, but without success. I went around and around this sea of tents and asked hundreds of people, but no one knew anything. It was as though they vanished without a trace.

Malaria, typhoid, dysentery, and other diseases were rampant. Almost everyone in the tents was sick from one of these diseases. It seemed that changes in our diet and living conditions caused such a shock to our bodies that we succumbed to these terrible diseases. We were used to eating only bread and water for all our years in captivity. We were frail, and our health was very fragile. Some of the Red Cross workers did not maintain any hygiene, and this caused the spread of more disease. Some of the military were trying to help us, but they were so overworked, they could not possibly help everyone. Many patients slipped through their fingers and died. People were dropping like flies, in such quantities that it was impossible to even guess their number, much less get a list of the dead. Everyone was overwhelmed with sorrow and mourning for loved ones. It reminded me of what the commandant of our Siberian camp warned us of before we left: the sickness and disease. But I would rather die here in freedom than as a prisoner of war in Siberia.

As the days went by, I grew somewhat stronger; although I was still weak, I started searching for my family again, but still I had no luck. Other ships arrived, and the population was so large, it made the search extremely difficult. I also tried again to find the nurse who stole the gold spoons, but I had no luck finding her, either.

The Beautiful Beaches
of Pahlevi

From time to time, we heard about bodies being washed up onto the beautiful white sandy beaches of Pahlevi. The bodies that were thrown overboard from the ship were following us, haunting us. People who were looking for their relatives, friends, or neighbors walked along the beach and examined the corpses for their loved ones. I heard about this, and because I was curious, I walked to the beach early one morning. The sand was cool, and the air was warm but pleasant. As the waves crashed onto the beach, they dissolved into white sudsy foam. I saw an unpleasant, sad, and terrible sight: Soldiers were taking bodies out of the foam on the beach. Around them, a group of emaciated people with sad faces waited to see if they could identify any of the washed-up corpses.

These people looked tense and worried, anticipating who might be washed ashore next. They looked for their relatives as they stared into the dead faces. The soldiers took another small body from the water; it was the body of a little girl. A woman from the group recognized this body as her daughter; she screamed and fell to her knees, with tears running down her face. She rocked on the sand, sobbing and moaning loudly. I started to cry and had to run away. A feeling of pain exploded inside me. I had to be strong. I had to endure. I must survive.

I walked farther along the beach, away from this sadness, and stared into the clear water. After a few minutes, I noticed beautiful fish swimming in the foamy water. The wild waves had beached these lovely fish on the shore. I decided to go fishing. I was terribly hungry and wanted to catch one of them and take it home for my supper. I went into the water, picked out a fish, and grabbed it, but it slipped out of my hand. But I needed to catch a fish. I had to catch a fish. I looked again and picked out a second fish; as I grabbed it, it also slipped out of my hands. I tried to catch a third one, but again it slipped away, falling onto the sand and then swimming away. I had to catch at least one of these fish. Looking at them, I thought they almost wanted me to catch them.

I heard someone behind me, saying these fish were coming to shore because they were full of eggs, and they wanted to lay them in the sand. I was not really interested in why the fish were so close to shore. I only knew I was hungry, and they were food to eat. I tried again. This time, I managed to catch a fish that was about two feet long. It wiggled and slapped at me with its tail. It slapped me so hard I could not hold onto it. It slipped right out of my hand and swam away. I wanted to cry. I was so weak, I could not even hold onto a fish.

I gave up and returned to my tent, full of tears. I was very hungry. The food they served us, especially the lamb, was so fatty and oily that I could not eat it. Instead of helping me, it only harmed me. I could only eat the dried bread and drink the coffee. I knew I would be at death's door if I did not get some nourishment soon. When I entered our tent, I told them about my fishing escapade. They felt sorry for me but then called me a clumsy clod.

The woman in the bed next to mine was sick and barely alive; I told her about trying to catch the fish and how it slipped out of my hands. My friend whispered something to me, and when I bent down to listen to her, she asked me to go and catch at least one fish for her. She said she would like to eat a fish before she died. She said that I could light a fire on the sandy beach and cook the fish right there. I promised her I would go and catch a fish and cook it for her on the beach.

I went back to the beach, making up my mind that as worn out as I was, I would catch a fish and bring it back to her. It was not lunchtime yet, but the sun was quite high overhead. As I walked along the sand, it burned my feet, so I walked as quickly as I could. When I walked into the water, it was cool and pleasant. As before, I spotted the fish and tried to catch one. I set a trap to catch one, but it slipped out of my grasp again. Again and again I tried, using all my strength. I scooped one into my hands and threw it, but it slipped out. I was clumsy, very clumsy, as though I had a physical disability because I could not catch a single fish.

Finally, I managed to catch one. I was determined this one would not escape from my hands. I threw it out of the water onto the sandy beach. It was too late for this fish now because we were too far from the water. It would soon be cooked and eaten. The fish was still covered with sand when I returned with it to the tent city. Many people stared at what I carried. They said they also wanted to catch some fish. I brought the fish into the tent. Everyone was happy, and we started a fire. We got a basin with water and put it on the fire after rinsing the sand off the fish. We put the whole fish into the basin, without removing the scales or insides. We made fish soup. In a short time, we were eating this soup, a wonderful fish soup, each of us having a piece of fish and a piece of dried bread. I fed my sick friend, and she ate it with gusto; as she slurped the soup, I got great pleasure listening to her as she enjoyed the meal.

I got up early the next morning; it was a cool but beautiful sunny day. After yesterday's tasty fish soup, I felt great. I went back to the beach and walked on the white sand. This time, I noticed Persian vendors walking around, carrying their goods. I could not believe what I saw with my still-hungry eyes. They had different kinds of foods, baked fish, many different fruits, different kinds of dates, and boiled eggs. Coming out of a life of hunger, this was the most beautiful sight in the world. Tears fell down my cheeks, and I did not know why. I was crying with happiness, probably because I was so taken in by this sight. So many goodies; it was like a dream come true. I wanted to swallow everything with my eyes. But I knew I must restrain myself because people in the camp often got sick from eating too much, too soon. With the freedom to eat as much as they wanted, they did not care about their health; they just wanted to fill their empty stomachs. I knew I must be careful and not eat too much so I would not get sick and suffer terribly, as they did.

I saw Persians sitting around, selling cooked eggs. I wondered how they could cook the eggs. It turned out that the sand was so hot from the sun, the eggs cooked right there in the sand. I thought I would get a few of these eggs and cook them in the sand myself. I only had to bury them for a few moments, and the eggs would cook. When was the last time I ate an egg? I couldn't remember, but I was compelled to do so. In the blink of an eye, I got an idea. I ran back to the tent, and without saying a word to anyone, I yanked the blanket off my bed and raced back to the beach. I started to bargain with one of the Persians, and we soon came to an agreement: I got ten beautiful eggs by trading my blanket. I sat next to the Persian in the shade and peeled two eggs right away, eating them there on the spot. Then I started walking along slowly, looking for my family. This meal had given me new strength. From time to time, I stopped to peel and eat another egg, savoring the delicious taste and flavor.

When the sun started moving toward the west, I knew night was coming. It would be dark soon. Nights were cool there, and I would be without a blanket. So I went to the Red Cross and asked for a new blanket. They gave me a new one without a problem. The eggs were so delicious that I made a deal with the Persian several days in a row to trade my blanket. I went back to the Red Cross and got a new one every time, with no trouble. He got the blanket; I got ten eggs. After a few days, though, someone at the Red Cross recognized me and warned me this was the last blanket they would give me. I must forget about the eggs.

I slowly regained my health; I felt stronger and stronger. I knew it would still take some time to regain my full strength, but I was in much better shape. My thoughts continually revolved around my missing family. I lived in a tent with strangers who asked about my family and how we lost each other. I explained that we were segregated before we were scrubbed down and showered and had our heads shaved. We were separated then and had not found each other since. Like many other people in the same situation, we prowled around the camp every day in search of our missing family members. I did not know what happened to my father and brothers. I could not find them; they disappeared. Many families were torn apart and looking for their relatives.

I decided that I would make my way to the general hospital

in Tehran to visit my mother, Alex, and Josephine. I did not even know if they were still alive. I asked some soldiers who delivered supplies to the hospital if they would give me ride there. They asked me if I realized how far it was to Tehran. They said it was three hundred and fifty kilometers, a difficult journey through the mountains, but they agreed to take me, and we set out in an army truck. When we got to the hospital, I saw a huge sign that said "Tehran General Civilian Hospital" with red crosses and the three huge letters, PCK.

A guard asked if I had any documents to enter the hospital. I didn't, so I had to get out of the truck and wait. The guard asked for the name of the patient I wanted to visit and then checked his list. He said someone would contact my mother, and she would come to the gate to meet me. After a while, I saw Mother walking toward me from a distance. She looked quite sad and was dressed in a white lab coat with the Red Cross patch on the sleeve. She held Josephine's hand. *Oh, God, I thought, where is Alex?* Scary thoughts ran through my mind; what happened to him? As she approached the gate, I could see she was sick herself; she did not look well. She took me to the ward where Alex was laying in a bed. I could see he was in very poor health and didn't know if he would get better. I did not know what was wrong with him.

Mother told me about all the sick people in the hospital. I could see that death was taking many lives, not just adults but children, as well. In the evening, I prayed for the health of Mother and Alex and went to sleep in a waiting room. The following morning, I said goodbye to Mother, Josephine, and Alex and returned with the same soldiers. When we finally got back to Pahlevi, it was getting dark, and I returned to my tent feeling tired, anxious, and worried.

Moving to Tehran

As time went on, thousands of us were told we must pack our few belongings and prepare to go to Tehran, where a better life supposedly awaited us. They packed us into army trucks, and we departed. As we left Pahlevi behind, we entered the mountains of El-Burz. The endless column of trucks moved at a snail's pace on these narrow mountain roads, which wound along deep, steep gorges. The Persian drivers of the trucks knew how to navigate these treacherous roads, but I was still frightened. At times, we drove along the edges of the roads, knocking stones out from under the wheels. These stones fell down into the ravine and disappeared somewhere in the abyss. I was so scared, I could not look out the windows.

We finally arrived in Tehran and pulled into an airfield. We stopped at a huge hangar that was known as Camp Number Two. As usual, we started with registration, one after another. They asked me for identification, but I did not have any. They asked where my parents were and how old I was. I could only remember that my mother, brother, and sister were here in Tehran in the hospital, and my father and my other brothers had disappeared. They asked me if I had any identification or any papers at all. I explained that we had the spišská from

Siberia and the document that he was given from Kokanda. But it was all with Father, and he was missing in Pahlevi. I was so confused that I couldn't even remember the date of my birth. I remember Mother changed my birthdate several times in Siberia, so we could get more food or so I could go to school instead of cutting down trees to earn food. Eventually, I picked a date for my birthday, and that was how I finally got registered in the camp.

They gave each of us a little carpet and a small blanket and pillow, they told us to prepare a place to sleep on the floor. I looked at these new surroundings; I was afraid because we seemed so small in this huge hanger. I had never been to such a place. In this camp, there were likely thousands of people gathered together. In the building I was assigned to, there were hundreds, maybe thousands of women. Men were in a separate building. We lay down, one next to the other. We did not know how long we would be living there but were told it would be for a lengthy time. They said there was not enough room in Camp Number One.

I felt like a lost orphan as I wandered about the hangar over the next few days. I could not seem to settle. But there were plenty of us here feeling the same way: sad and crying for days.

A priest arrived, and they announced Confessions would be heard and a Mass celebrated. I went to Confession. I could not remember the last time I went, it was so long ago. I told the priest how I stole cheese, bread, and other items of food because I was so hungry. The priest reassured me that I had no other choice; I had to save my life and the lives of my family. I did not understand how this could be; how could I be forgiven for stealing? My father always said it was wrong to steal, but the priest told me that it was okay and absolved me. I left the confessional confused, but after attending Mass, I felt a little better.

The Red Cross continued to care for all of us. The food was better here than in Pahlevi. Every day, we were given some halva, a sweet treat made from ground sesame seeds and sugar, shaped into bars. They said it was very healthy, and we should eat it. The Red Cross put up a list of hospitalized patients in the hanger. I looked for Alex's name and spotted it on the list. I learned there would be an army transport going to the hospital in a few days.

A White Dove

That evening, I went to sleep, and during the night, I felt a gentle breeze on my face. It woke me up. I felt like someone was pulling my blanket off. When I opened my eyes, I saw a white dove. It had a pink beak and beautiful blue eyes. It looked at me and started to quietly coo. Was it a dream? No, I knew I was not asleep. I clearly saw his beautiful eyes staring at me, as if he wanted to show me something. I saw another dove sitting a little farther away; it was also cooing. Both doves made me feel that Alexander and my cousin, the son of my Uncle Paul, were happy. I asked the doves to come closer to me so I could pet them. They acted as if they were waiting for something. I woke my new friend Jackie, who was in the bed next to mine. When she opened her eyes, I told her I saw two doves, but now they were gone. I told her I wanted to say something to the doves; I felt like they were from Uncle Paul's son and Alexander. I was certain they came to say goodbye to me. I could not sleep the rest of the night because I was praying for the two of them.

In the morning, I tried to get a pass as soon as possible to go to the hospital in an army truck. As before, I had to wait at the gate until they found Mother's name on the list and notified her she had a visitor. As before, she must come to the gate to meet me. I saw Mother walking toward me, and she looked so tired, sad, and devastated. We hugged each other tightly, and she said she was so happy to see that I was still alive. She told me Alexander had died. His body was buried the next day, but she didn't know where. I tried to get a pass as soon as possible to go to the hospital in an army truck.

I could not believe my brother was dead. I felt such sorrow and remorse. Why did he have to go? He was so very young, the youngest of all my brothers. Where was the justice? He wanted to live. Through my tears, I told Mother I experienced a visit from him last night. She said that was impossible; how could I have seen him? He was dead. I told her he came to me in the form of a dove, together with Uncle Paul's son. The two of them visited me.

As we continued to walk, she showed me where Josephine was in the girls' emergency room. After a few hours, I returned to the camp, filled with grief and sorrow.

A few days later, I returned to the hospital. Because I knew the guards, I could go straight into the hospital. I didn't have to wait to have my pass checked or for Mother to come to the gate. I looked for Mother and saw her walking toward me. She seemed even thinner than before; her eyes were sunken, and she looked pale and weak. Josephine was feeling better now and walked behind her, holding onto her dress. We greeted each other with a hug, and I gave her a piece of halva I had brought with me. She immediately told me that Father had been found. What a joy! I was not expecting to hear such good news. But that's not all Mother said. Father told her that my other brother, Godfrey, died in the military hospital in Pahlevi, just prior to the first evacuation.

This news makes me sick. *No*, I thought. *I don't want to hear this. How can this be?* I buried my face in my hands and cried. After sharing our grief and tears for a time, Mother told me about our separation in Pahlevi. Father was assigned a tent with the boys, and they were constantly looking for me. One day, they walked past a vendor selling pork sausages. Father explained to Godfrey that he should not eat these delicious-smelling sausages. But Godfrey begged and begged until Father finally gave in to him. He bought a piece, and Godfrey swallowed it in a heartbeat. He enjoyed the taste of the sausage so much he wanted more; he did not want to stop eating them. He said it tasted so good and reminded him of home.

Soon, however, he began to complain about pains in his stomach, and after only a few hours, he was suffering so much, Father had to take him to the field hospital. Shortly thereafter, he died. Godfrey died on September 25 and was buried the same day in the Polish cemetery.

I had four brothers. Two were dead. I had not heard anything about Tony since he left Siberia. My last brother, Chester, was now sick in the hospital. Mother took me to see him, pushing our way through the crowded hallways. They segregated the patients, keeping the children away from the adults and the boys away from the girls. Many people were volunteering, taking care of their relatives, just as Mother was doing with Chester. We went into the room for boys, looking for Chester, and found him lying in a bed.

I walked up to him and asked how he was feeling. He opened his eyes and smiled at me. I saw he was weak but happy to see me. He stared at the chain with the medal around my neck and said he liked it; he asked me to give it to him. I didn't want to part with the gift from the soldier on the ship, so I changed the subject and tried to talk about something else. But Chester was not so easily fooled and insisted I give it to him. I felt so sorry for him that eventually I gave up, took the chain and pendant off, and put it around his neck.

He pointed at his soldier's uniform and told me not to take it away because he was going to get better soon and return to the labor battalions. Time went by so fast, and the hour was getting late. I had to go back to my camp. Mother asked me to take Josephine with me back to the camp; she could not cope with her anymore. I said I would gladly take her and promised to figure out a way to move closer to the hospital. Anyway, I felt much better and was happy I could help my parents by taking Josephine with me. Mother said she would talk to Father about moving all of us closer to the hospital.

In the camp, Josephine and I were given good food. Every morning, we got black coffee and halva. They gave us meat as well, but I still could not look at it.

The Third Fatal Blow

Time passed. One day, Josephine and I got a pass and met Mother at the gate. She looked terrible, barely alive. She asked us to accompany her because she wanted to show us something. She led us to a large room. The sign above the doorway read "Morgue." Inside the room were many, many bags filled with something with little cards attached to them. Mother said in a quiet voice, breaking with sobs and tears, that yesterday, Chester had been laughing and joking around and even teased someone about wanting a piece of a cracker. That morning, he was dead. Chester Nykiel died on October 15. I looked at the bag with his name attached to the card. Mother said some soldiers would come soon and load the bodies into army trucks and take them somewhere. She didn't know where.

Tears fell from my eyes; I couldn't control myself. I felt terrible anger and resentment against God and against the Russians. In such a short time, I had lost my third brother. God, that was not fair. So many died. They survived the famine in Siberia, and now that we were here in this country, where there was so much food, we must say goodbye to them. Why? I could not understand. Why? I had so much grief and sorrow, I cried uncontrollably, with huge sobs and tears, for all three of my brothers. I thought to myself, *After these terrible times we have gone through, this is the freedom we have.* The three of us cried as we left the morgue. I told Mother we had to visit their graves. She said she wanted to know where they would be buried.

First, she had to talk with Father, but she was not sure whether he would be able to help the burial sites. He was depressed and unable to talk about his sons. He was resigned to the way our life had become. I asked Mother what was happening with Father because I had not seen him for a long time. She said he was walking around blindly, as though in a daze, looking for work, and he was in bad shape mentally. She told me to go back to the camp with Josephine and keep her with me for a few more weeks while she stayed in the hospital, helping others. That way, she might regain some of her health. So Josephine and I returned to camp later that evening. Returning in the army truck, I continued to think of my family and how it had broken up. I thought of all the reasons for this pain; my mind wouldn't stop wondering, *Why, why, why?*

Cemetery

As time passed, we were finally united as a family and given a house to live in. Father met a priest who turned out to be a good friend of Uncle Martin. The priest presided over the Catholic Mass, and Father helped him in the chapel, performing a variety of tasks there. Mother washed the priest's shirts and starched his collars to earn extra money. Father became quite close with the priest, who agreed to help find the graves of my brothers. He went with my father to the cemetery where the Poles were buried, but he warned Father they would be difficult to find because they were only labelled with numbers or crosses marked "NN" (Name unknown).

The cemetery was located next to the hospital, near the city dump. The priest, Father, and I walked through the graves, looking for our family, but found few graves with names. We met many people who were also looking for names. We asked them if they knew who was buried where, but no one knew anything. We wandered around the cemetery, but without results, even among the freshly dug graves. The number of people who were dying here each day was increasing, and more and more graves were marked "NN."

The priest came up with an idea that perhaps the office of

the Head of the Catholic Chaplaincy in Tehran could help us. We went with the priest to the garrison, but there was a long queue. All the people in the line were looking for the same answers we were. The line moved at a snail's pace. Some of the people said they had been waiting in this line for a few days. The priest suggested we take turns standing and waiting in the lineup. That way, we could rest and get something to eat and then return to the lineup, since it was likely a few days before we got our turn.

After a few days, our turn came up. When we got inside the building, they asked for the names of our dead relatives, and Father gave the names: Alexander, Chester, and Godfrey Nykiel. After searching through the books for a few hours, they found Alexander's registration in the main book of the dead from the year 1942, Volume II, page 79. He was buried in the Catholic cemetery in Tehran, in the Polish lot, Section 9, the number of the grave being 509. After more searching in the same book, they found Chester's name; he was also buried in the same cemetery, Section 10, with his grave number being 856. They could not find Godfrey's name. They asked where he died, and Father told them that he died in a military hospital in Pahlevi. They said they could not get this information because he was buried there and not here in Tehran.

Father then asked for their death certificates. An official told him with a polite smile there was such a huge backlog of death certificates, it could take up to a year to receive them. Father asked why it would take so long and was told that the Russians removed 1,500,000 Polish people from the eastern part of Poland, but only 120,000 people came back, and many of the remaining people died on the way to Tehran. Father was astonished at these facts; so many Poles had died. They said finding these documents could take up to a year because so many died.

After leaving the garrison, Father declared he wanted to go Pahlevi in search of Godfrey's grave. The priest said he would borrow a military car from a friend so we could go to Pahlevi. Early the next morning, we departed. Since we knew the road and what to expect, we arrived without problems. The priest also knew the hospital chaplain, who welcomed us warmly. He quickly found that Fred was registered in the Main Book of Deaths in 1942, Volume II, page 174. He was buried in the Polish cemetery in Pahlevi in tomb 542. Father was happy to get this information and then asked about the death certificate. But the response was the same as in Tehran. We must wait at least six months to get it. Father then asked the priest's driver if he could visit the grave before returning to Tehran. He answered yes, so we went to the cemetery to see Godfrey's grave. And there, at the grave of his son, Father, this grown man, wept bitter tears, unable to forgive himself over a piece of sausage. Somberly, we returned to Tehran.

Unpleasant News

One day, I visited Mother at the hospital, where she worked as a volunteer. I barely recognized her as she walked down the hall to meet me; she looked like a human shadow. She immediately started crying. I tried to calm her down and find out what happened. In a barely audible whisper, she told me that yesterday, as she walked to her friend's house in the camp, she met another friend, who immediately began to express her sympathy on the death of Mother's eldest son, Tony, who was killed in the military.

The message shocked Mother to such an extent that she fainted and fell to the ground. Mother's friend started shouting for help, and many people gathered and eventually helped to bring her around. Realizing that Mother had not heard about Tony's death, the friend apologized, explaining that she thought Mother already knew about this tragic news. She said her husband had come home on leave from the army and mentioned to her about the so-called valley of death in Kirmine, Uzbekistan. He told her this was where all the dead soldiers were buried, and he saw one of the corpses being carried out was Tony. After Mother was escorted back to our house, Father wanted to know if it was proven that it actually was Tony. Father went with the priest to the Red Cross trying to find out if this was true, that Tony was actually killed. After looking through all the documents and daily postings, Father filled out the necessary forms, but they could find no mention of Tony's death. We were grieving anew.

Fortunately, the priest had given Father a job at the church, so he had less time to dwell on the painful memories of all his lost sons. The Red Cross allocated free housing to families in which both parents worked. Since he and Mother worked with the priest in the church, we got free housing. Our apartment was located in a two-story building. We would stay in a large house next to the church until it was ready for us to move into. Soon, we would all be together in an apartment: my parents and their two surviving daughters, Josephine and me.

Happy Letter

Before the apartment was be ready, Josephine and I traveled by army truck to the hospital to visit Mother and found her very happy. She was exuding happiness. What happened to make her so ecstatic? Was it because the apartment was almost ready? She grabbed us and squeezed us tightly, saying that she had a surprise for us. She was singing and dancing. We stared at her, waiting for the news. She finally told us Tony was alive. He actually sent us a letter. He did not know where we were but hoped that in spite of this, with the excellent work of the Red Cross, his words would reach us. He wrote he had done a lot of work and a lot of traveling, with many difficulties. It took him much effort to cross from Siberia to Gorchakov, to reach the main centers of the Polish army. It took him and his friends three months before they arrived. From there, he was transferred to Karaganda and then to Kirmine. There he became very ill and was transferred to Krasnovodsk and then continued by ship across the Caspian Sea to Pahlevi. And this was still not the end of his journey. First, he went to Tehran, and then he was moved to Basra in Iraq. That was where he received his letter accepting him as a soldier in the Polish army under General Anders.

In Kirmine, he contracted pneumonia. He was in such a bad state that at some point, he stopped breathing. It was then they determined he was dead. Doctors did not take the time to evaluate him. They believed if a patient did not breathe or move, he was dead. And so the doctors ordered him removed from the hospital to make room for the next patient. Army personnel threw him on a truck among the other dead bodies which were to be thrown into a deep pit for burial. While loading more dead bodies onto the truck, they noticed that Tony moved. They immediately rescued him from among the corpses and brought him back into the hospital, where he eventually recovered. This explained the tragic but happily false information about his death. Tony wrote that he hoped we'd get this letter and that he had faith the Red Cross would find his family. We were overjoyed.

Father was very happy and told the priest that we were ready right now to pack our few meager belongings and go in search of Tony, wherever he was. The priest, however, discouraged us from doing this. He said we should not be in a hurry to leave; we should not forget there was a war on. He then explained that because Father worked for the church, he could not be released. He asked us to postpone the trip whenever the Polish and other governments put pressure on our family to leave. The Polish government wanted all the Poles to return to Poland. However, when they returned, they would not have any rights to the land they left behind. They would be just as poor in Poland as they were in Tehran. The priest assured us he would tell us when the time was right to make such a move.

Every time Father was notified about returning to our homeland, the priest told us to wait. Other people were traveling to many different parts of the world, but Father abided by the priest's advice. However, we didn't lose hope of returning to our homeland with other Poles, so Mother enrolled Josephine in the Polish school to learn the language, along with other children. Josephine brought home quarterly report cards and was proud of her good grades. Her teacher was Miss Krysia, a young Polish orphan. Miss Krysia often looked in on us, and we taught her how to cook Polish food. Like many other Polish girls, she married a Persian captain and lived there. She was very fond of Josephine, and she and her husband often took her for walks or horseback riding.

I Go to Work

I looked for work, any kind of work, maybe even something with a future or something that would give me an education. I loved the army uniform and wondered if I should go to the Polish Fourth National Service camp to register myself with the PSK. After I talked with Mother, I decided to look for work in a hospital, so I went with her to the main civilian hospital in Tehran. Right away, I was hired by the PCK to work with sick children. I was assured I would be taught how to do this new job. I worked with Margo, a Russian nurse, who taught me how to care for the sick children. Since I knew the Russian language, I could understand what Margo taught me. She told me how she was taken away from her homeland. When I got my first paycheck, I went to a shop and spent all of it on toys that I took to the hospital and gave to the children. The work was very demanding, physically and mentally, helping these young sick children as well as some adults who were affected by the trauma of war experiences

Lost Friend

One day while busy helping a patient, I noticed a young girl walking from bed to bed. At first, I paid no attention to her, but after another look, something seemed familiar about her. She reminded me of someone. She was of medium height and had an olive complexion and black hair, and of course, she was terribly thin. I looked at her, trying to remember who she was, and decided to approach her. I walked over to her to get a better look, and to my amazement, I realized it was Stella, my friend from Poland. She recognized me too. We threw our arms around each other, hugging like two lost sisters. She asked me what I was doing here, all dressed in white, so I said I was in training to be a nurse. Stella said she was looking for her family: her parents and three younger sisters. She said they all contracted a severe illness, and she, being the only healthy one, had to care for them. Their condition deteriorated so much that eventually, they were taken to a hospital. She did not know exactly where, so she went to all the hospitals, searching for her loved ones.

My shift ended soon, so I asked her to wait for me. We had a lot to talk about, to catch up on everything we'd gone through during the years we were separated. She agreed to wait, and we met after I finished work. She said she felt like an orphan because her parents and sisters were in a hospital somewhere; she was in such terrible shape, she didn't know if she could survive.

I tried to comfort her; after all, we were almost the same age (she was older than me by only nine months). She said she would like to be my sister. I promised that I would help her search for her parents. I asked where she was living, and she said she lived in another camp but wanted to live with me. I asked her where she was taken to in Siberia. She answered she was taken to Ciurga, not to far from Archangielsk, to cut down trees, just like I was.

We tried to find her family, and when the occasion arose, we explored the city. We saw the sights together. We both slowly returned to health. We met a lot of guys: Polish, British, and American soldiers. We were young and had fun joking around with the men we met. The joy of life was returning to us, especially after we found her family. We made friends with a lot of the girls we met. We even started going to dances. We had to get a pass to go into the city. Curfew restrictions forced us to return to our camps by ten o'clock in the evening.

One day, we met a young American pilot, who said he wanted to take us in his plane to show us what Tehran looked like from the air. We had never been in an airplane, and being young, brave, and foolish, we agreed to go. We met him and his friend, who took us to an airfield. We got into the plane, and within one minute after leaving the ground, my heart was in my throat. The plane climbed up above the city, and after I calmed down, I look out the window. I felt like an eagle, soaring high above the ground, looking at the beautiful city below. After we landed and got out of the plane, our knees felt like jelly, and we could hardly walk. When the feeling passed, we returned to camp, happy again.

Stella and I often wandered around the city in the evening, after I finished my shift at the hospital; it was a happy life. One evening, as we walked along the road, we started laughing and singing in Russian, *"Strana maja, Moskwa maja"* (My city, Moscow is my city). The sun was beginning to set on this pleasant, warm evening, and we were in no hurry to make our way back to camp because we had lots of time before curfew.

Suddenly, a limousine pulled up beside us and stopped. The chauffer said he would give us a ride back to the camp. Completely unaware of the risks we were now exposed to, we got inside. We settled in the back seat next to a fat, elegantly dressed Persian man. Stella sat in the middle, between me and the fat man. All too quickly, we realized something was wrong; the car was moving in a different direction than we had expected. We knew our way back to the camp, and this was not the direction.

First, we asked the Persian man to take us to the camp. Then we asked the chauffer to take us back. The chauffer said they were taking us back to the camp a different way. Shortly, I realized the road we were on was going somewhere we did not want to go. I asked the chauffer again to stop and let us get out of the car. He ignored me and accelerated the car even faster. I knew these men did not understand the Polish language, so I said to Stella that we had no choice but to jump out the door. I told her to put her arms around my waist and hold on tight as I tried to open the car door. As she put her arms around me, the fat man grabbed her with his hands and tried to stop her from jumping out with me. I opened the door again, and the chauffer sped up even faster.

I didn't know what to do and was really afraid. I made the

sign of the cross and yelled at Stella in Polish that whatever happened, we had to jump out of the car. She screamed that the Persian would not let go of her; she was being pulled in both directions. I told her that if we cared anything about ourselves, we had to jump out of this limousine right away. I managed to free Stella from the fat man's grasp, and we jumped together. We landed on the road and rolled like two balls into a ditch.

It was very dark and quiet. I called to Stella, and she answered in a frightened voice that she thought we would break our necks. My shoulder ached, so I asked her if she had any pains. She said no, she had none at all. She said she thought the fat man would jump out after us. After we climbed up out of the ditch, she said her leg hurt. We knew it was too late to go to our camp now and decided to spend the night in the ditch. Once daybreak came, we started walking back to the camp.

Announcements were being made for the mobilization of young volunteers into the Polish National Service. I still wanted to wear the PSK uniform. I thought about the rewarding work at the hospital and the white uniform I wore there. When I talked to my girlfriends, however, I found I was being pulled by the PSK uniform. I felt split between both uniforms; how could I decide? I went to the PSK office to register myself and take part in their services for one year. They called us "seeds." They were organizing an outing to the PSK in Palestine. I asked my parents if I could go, but they said I was too young. Upset with that decision, I resigned my post from PSK and returned to work at the hospital. They paid me a good wage in British pounds.

Shortly after this, the camp where Stella and her family lived, known as Camp Number Four, was eliminated. The entire assembly left. Stella came to say goodbye. She said her parents gave her permission to become a nun in a convent in

Isfahan. I told her I didn't know when, but I was certain we'd see each other again, maybe even in Poland.

Time passed, one day into the next. The war was now ended, but nothing changed in Iran. One night, I went to a dance with some of my girlfriends and saw a man playing the violin. His name was Joseph. He danced and jumped around and sang. He was so handsome that I stared at him, as if I were hypnotized. The young boys and girls surrounded him and pulled him into a dance right away. He was so mature, eight years older than I was. I spent more and more time with him. He was like a wizard, my wizard, and slowly, we began to weave plans for a future together.

Some of Joseph's and my friends were leaving to go to different countries around the world. There were now open borders to accept the Poles who had been forced from their country and taken to Siberia, countries like Great Britain, the United States, India, Mexico, Australia, and New Zealand.

But many spies from the Communist government encouraged us to return to our homeland, using all types of tactics to force us to return. They urged us to return by saying the country was rapidly recovering and there was a lot of work to be done, now that the war was over. They promised a fantastic life with tremendous career opportunities for the younger generation. They said Poland needed many people, especially young people, who would have a great life there, with no hindrances to return.

It sounded beautiful, but on the other hand, we often heard that many of those who did return to Poland were deported to Siberia again. If this was true and we were forcefully deported a second time, we would not survive so great a torment. We wanted to go back to our home country but were too afraid to do so.

The enthusiastic younger generation was looking for a new life, even in a strange country. They were hungry for adventure and open to meet new challenges and travel away from this way of life. Many of our friends were going to India and asked us to follow them. I asked my parents if they wanted to move somewhere else. I asked what they thought about our leaving Persia and settling somewhere else, maybe in India. But Father insisted on waiting for the priest to advise him, and so he waited for the last transport.

Joseph asked me to marry him, and I happily accepted his proposal; we decided to get married. Friends helped me with the preparations for the ceremony. I had a lightweight wedding dress and even had nice red shoes. Nylon stockings, unfortunately, were not available. So a friend of mine drew seam lines on the back of my bare legs to look like I was wearing elegant nylons. Everything was done very modestly. Our wedding ceremony took place in a field next to the Catholic church, under a huge tent. The tent was actually constructed from several other smaller tents joined together to form one large tent. This was done to accommodate at least one hundred participants for the Mass. Our marriage ceremony was not as large; a handful of our invited friends were lost in this great space.

My new husband and I joined a group of other young people with the intention of going to India. My parents were angry and unhappy about this decision and did not accept it. My father was so livid that he tried to stop me from leaving. But I was sick of living there and was determined to have a better life. Joseph learned of my father's intention to stop me from leaving, so he hid me in a train car and had a few of his friends guard the door. I could not leave, and Father could not find me. I found myself being a prisoner again, only this time, my husband was my jailer.

Joseph and I got into an army truck and headed to Ahwaz in the southern part of Persia, a seven-hundred-kilometer journey. Ahwaz was the main point for people leaving the country. We traveled through beautiful mountains, but I did not feel so enthralled by their beauty this time. I saw similar peaks many times in my travels from Siberia. Everywhere, I saw only rocks and sand. Being held against my will by my husband was still fresh in my mind. I thought about running away once we reached Ahwaz, but I didn't know where I would run in a strange city.

In Ahwaz, they put us in a temporary camp, saying it was only for a short time until we left. Tents were set up in the middle of the desert wilderness. In the distance, I could see huge mountain ranges. We made new friends who told us they were also waiting for further transport; they had been waiting there for at least a month. Finally, our turn came. We had to load ourselves into canvas-covered army trucks for the trip to Karachi, India, more than three thousand kilometers away.

Karachi, India

Everything had changed. The country was different, the people were different, and their unusual customs were different. This was another world, but unfortunately, it was not a better one. We were aware of the immensity of human tragedy. Many there were orphans, children whose parents died or disappeared in Siberia or died on the way to India. Many of the mothers found themselves alone because their husbands had not returned from war. Conditions here were much worse than in Tehran.

We were cut off from the rest of the world, and it was hard to believe the war was over. We were not shown any pity, compassion, or mercy, even though we were still suffering. We were living in another camp, consisting of thousands of tents. The tents were so close to each other that we had difficulty walking between them without stumbling over the pegs or the stretched ropes holding them up. We had no furniture except for military bunks to sleep on. The bunks consisted of wooden frames with interwoven ropes. The mattress was stuffed with grass and thrown onto the bed frame. We also had one blanket. Mosquito nets hung over the bed to protect us from the billions of mosquitoes circling around us. These insects bit mercilessly, especially at night. They were so annoying that when some people went out in the evening, they wore a mosquito net wrapped around their faces.

Unfortunately, because of shortages, not everyone had the luxury of mosquito protection. I didn't know when, but a mosquito bit my leg. It swelled up and started to leak fluid. Within hours, I developed a fever and chills, my bones ached, my head was pounding, and my whole body hurt. My temperature continued to rise until I became delirious. After losing consciousness, I was taken to the hospital. Once I revived, the doctor told me I had malaria. He prescribed some tablets for me because I still had terrible attacks of high fever. He said I must swallow these bitter quinine and atabrine tablets, even though I learned I was now pregnant. The tablets helped me, but only with the fever, not the actual disease. The doctor said I would never be rid of this disease; I would have it for the rest of my life.

After leaving the hospital, I learned that the Red Cross was asking for blood donors. I volunteered to donate my blood because I wanted to help. The Red Cross doctor interviewed me and asked about my history and illnesses. They refused my blood, saying it was because of the malaria. I would never be able to give blood. They told me the malaria germ would only harm, not help, others.

While I was at the Red Cross hospital, I learned they needed help. I applied and registered, and because I already had experience, I was hired and told to report at the beginning of the week. I returned to our tent, overjoyed, but in the evening, I got another attack of malaria. I got a high fever and a severe headache; I passed out for a few days. I was unconscious, not knowing anything happening in God's world. At the start of the following week, I regained consciousness. Sadly, the hospital could not wait for me to recover and hired someone to take my place.

What a surprise to meet Stella in India. The last time my friend from Poland and I were together was in Tehran. We hugged again like two long-lost sisters. She said she barely recognized me, and no wonder: I was pregnant, and my stomach was as big as an inflated balloon. She asked my due date, and I told her it was in August. Happily, we lived not far from each other in the same camp. She went to a school in the camp and was learning how to sew. She was going to sew something for the christening of my child. She said she would rather learn some other skill, but her mother told her to take the sewing course.

I invited her to visit us so we could talk and catch up on all our news. She said she would love to come over after dinner. When she came over, I introduced her to my husband, Joseph. When she looked at him, she could tell he was a little older than me, and I told her he was eight years older. I asked her to be the godmother of my child if she was still in India when my child was born. I asked her because we had been friends since our younger years; we'd been through many difficult things together and lived in many of the same countries.

Stella told her mother she wanted to be the godmother of my child and asked her to help sew some clothes for the christening. But her mother disagreed; she said she should not be the godmother, and she would not help her sew any clothes. Stella did not want to have problems at home, but it was a great honor to be asked, and she really wanted to do it. She hesitated but finally accepted my request, despite her mother's protests. She said she would ask her teacher for help with the sewing. She said her brothers and sisters were with her in Uzbekistan. Her brothers registered in the Polish army in Uzbekistan, but she had not heard from them since. She arrived with her sisters in Isfahan, where they were taken to a great school, a convent, where they were taught by nuns who not only gave them a very good education but also lovingly cared for them.

Stella and I talked every day now. She told me about a man named Michael, a handsome, dark-haired guy who was our age. Interestingly, it turned out that he came from the same area in Poland that we did. Joseph and I met Michael and got to know him; he said he would like to be the godfather. He talked about the area he came from, and it was true: He lived not far from our colony.

I Give Birth to a Son

The date of my delivery arrived. I was having pains, so they took me to the hospital. It was an English hospital, where only white people were accepted as patients. The nurses were either English or Indian. I called for *aja* (water) because I was very, very thirsty. I could not communicate with them. The doctor was an Englishman, and when he determined that I was Polish, he sent for a Polish nurse.

Her name was Sabina, and she lovingly cared for me and was a great help during the birth of my child. On August 9, 1944, I gave birth to a son. We called him Jon, and I was proud of my new role as mother. Many people visited me: my husband, our friends, and of course, Stella and Michael. She congratulated me and said she was going to start sewing some clothes for my new son right away. I was given a variety of juices and fruits. I opted for a pear, and as I slowly ate it, I heard about a terrible storm that passed through our camp. In the hospital, I could hear the wind and some breaking glass. I did not realize the power of this storm. It turned out this was a cyclone with a terrible tropical downpour. The storm destroyed our whole settlement. No one knew where all the tents went, and even the small buildings were just gone. Only the stone hospital was able to withstand the storm. The city suffered huge losses, leaving many people homeless, and a great number lost their lives. I thanked and praised God that he looked after me and protected my new son.

As I listened to the story of the storm, I suddenly got a terrible pain in my stomach. I could not cope with the pain, so I yelled for a nurse. After a quick examination, the nurse got on my belly and started bouncing up and down. It was an agonizing ordeal, but thankfully, the pain soon subsided. The nurse told me to relax and then advised the guests to return tomorrow.

Stella returned with Michael the next day. She showed me a beautiful white and blue christening gown she and her teacher sewed. I noticed the bonds between Stella and Michael were growing stronger every day. After two weeks, I was allowed to return to a new tent in our hastily rebuilt settlement, and Stella came to help me, but this time with another guy. His name was also Michael, and he was very tall. I could see that this second Michael was coming around more and more to visit Stella, so I asked her what was happening. She said she had found a second boyfriend, and both were competing for her. She started to sing a song about two Michaels: one was tall, and one was short. Finally, one of the Michaels asked for Stella's hand in marriage. But she refused and explained to him that she had to look after her younger siblings, who still needed her. She had done this her whole life.

One day, something was wrong with my infant son Jon. He was shaking, and his skin was covered in goose bumps. He would not stop crying, so I took him to the doctor. I found out he had malaria. I was very worried about my son and this diagnosis. I tell the doctor I don't know when a mosquito bit him because he was always under a mosquito net.

All too soon, Stella came to see me with tears in her eyes. She was saying goodbye. Her family was preparing to leave for another part of India. We promised to write to each other to stay in contact and send our letters through the Red Cross.

A few days later, I had another farewell. Little Michael, who became my son's godfather, told me he was going to Australia. I was sad to hear this and thought Stella should be going with him. He said he could not forgive himself for not stopping Stella from leaving; he should have insisted she marry him.

For many nights, Jon had been crying, and I didn't know why. He had recovered from his bout of malaria. When I got up and took him in my arms, he stopped crying, but as soon as I lay him down, he started crying again. This happened night after night. Then one particular night when he was crying again, I got up, lit a paraffin lamp, and took my son into my arms. I looked at his bed and rearranged the blankets in his crib, thinking he may be crying because he was uncomfortable. To my horror, I saw a snake lying there, twisted and coiled in Jon's bed. The snake had gotten comfortable from Jon's body heat.

Terrified, I started to scream. Joseph woke up and ran into our son's room. The black snake lifted up its head, stuck out its tongue, and hissed. We didn't know what to do. Slowly, the snake slid off Jon's bed. It was about a meter in length. People came running into our tent and grabbed the snake and killed it. They told us to sell the snake to an Indian man because there are many snake charmers who bought reptiles.

We lived, or rather existed, in this camp in Karachi for almost a year. Stella sent me a letter that she had gone with her family to Valivade, Kolhapur, in northern India. She was going to school again and was very happy. She was learning how to work in a print shop and hoped this would allow her to find a good job.

A few more months went by, and Joseph and I decided to leave for Bombay with our son. We would travel from Karachi to Bombay by ship because going over the mountains was too dangerous. We were told the name Bombay means "Gateway to India," named by the English when they first arrived here. Before we went to Bombay, we had to wait for a ship in another tent camp; we waited in this camp for seven months.

Leaving Bombay

Because of the continuing violence in India we were informed we would be leaving Bombay and traveling to the continent of Africa. We lived in Bombay for only a short time, but perhaps a new country would have better living conditions. Many people traveling with us panicked because they didn't know what to expect. They heard Africa was not a healthy country, and there were many wild people and wild animals. Again, we were loaded into army trucks that took us to the port. There were hundreds of soldiers, who had priority for the journey. They walked in columns, carrying their equipment onto the ship. Once the soldiers were on board, they helped the civilians to board. In total, there were about three thousand people. Everything looked much better organized than in Krasnovodsk.

Our ship was a British steamship. When we left the port, we were in the open Indian Ocean. The wind was quite strong, and the waves were very high and rocked the ship. Many people were throwing up. My stomach was turning over and over, bringing what little food I ate into my throat. I rushed to the side of the ship and vomited over the rail into the water. I was so sick that I returned to the side of the ship to vomit again and again. After several rounds of this, my stomach was completely empty. I felt loathsome and horrid. But then, my stomach had the dry heaves. I tried to get some fresh air into my lungs, and I felt a bit better, but still not very well. In addition, I could not leave the deck for fear of more vomiting, but the sun was burning my skin. I looked for an umbrella or some kind of shade, but I could not see any place where I could duck into to hide from the scorching heat. The people who were throwing up had already taken the shady spots.

I looked down, watching the waves crash against the ship and then break up into foam. They said we were approaching the equator. Not understanding what that meant, I didn't know what to expect. Thankfully, Jon was happily playing with other children. The sun started to set and changed into a huge red ball. On the distant horizon, there was a beautiful sunset. Night fell. I still felt my stomach churning and was afraid to go to sleep. I dozed through the night, clinging to the railing.

In the early morning, the wind died down. The sun rose, announcing the start of a beautiful, sunny day. There was not the slightest movement of air. I looked over the side of the deck and saw incredibly calm water. It was smooth, shiny, and flat, like a piece of glass or a mirror reflecting the sun's rays. There was not a single wave. It was as if someone grabbed the edges of the ocean and spread it out like a piece of cloth.

We were on the equator. I was thankful my stomach settled, and it started making growling noises. I was hungry. The sun began to bake my skin, so I tried to find some shade. Everyone was suffering in the intense heat at the equator. All day long, people complained about it. We all tried to hide from the burning rays. We could not wait for the cool of the evening and nightfall. Finally, once again, the sun turned into a fiery ball and disappeared into the ocean. I had never seen such incredibly beautiful sunsets in my life.

Impact of a Mine

Night passed peacefully, and I slept well. In the morning, after breakfast, we all suddenly heard a loud bang. The ship jolted, and the passengers were thrown off balance, falling to the floor of the deck. Everything was thrown toward the front of the ship. Things in the cabins bounced off the walls and broke. I found myself on the floor in the cabin. As soon as I gathered my wits about me, my first thought was of my baby. I jumped to my feet, grabbed Jon into my arms, and ran up the stairs to the main deck. I needed to find my husband. I knew he was gambling with some friends. I was full of foreboding and heard the sound of cursing because of this sudden banging and jolting.

On the main deck, there was total panic; people were screaming and crying. Many were coming up to the main deck; it was so crowded, you could not move.

Someone shouted, "It's a mine!"

I grew scared and wondered if this was possible. Fear paralyzed me completely. Were we sinking? Suddenly, the ship began to blow ear-shattering blasts from the chimneys, again and again. The blasts were so loud that everything was shaking. The steam from the chimneys rose high into the clear blue sky, making dense columns of steam. People were saying these blasts were a call for help, an SOS call.

Someone said they saw a huge hole torn out of the bow. Others assured us the damage was minor and said not to panic. We did not know who to believe. Panic and confusion deepened with every passing moment.

The soldiers asked among themselves if it was possible that a mine could have been missed by the minesweepers who cleared these waters. They said they were assured all the mines were destroyed in these waters when the war was over. Now, they were questioning whether one of the mines was overlooked, and we sailed into it.

We waited impatiently for a formal communication from the captain. The ship's sailors wandered around, trying to explain the situation. Finally, they came with translators to try to calm everyone down, saying everything was fine, the mechanics were working on repairing the damage, and an international call for help had been sent. They said help was already on the way. The engines were shut down so the situation did not get worse. The crew asked people not to panic and said they would hand out life jackets and demonstrate how to put them on.

One of the passengers was a priest. He started to pray and began with Hail Mary. One by one, everyone calmed down, and it got very quiet. People knelt on the deck and started to pray to Mary for help. In between the words of the prayer, I heard only sobbing.

The ship was not moving, just standing still. I knew for certain now that we were sinking, but it was very slow. Everyone was praying, but as we looked around us, we saw only the expanse of water, the vastness of the open ocean, and the blue sky. If someone was coming to rescue us, we would see them on the horizon, but there was no one. All day went by, and we saw nothing; no one was coming. When the sun went down, it got dark, and some people lit candles. The priest insisted on celebrating Mass. After the Mass, we prayed and sang a few hymns to Mary, mother of God. We asked her to save us and to send help, to rescue us. What else was left for us to do?

Although the night was cool, it dragged on and on. After what seemed like an eternity, the sun came up. With the sunrise, we heard shouting. Someone saw something on the horizon, a tiny speck. We got our hopes raised and started smiling and thanking God for answering our prayers. Our ship started to blow its horns full blast to signal for help. Everything shook and rumbled. The steamer in the distance sent up a column of smoke. It was approaching us, but was it coming to rescue us? It was headed right for us. We were so impatient; we could hardly wait for it to reach us. We were sinking, yet we knew that help was coming.

The rescue ship finally reached us. When it was close enough, it stopped; lifeboats from our ship were loaded with passengers and lowered into the water. The passengers were then loaded onto the rescue ship. After taking some of the passengers from our sinking ship onto their rescue ship, they checked the condition of our vessel and could see it was damaged. They worried there would be trouble if our steam boilers exploded. Then we heard a powerful explosion from the steam boilers. They were blowing up, and we saw gigantic clouds of steam climbing into the sky. Our ship was going down. The back of the ship was way above the water, with the propeller showing. Another ship arrived to help with the rescue. Thankfully, we would all survive. The ocean water was quite still, and both rescue vessels departed as soon as everyone was safe. Shortly after, our ship began to sink, with only the back of a large turbine visible. Soon, she was immersed in the depths of the Indian Ocean, and we could see it no more.

After our ship sank, the water was calm, almost like glass. An announcement was made over the loudspeakers that a thanksgiving Mass would be celebrated to give thanks to God and Mary for saving us from disaster. We gathered on the main deck and waited for the Mass to begin. We tried to forget about the tragedy that could have buried all of us in the depths of the Indian Ocean.

After a few days, we spotted huge fish circling the ship. The personnel on the rescue ship said these fish were African dolphins and would likely accompany us all the way to the coast of Africa. The fish jumped out of the water and dove back in, swimming like lightning on top of the water, and disappeared again, like they were playing with us. They were most charming. Watching them play, I could see far away on the horizon an outline of land. This was Kenya, the next country on our journey.

Kenya, Africa

Far on the horizon, I saw land and was told it was Kenya, one of the countries of the huge African continent. I wondered what kind of life we would have there. I heard people talking about jungles, different wild animals, unusual fruits, things I had not seen or heard of before. I overheard people talking about horrible diseases and plagues of all kinds. We saw a huge city; it was Mombasa. We approached a port called Kilindini.

We reached the shore and quickly descended a long staircase to land. Some people fell to their knees and kissed the ground in gratitude for their safe arrival after our near-drowning. We had to wait for the transport to take us to Nyali, a temporary transient camp in the suburbs of Mombasa.

For the first time in my life, I saw black-skinned people; they had skin as black as coal. I watched them and saw how they carried packages and all kinds of things on their heads. What a new world this was to me. Maybe it would be better than the previous ones.

Our transport arrived. We got into a row of army trucks that weaved in and out like snakes as we headed to our new destination. Polish army drivers welcomed us to this British colony. We asked them where we were going. They replied,

"To an English camp in the British colonies." The Polish drivers said there were over twenty scattered Polish settlements in eastern and southern Africa. Most were founded by the English after the first evacuation from Siberia in 1942. The driver jokingly asked what kind of demands we had.

As we left the port, I saw many black-skinned people walking in every direction. In between them were black policemen, wearing white uniforms with white helmets on their heads. The women wore wonderful dresses in all the colors of the rainbow. The roads and sidewalks were planted with beautiful shrubs and flowers of all colors; the species were unknown to me. There were groups of people standing around or sitting down in the shade of spreading trees and coconut palms, just like in India, talking in incomprehensible gibberish that I didn't understand.

We arrived at a camp and were told we wouldn't be there long. The rest of the day was spent resting and eating supper. We slept wherever we could find a place. In the morning, we set off on a journey into the depths of Africa.

Tangero, Tanganyika

We traveled through different parts of Kenya and across the border into Lake Tanganyika, a distance of over four hundred kilometers. As we drove, the landscape constantly changed. We stopped at the border of the two countries to stretch our legs and enjoyed a dinner consisting of hot soup and sandwiches. We spent the night on the African steppes, in an open field with lit fires around us. The native guards kept watch over us to protect us from the wild animals.

Early in the morning, after a quick breakfast, we were on the road again. The system was now in English miles, not kilometers. The road to the west went into the depths of Africa and led us through extraordinarily beautiful landscape, with stunning, lush forests and jungles. We traveled through beautiful clearings covered with elephant grass reaching up to four meters high. Riding in the army trucks was sometimes worrisome. Although the road was paved with asphalt in places, most of the roads were not. We stopped for a break and got a couple of sandwiches each. They warned us to keep together in a group and not to wander away because of the animals hiding in the bush.

I asked the driver about the two huge mountains in the

distance. He pointed to them and explained the smaller one was called Mount Meru; we would travel around it. The higher peak was Mount Kilimanjaro, and we would not reach it because we needed to rest. As we traveled around Mount Meru, I saw an unusual sight: There were strange black spots moving on the sides of the slopes. I asked one of the soldiers what they were. He answered they were shadows of clouds moving alongside the mountain. They were so black; you could not imagine how black they were. The soldiers explained that we were so close to the equator, and the sun was so bright, it threw unusually dark shadows on the side of the mountain. I admired this unusual sight. Wherever I looked, I saw lush green landscapes.

We traveled on, toward the settlement of Tangero. The drivers explained that the name was derived from Tanganyika and Meru. Traveling into the settlement, we saw it turned out to be an unusually charming town, filled with hundreds of different whitewashed mud houses. I learned later that the whitewash was painted with lime. In the sun, the white looked like snow. There were a variety of house shapes: some round, some square, some small, and others large. The roofs were covered with leaves from banana trees, palm leaves, or long elephant grass. I saw many gorgeous flowers, giant cacti, and trees. There was a large church and a few other large buildings in the distance. The settlement was quite large; it turned out this was one of the largest settlements in Africa. It housed more than four thousand displaced Poles.

It was very hot. The air was so hot that everything around seemed to shimmer. They said the sun rose here at five thirty in the morning, and by nine o'clock, it was almost unbearable, and yet the worst heat of the day was around midday. There was a pleasant light breeze that blew from time to time, cooling us off.

The army transport stopped in front of the church, and we all got out of the trucks. Waiting for us was the quartermaster and his delegation. After a short welcome, they explained the layout of the settlement to us. There was a parish community center, a theater, government buildings, schools, warehouses, stores, and a hospital, all whitewashed with lime. The church was surrounded by a neat lawn and was dominated by a lovely manicured green hedge. As I walked up to the hedge, I saw it had letters that read "POLAND 1942." They told us this was our Poland for now, but it was only temporary. They said that everything would be explained in a general meeting after dinner in the community center.

They designated different mud huts according to the size of the family. We were given two small round huts. The smaller one was our bedroom. It was furnished with wooden army cots with straw mattresses. This hut was so small, you could barely turn around in it. The second hut was the kitchen, but for now, it was completely empty. There were no ceilings in either of the huts. Above the wall was a large open space. Looking up, I was astonished to see the roof was constructed of logs that came to a point in the center at the top of the roof. These logs were then covered with leaves and overlaid with elephant grass. There was a wide gap in between the walls and the roof. We were not sure what it was for; I guessed it might be for better ventilation.

The floors were of packed clay mud. Each hut had one window for ventilation but did not have any glass. They were not sealed in, anyway. The shutters did not close properly, even on a windy day. If the rain came in, it would soak you. The doors to enter the huts were also not sealed and had cracks. But it seemed to me the water would not get inside because the overhang of the roof was very wide around the entire hut, which protected the inside from rain and the scorching sun. As we left our mud hut, we walked along to the community center and passed a huge tree. I asked some people the name of this tree. They said it was a baobab. They said it was the grandfather of all trees and was more than one thousand years old. I'm not sure if even twenty-five people circling the tree arm in arm could manage to join hands. During our lunch, they reminded us about the important meeting.

The First General Meeting

In this orientation meeting at the community center, the quartermaster said there were about four thousand people there in Tangero. About half of them were children, and half of these children were orphans. He said we would not be forced to work; we could rest after our Russian captivity. There was a lot of work here in the settlement, however, for people who wanted to volunteer. There were opportunities in the hospital, kitchen, warehouses, and farms. He warned about the many tropical diseases and said that we must be careful to avoid them as much as possible. There were shortages of formally qualified teachers in our schools and orphanages. People would be given help with household tasks, cleaning, laundry, cooking, and looking after little children. After the meeting, we registered to get help from the local natives.

The quartermaster assured us our children would return to Poland with an excellent education. He continued by saying the youngsters needed to register for schools and higher education as well as taking part in scouts. He explained that Poland had been destroyed. The schools were destroyed, teachers were not available to teach the youngsters, and if we returned now, the children would not get an education. So we had to make use of the English government, which provided this service to us. He said the youngsters would study in groups after-hours in the teachers' mud huts.

Each Saturday, there were dances at the center, and they had their own orchestra. Joseph was happy to learn he could play his violin at the dances and in the theater. There would be staged performances in the theater, as well as plays and dances wearing national costumes. Also, there would be different religious performances, and a choir would entertain us quite often. We would also have volleyball and soccer games. Sometimes, we would even have tournaments with teams from other camps.

Next to the soccer field was a farm where anyone who wished to could plant their own garden, watch it grow, and collect the harvest. Across the road from the farm was a field surrounded by plantations of coffee, corn, cacao, and papaya trees. Just off the settlement was a lovely lake called Duluti. It was surrounded by picturesque hills. The water was clean and cool. The quartermaster asked us not to pollute the water and to keep a close eye on our children because the lake was very deep.

The hospital, unfortunately, was filled with people who had not yet recovered from the hardships of Siberia and their subsequent exile. Some already picked up tropical diseases, mainly malaria. Behind the hospital was a cemetery for those who had died.

Walking to our supper the first night, we heard people telling a horror story of two brothers, fourteen-year-old Jack and sixteen-year-old Michael, whose parents died in Uzbekistan. They were being raised their grandmother. They wanted to go swimming in the lake, even after the warnings. They jumped in and had a wonderful time, playing as young boys do, but suddenly, emerging from the depths of the lake came a mighty crocodile. While other children were playing on the shore and watching, the monster crocodile opened its huge mouth, snatched Jack's leg, and pulled him under the water. The boy struggled for a moment and cried out for help, but no one was able to save him. He never surfaced again.

A couple of men decided to find Jack's remains and kill the crocodile. Hours passed, and later days, but all in vain. No sign of the boy or the animal. Their grandmother sat day and night on the shore, crying and praying. Michael promised himself he was going to kill that crocodile. One day, he went out with a dagger, determined to find it. He went swimming and splashing, hoping to attract the beast. It was as if the crocodile were waiting for him. It appeared this time in front of a whole crowd of onlookers. In only a few seconds, Michael was grabbed and disappeared below the surface. At the end of the day, the men gave up looking for their bodies. They announced they would try to somehow poison the man-eater.

Walking to the storage buildings, we had to wait in a lineup. I listened as people complained that the Russians had stolen the best years of their lives. They said we had to go to many different countries, so why did we need a school and an education? They felt they did not need to be educated and thought the government would always give them everything for free. After I gathered all my supplies from the storage area, I heard different parents wondering how they could coax their children into attending school and scout functions, since none of them had attended school in a very long time, if at all.

The quartermaster said we were to pick up mosquito nets, bed linen, oil lamps, little spirit stoves for cooking, and lots of pots. They gave us everything we needed: blankets, pillows, and some other items to help us get settled, like towels, soap, and dishes. We brought it all home, and the first thing I did was hang the mosquito nets over our beds so we could sleep without the threat of disease-carrying mosquitoes. Once the nets were in place, it was time to go to the main kitchen for supper. Right after supper, it started to get dark. With the darkness, we saw there were poles with electric lamps lighting up several streets as well as the main square of our settlement. I explained to Jon that tonight we had to go to bed with the chickens, because we did not have any light in our hut, but tomorrow, they would give us paraffin for the lamps.

The first night, I fell asleep quickly from fatigue, but I soon woke after hearing strange noises coming from outside. I didn't know what was lurking in the dark. I listened to strange noises, roars from lions, barking and howling from hyenas, and screams from other animals. These sounds were so loud and clear, it was like we were sleeping outside. My imagination told me these screaming animals could come inside our hut at any time through the many holes in the walls. I was afraid for my son and did not want to admit my fear or cowardice to my husband, so I covered my head with a blanket, shaking and trembling all over with fear. Finally, I fell asleep, exhausted.

In the morning, I went out into the yard to see what happened during the night but found nothing, not a single sign of animals or anything out of place. We went for breakfast, and while eating at the table, I heard stories about the wild animals and their activity during the night. Every day, I learned something new about the local fauna.

While eating, I started furiously scratching my calves. I thought I may have been bitten by mosquitoes, but a neighbor at the table said it was most likely bloodsucker bugs. The only way to be rid of them was to go to the storage building and get a sprayer filled with a substance called Flit. He said it must be sprayed on all the walls and floor; that was the only way to keep these vermin under control.

Right after we finished eating breakfast, we went to the office to ask for help with the work in our hut and then went on to the storage building to get a supply of paraffin for the lamps and Flit for the bugs. We wanted to be prepared for the coming night. The day was so hot and dry; the earth was parched and cracked and could cause terrible burns on bare feet, so we always wore shoes.

When we returned to our hut with the sprayer, I didn't know exactly where the bugs were hiding, so I started searching with determination. I removed the pictures of Mary and Jesus I hung on the walls and saw bugs running around, trying to escape. I found more of these nocturnal vermin emerging from cracks in the doors and walls and holes in the roof. The bloodsuckers and termites marched briskly along the walls and floor. I shook at the sight of all these bugs. I quickly grabbed the Flit and headed into battle. I sprayed the deadly cloud directly on the insects and the walls and floor. The intruding bugs immediately died. Jon and I spent some time trying to kill them all. This reminded me of what I had to endure in Siberia.

After lunch, everyone went for a restuntil at least three o'clock in the afternoon because of the intense heat; it was much too hot to do anything except rest and stay out of the sun. Fortunately, the hut was a great place to escape from the blazing sun.

Slowly, I began to distinguish between the individual African sounds: the crying, howling hyenas, the roar of the lions, and the shrill cries of monkeys, birds, jackals, and vultures. I also found there were many different species of ants. Ants, it turned out, were the most dangerous of all; children especially had to watch out for them as they played.

Around six in the evening, Jon and I took a walk to look at the beautiful sunset. The air was filled with the fragrance of oleander bushes growing along the broad street. They had all sorts of colors: white, pink, red. The scent seemed even more beautiful and intense after sunset.

On Sundays, I went to church and celebrated Catholic Mass. I observed this day as holy. I thanked God for surviving difficult times and for our freedom. I tried to faithfully fulfill my religious responsibilities. I learned that an English bishop would be visiting our settlement for two days to welcome the new settlers. He would preside over the Mass, and when he arrived, I went to see him. The ceremony was very solemn and beautiful, but it was spoken in English. I liked the language but did not understand it. The priest saved the situation by translating the bishop's words into Polish.

I heard a lot of talk about the town of Arusha. It was in a valley about seven miles from our settlement. I made arrangements with my new friend, Kristen, to visit this town. There were only a few shops, a railway station, and a bus station. We walked around the shops all day long, feeling like we were on holiday. We had a wonderful time. I left Jon with my new black-skinned helper named Yona. They got along very well together, so I was not worried.

Every time we went for a meal, I noticed unusual long-legged birds near the main kitchen. They reminded me of storks. Jon always ran toward them and scared them away. They were taller than him, and I wondered if they were vultures. One day, when I went into the kitchen, I asked about these birds. They told me they were called marabouts. These birds were always begging for any food discarded from the kitchen. After a closer look at them, I concluded they were quite funny. They had a large, bald head on a long, bare neck, and their huge body was covered with lovely, dark green feathers. Anything they caught in their beaks just disappeared in the blink of an eye down their deep throats.

I found we needed to be very vigilant about the different types of ants, especially the warrior ants and the dangerous termites that lived in walls, in trees, or in mounds that were built like fortresses on the land. Red ants were tiny and difficult to see and lived just under the ground. Their nests were hard to see, and if you stepped on one, they attacked by the thousands. Their bites were extremely painful. There were wanderer ants, which were constantly moving, attacking and destroying everything they encountered on their way. I heard a story about a twelve-year-old girl who was playing near an ant nest without realizing it. Within seconds, she started to cry and scream because she was covered with millions of biting ants. Hearing her scream, people came running to try to help but were unable to get the ants off her. They had to douse the girl with paraffin and rushed her to the hospital.

After hearing of this incident, it makes us wary of any kind of ant. And not only ants, but snakes, many of which were poisonous. They said size did not matter; little snakes the size of small woman's belt could be as dangerous as giant pythons. One woman who was walking along a pathway spotted a pretty colored belt lying on the ground. She bent down and picked it up, and it was a snake, which bit her. She had no chance to even call for help before she died.

Another woman was also walking along a pathway and encountered a giant snake. Terrified, she began to back away, and when she was a short distance from the snake, she screamed. People ran in her direction. I also heard the woman scream, so I took Jon's hand and went to see what was happening. When we came upon the snake, it turned out to be a boa constrictor about ten meters long, lying motionless on the ground. It was very thick. A man ran over with a rifle and fired a few shots into the snake's head. Then he cut the belly open and found a small deer inside, still half-alive. Apparently, the snake had the deer for lunch; luckily, we were able to save its life and let it go free. But it could have been a catastrophe for the woman if the snake had not already eaten.

There were many dangers in this beautiful land of Africa. Ground fleas laid their eggs under your toenails. Once the larva hatched, they became parasites and lived in your body, causing infection. Then your legs would fester and become painful, and by then, not even the hospital could help. The only remedy was to visit a local healer. They were so familiar with this condition that they used a needle to extract the eggs from under the toenails. They were so efficient at doing this procedure, it was painless.

Black Help

To help in the house, I got two young native black boys, sixteen-year-old Yona and eighteen-year-old Kuda. Their pay was two shillings and a sixpence a week and a pound of *mili-mili*, which means coconut flour. I was trying to learn Swahili, but I mostly communicated with them in Polish, with a lot of gestures and waving of hands. I was also having a tough time with the English money as well as the English weights and measures. I asked the boys if they were Masai, like most of the natives who worked in the area. They said they were from a different tribe of the Masai. They said their tribe mainly worked with goats and raised fruit, but they had many disagreements and fights with other tribes who raised cattle. Many of these fights turned into bloody wars among the tribes.

Yona talked happily about working for a Polish teacher who recently left for Mexico. She taught him how to work with children. He had been taught good manners and had a good sense of humor. His duty was taking care of Jon. Kuda was more serious. He spoke very gently and respectfully. He previously worked for a doctor, who trained him to cook and clean the house. Those were his duties for us.

To be honest, I felt uncomfortable about the help situation.

Black natives worked everywhere around the settlement, and it made me upset that they were being exploited by whites, not only by the colonists, but also by our Polish people. I felt sorry for them because I saw they lived very modestly; when I could, I gave them clothes or food to take home. Such gestures created good friendships.

Yona played with Jon, teaching him how to climb the small tree growing beside our hut. Jon learned quickly, as if he were a monkey. As he climbed the tree, he learned more about nature. He caught and played with chameleons. Yona showed Jon how they changed the color of their skin, depending on the surface they were on. He warned Jon about putting these chameleons on a red surface because they would die. He claimed their blood would come through their skin and cause their death.

A large black bird often came by to be fed by Jon and Yona. They always fed him bread crumbs or sunflower seeds. Jon wanted Yona to catch this bird so he could have it for his pet. Since they fed the bird regularly, it was used to them and trusted them. So Yona caught the bird and tied its wings so it could not fly away. He also tied a string to one of its legs, preventing it from running away. Eventually, the bird got used to its new situation, and Yona took the rope from its leg and released its wings.

Jon played with his pet all day. He lay down on his back with his hands behind his head, and the bird hopped onto Jon's chest. After eating a sandwich, Jon would grin, showing his teeth, and the bird, still sitting on his chest, gently pecked at the crumbs from Jon's chest. Then the bird pecked at his teeth. It cleaned Jon's teeth by gently pecking the crumbs from between his teeth. Jon proudly boasted to me that his pet cleaned his teeth. I was afraid the bird might peck out Jon's eyes, but Yona assured me there was no danger of that happening; the bird was really peaceful. We had a little dog, a dachshund called Reno, who tried to grab the bird (to protect Jon, or perhaps out of jealousy). Even though Reno was tied up, he still tried to grab the bird.

One day, I received a letter from Stella via the Red Cross. She wrote that she had no information about her brothers but added that she managed to get on a list to go to England. She said she would be leaving for England soon.

Kilimanjaro

I often looked at the beautiful Kilimanjaro Mountain; it was a lovely white color. The people here said it was covered with an ice glacier, and it shone so brilliantly in the sunshine. I wondered if this ice would ever melt under this very hot sun.

I asked Yona why this mountain was called Kilamanjaro. He said it is was called Kilamanjaro because it was like a torte covered with white icing. He said the mountain was about fifty miles away, and it was about fifteen thousand feet in height. According to legend, the mountain peak was always white. It was covered with glaciers and therefore shone like a diamond in the sun. It amazed me how the ice did not melt from the heat and sunlight. "*Kilima-ya-Njaro*" in Swahili means "Shining Mountain." Yona said that the old people in his village told many stories about the mountain. They said the name dated back a thousand years and that the white icing was a magic medicine called "*Ngaje-Nga*," meaning it was their house of God. A long time ago, it was an active, dangerous volcano. It spewed flames, lava, smoke, and ashes that covered the whole area. Now, fortunately, Kibo was asleep. This mountain was an attraction where daredevils and expeditions came to get a close-up view of the volcano. Anyone who felt strong enough would visit this mountain peak, people like doctors, priests, scouts, and teachers. From sunrise to sunset, it was always a beautiful sight. In fact, it did look like a cake drenched in white icing.

My friend Kristen and I wanted to see wild animals. We asked Yona to take us to see some animals, even if only from a distance. He agreed, and the three of us traveled some distance outside our settlement. Soon, we came to a flock of lovely colorful birds. A little farther along, we found zebras, giraffes, and ostriches. We watched how easily the giraffes could reach the leaves from the tall acacia trees. They pulled the leaves into their mouths with their long tongues. Surprised, they looked at us with their big, brown eyes, as if to ask what we were doing here. The zebras fed themselves on the grass, just like horses do in a pasture. They snorted and waved their tails, trying to get rid of the flies that buzzed around them. They paid no attention to us. Ostriches, with their tiny bare heads, looked as though their beaks were glued onto their heads. They appeared to be straining, with naked necks stretched over the bird's body. Their wings were covered in beautiful feathers, and their tail was a plume of large lovely feathers. They stood proudly on high stilted legs, staring intently at the intruders.

The view of all these animals was impressive, but it scared me a little. I didn't know if we were safe here. We tried to keep quiet and peaceful so we did not frighten them. But as we got closer and closer to them, they suspected danger. Suddenly, they broke into a run. The zebras escaped at a gallop, the giraffes escaped with their powerful jumps, and the ostriches picked themselves up with their wings and ran off. For a while, the earth rumbled with the sound of all these great hooves pounding the ground, but then, everything stopped. They did not run far before they stopped and looked back in our direction, almost as if they wanted to talk to us. We did not want to bother them further. Yona brought us back to our settlement, and that was how he ended his day's work.

Yona often took Jon for walks outside of the settlement, going to sugar cane, corn, and mango plantations. He also brought him to the Masai village. Many times, Jon came back with something in his teeth or sucking on a stick of some kind. Initially, I tried to tell him to get rid of this garbage stick from his mouth, but he kept sucking on it, teasing me, trying to play a game with me. He laughed, explained that it was sugar cane, and gave me some to try. It was tasty. He got these sticks from the Masai on the plantation. He gave them a crust from white bread, which was a rare treat for them, and they in turn gave him small sacks of corn.

The natives were very proud, though mostly naked, and they were always armed with knives and spears: ready for war, to fight wild animals, or to defend their animals, their land, and their family. They brought their cattle to graze in a field near a village. The cattle often fell prey to lions, leopards, and other large wild cats that waited to attack any animal. They lurked in the tall grasses at the edge of the forest. Masai people drank a lot of milk and fed mostly on red meat. They pointed to a wounded steer and said the men had to drink a lot of fresh, warm blood to give them courage and strength, and it increased their manhood.

Along the edge of the forest, I saw some trees with huge stumps hanging from them. These stumps had been hollowed out, and inside them were large bee hives. The natives gather lots of honey from these hives.

Jon sat with the Masai in a circle in front of a fire. They were frying termites and grasshoppers on a piece of tin. Once they pulled the wings off, they stuffed these delicacies into their mouths. Once their mouths were full, they patted their bellies and said, *"Mzuri, Bwana, mzuri"* (Good, man, good.). I could hardly believe my son was really enjoying this Masai delicacy, smacking his lips. Initially, I was disgusted; I grabbed his hand and told him to spit the stuff out of his mouth. The Masai roared with laughter, for they were convinced it was good food. They asked me to try some also. Jon laughed with them and said he was learning the natives' manners and their Swahili language.

Jon was becoming more independent. After we returned from the Masai village, he went to the brick oven built in the middle of the settlement near our hut. The furnace was usually fired up; every housewife from the settlement used it for cooking and baking. Jon opened the oven door and briskly pushed corn into the hot coals and ashes. After a few minutes, he returned to the hut, jumping up and down, anticipating this treat, while blowing on the corn to cool it off. He sat on the doorstep and smacked his lips while he ATE the corn.

One day, we heard some drumming music. Jon called me and pointed to a marching scouting troop. In the lead was a boy proudly carrying a white flag with an embroidered gold cross and a red inscription reading "Tangier Polish Brigade." Under the cross was written one word: "Vigilant." In the corners of the flag were green fleur-de-lis. On each side of the parade, marching percussionists beat their sticks on drums. In rows behind them, a regiment of scouts loudly sang "The Marching Soldier," a Polish song. Jon was delighted with this music. He said as soon as he was a little older, he wanted to join the scouts. I had no problems with that. I liked that the scouts taught the young people discipline, cooperation, and respect for nature.

The youngsters learned in groups. Many of these groups studied into the night in homes of the teachers. Some of the youngsters who were interested in their futures began to walk to the British vocational schools.

One day, the young students cleaned the entire settlement, repairing and whitewashing the mud huts. We asked what the occasion was for the big cleanup and were told that we would have visitors. Soon, the guests arrived; they were from Nairobi. They turned out to be the minister of science and education, along with his delegation. I snooped around and heard them talking in my native language. I was convinced they were Poles.

Some of our neighbors heard about high wages in the nearby towns like Moshi, Arusha, Kampala, Dar Es Salaam, and Nairobi. Travel to these towns was a problem, and so they were given other accommodations there. Many of them chose to move to these towns.

A Letter from Stella

I received a letter from Stella through the Red Cross. She said she made it onto the list to exit to England and already managed to get there safely. She described her voyage on a cargo freighter through the Indian Ocean. They did not have a cabin so they had to sit and sleep on the main deck. The weather was nasty and so terrible that everyone was seasick, vomiting all the time. She said they were told to just lay on the deck and pray. It was only when they reached the Red Sea that the storm subsided, and the rest of the journey was pleasant. The ship docked in the port of Southampton in Great Britain. From there, Stella was transferred in army trucks that drove smoothly to the town of Leamington in Warwickshire. She wrote the whole journey through England was amazing, but she was unable to believe how overcast and gloomy this country was. She was accustomed to the landscape of India and the hot burning sun and forgot about rainy weather. She described England as being slightly hilly and very green. The towns and villages were close together. She was so used to sandy desert; she didn't remember what the rest of the world was like. Once she reached the army camp, she realized she had a problem: Everyone was speaking the English language, and she did not understand a thing they were saying. She met some Polish soldiers who translated the language for her. She said she got to know a Polish sergeant whose name was Walter. After only two months, she married him.

The English army personnel didn't waste any time; they found jobs for the Polish immigrants in a munitions factory. Stella said that before she was accepted for this job, she had to swear to keep everything regarding the job secret. She could only tell me she was working in the production of mines, bombs, and grenades.

She also wrote about the tragic story of her brother. After her arrival in England, she received a beautiful letter from him, sent from Monte Casino in Italy. She was so happy to get his letter, but her happiness only lasted for two days. Two days later, she received notification of his death. He stepped on a mine, and his body was torn to pieces. Stella wrote she was still in shock and mourning him. He had wandered the world for such a long time, and they were so close to seeing each other again, and at the last minute, he died.

My friend reminded me of our shared escapades in Karachi and Tehran, when the American pilot talked us into flying with him in an airplane over the city and the fateful limousine ride, where we had to escape by jumping into a ditch from the moving car. As I read the letter and recalled the stories she wrote of, I realized I miss her very much. She was my truest friend.

Female Masai Merchants

Although it was illegal for the Masai women to sell their goods, they came to our settlement and traded all kinds of commodities. They were dressed in long, colorful dresses, and their heads were shaved clean and smeared with grease that shone in the sun. They stealthily emerged from the forest and walked over to our mud huts. On their heads, they carried blankets, mats, and rolls of beautiful fabric. They also carried other goods. Their neck and ears were covered with chains and earrings, which they made by hand from brass and pretty colored beads. Their arms and legs sparkled with dozens of bracelets and glowing rings. They looked very attractive. I invited two of them into my home. They had beautiful material that I was fond of and definitely wanted to buy. We haggled over the price. I offered two English pounds in paper notes, but they did not accept this, so I raised the rate to three pounds. Again, they refused, saying something to me in Swahili. I could not understand what she was trying to tell me, so I used sign language to tell her I didn't understand. Then I offered them a five-pound note, and I saw they were clearly displeased.

One of them shook her head again, not agreeing to my price. Instead, she said something in Swahili and pointed to my wallet. I picked up my snakeskin wallet and emptied all the coins out of it, pennies and shillings made from copper, brass, and silver; some of the coins had holes in them. She picked out one with a hole and showed me by sign language that she would make a necklace, a bracelet, and earrings. It finally dawned on me what she meant. Although the paper money had a much higher value, this Masai lady did not want it because paper money could not be made into jewelery.

I saw she was pleased and happy. I showed her using sign language that she could drill holes into the coins and convert them into not only necklaces and bracelets but also earrings. She was delighted and happily grabbed all the pennies, giving me as much material as I wanted. They got up and disappeared into the jungle again. I could not believe that I got all that beautiful fabric for a few pennies. Now I understood if I wanted to buy something in Africa, I had to carry a lot of small coins with holes in them to bargain with.

I also learned from watching these Masai women how to carry my son Jon so that he was protected from the ugly ants, snakes, and fleas.

We lacked furniture, so Joseph brought home orange boxes and empty wooden tea boxes from China; they were three feet by three feet and lined with aluminum foil. The larger tea boxes we used as a kitchen table. We set the smaller, more fragrant orange boxes beside our bed as nightstands, and some we used for chairs. With my pockets full of coins, I set off in search of the Masai to buy material to make tablecloths and chair covers for our new furniture.

Looking at Mount Meru from Tangero, the landscape was absolutely beautiful. Gently rolling folds of the terrain rose higher and higher, eventually reaching Mount Meru. Looking at the picturesque landscape, my husband said there must be beautiful game with decorative horns and antlers living up there. He was anxious to go hunting for this game and bought himself a shotgun. I warned him that even though he had a rifle, he could still end up in the claws of a leopard or another wild animal. Joseph was not afraid, however, and often brought home various trophies from his nocturnal escapades: giant heads with horns and different skins that he stretched out on the walls or the floor. Some hunters shot the poor animals just for the love of the kill. I had mixed feelings about these hunts.

A safari was organized by our settlement to Lake Victoria. Expedition organizers said we could watch the animals in their natural hideouts and lairs. We would especially like to see lions, leopards, giraffes, elephants, ostriches, zebras, antelopes, buffaloes, and gazelles. We traveled by army trucks, looking at different jungle terrains and stopping along the way for supper and a rest. We spent the night in tents. In the morning, after breakfast, we continued our journey. On the shores of Lake Victoria, we had the opportunity to see crocodiles and hippopotami. We were looked after by guides armed with rifles; they asked us to keep a safe distance between us and the wildlife. Because they were wild, we had to be careful; although the animals were afraid of us and in most cases ran at the sight of humans, the guards didn't want any unfortunate accidents. We returned from this adventure happy that we were able to see so much African wildlife in their natural habitats.

I took a walk with my son Jon on the shores of nearby Lake Duluti, where we had more incredible viewing experiences. We admired the unique beauty of many birds. We liked the toucans the best. These birds had a powerful beak and reminded us of circus clowns; each part was different and full of intense colors. As we walked along the different pathways, we looked at the beautiful trees, called *tembu,* which was elephant wood.

We met several natives. They were cheerful and friendly, and they always greeted us with the word "*Jambo*," which means "Good day."

We went to a local African market, which was a stone's throw away from Lake Duluti. The Africans sold their colorful necklaces, earrings, and bracelets made with brass and colored beads. They also sold fabrics and fresh fruits. They looked at us as though they were interested in our dress and listened to our foreign language. I liked going there to buy whatever they sold. The fruit tasted so good to me, especially the sweet and fleshy mango, which grew there in large quantities. Walking around, I picked a few nice ripe mangos to bring back home to our mud hut. We ate them for breakfast or finished our meal with this beautiful, sweet fruit for dessert.

Meanwhile, I decided to change the route I walked with Jon. I did not want to tempt fate. I was afraid of the crocodiles, so we walked outside the orphanage buildings, where we watched the teams playing soccer. Yona often brought Jon there to play on the swings. This was where many fairs and festivals were held. It was also a great place to meet people and chat with them and exchange stories. We often heard good news. One morning, for example, we said goodbye to a group of children from our orphanage because they were going back to Poland to be reunited with their parents, who had recently been found in Poland.

In the valley near the mountain of Kilimanjaro, there was a town called Moszi. I heard people saying they were going to Moszi to shop because the bus transportation there was easy and excellent. I went there with my friend Kristen (or as she's called in Polish, Krysia) to look around the stores and perhaps buy some fabrics, maybe for a nice dress for me and a suit for

Jon. The bazaars were already hustling and bustling when we arrived, especially the fabric bazaars.

Before leaving for Africa, I was warned about the wildness of the jungle and the natives. I was shocked and surprised to see that many of the natives in this small town were well educated and held high positions. They were well versed in the culture and the economy. This colony was under British administration, and they were being protected by the British. The natives smiled, sang, and gave the impression they led a happy life. In fact, they didn't have much, but they were without the responsibility of possessions; they didn't have many worries, either. They were very friendly and honest.

In February, we had a great honor. The British colonies of Africa hosted a visit by the royal family, King George VI, Queen Elizabeth, and their daughters, Margaret and Elizabeth. There would be a great parade and festivities in their honor. The rulers were also going to Nairobi, and our scouts were attending the celebrations. We were so proud, we had our noses above the clouds.

Krysia and I arranged to take a bus to see the royal family. Even though it was a long way, we just had to see the parade. We traveled by army truck to Arusha, where we caught the bus to take us to Nairobi, nearly two hundred miles away. But we didn't mind; the scenery was beautiful, and we admired the African wilderness the whole time. At first, we passed fairly large German farms. When the bus went around the foot of Mount Meru, the countryside became a flat prairie, covered only with grass. Dotted along this flat land, we saw low, flat, wide-branched trees.

We also saw thousands of white storks. The driver said these birds would migrate in a few weeks. They were gathering here to fly away to different parts of Africa. Showing the birds to

Jon, I told him they would fly to my beloved Poland. I enjoyed the view, but on the other hand, I was sad because I would not be returning to Poland. What would happen to us when we evacuated this camp? What fate awaited us? Who would be interested in us, and where would they take us next?

In Nairobi, we discovered a true melting pot of natives, Indians, Arabs, British, and even a small colony of Poles, who settled there years ago. It was easy to see the natives were from various African tribes. They differed in height, skin tone, and clothes. Some of their heads were adorned with colorful peacock or ostrich feathers. One thing united them: everyone walked around barefoot.

Nairobi was teeming with life, and the shops were full of all kinds of different goods, all in abundance. We saw unusual creative fashions, bookstores, jewelry stores, restaurants with fragrant-smelling dishes, and even a movie theater. It showed films from England, America, and Italy. On the streets, the locals traded their crafts, and German farmers sold fruits and vegetables.

Unfortunately, we could not break through the crowd to see the royal family, but I went back to Tangero satisfied with my visit to Nairobi. As we returned in the bus, we chattered about what we had seen in Nairobi. We wanted to share all our impressions of the city and the royal visit with each other. Krysia suddenly told everyone to be quiet and listen to the thunder coming from afar. We looked up at the sky but could not see a single cloud. But everything was thundering so loudly that fear overwhelmed us. The bus driver saw our reaction and told us to stay calm; he said it was just a huge herd of wild animals stampeding because they had seen people. The animals were frightened, and the sound of their hooves was like thunder. That was what we heard: the sound of their hooves on the ground as they ran. The noise was so loud, it frightened all of us and worried me. Coming into view in the distance was an unusual cloud of dust. The driver slowed down, saying we had to stop and wait until the herd of elephants in front of us crossed the road. This was a typical scene of galloping wild animals in Africa. We finally arrived safely back in Tangero.

Lately, we had to be very careful and watch out for an ostrich that was on the loose in our camp. It would go into a hut and swallow all the food that had been prepared for supper. It seemed to prefer pierogi (noodles), *kluski* (dumplings), and fruit. And when it did not find food, it ate soap, small pictures, even picture frames, sealed cans of food, and children's shoes. One day, Jon sliced himself a piece of bread and put butter and jam on it. He went outside, sat on the threshold, and began to eat his bread and jam. The ostrich walked by and stared at Jon's bread. It finally decided to try this delicacy, so it ripped it right out of Jon's hand and swallowed it. Jon enjoyed watching the ostrich grab and swallow the bread. So he ran into the kitchen to cut more bread and began secretly feeding the ostrich. Finally, I noticed that not only were we out of bread, we were also out of butter, jam, fruit, and vegetables. I went outside and saw a strange sight: the ostrich was eating straight from the hand of my child.

After a year, I received another letter from Stella. She wrote that she had given birth to a daughter and named her Agnes. She wanted me to be the godmother of her baby girl, but she realized it was not possible. We could not get together for her child's baptism.

Stella's news coincided with a disease Jon came down with. He was very sick from a severe type of malaria called black malaria. He was taken to the hospital along with three other boys and quarantined in a locked ward. The doctor said the disease was so severe, I should be prepared for the worst. He said straight out my son was going to die. I was devastated. Jon was so carefree; he could not tolerate being in isolation, and one day, he jumped out a hospital window and ran home to our mud hut in his pajamas. He begged and pleaded with us to hide him, crying he did not want to go back to the hospital. Moments later, a jeep pulled up with a doctor and two nurses. They interrogated us and then started searching for Jon inside the mud hut. They found him hiding under the bed. They forcibly took him back to the hospital. Fortunately, the doctor's prediction did not come true, and after some time, Jon returned to us in good health.

For some time, we heard rumors that some of the families would be taken from our settlement and transferred to another settlement located farther south. When the list was posted, our name was on it. Again, we needed to pack. Army trucks would take us over a thousand miles to southern Rhodesia. The camp was called Marandellas and was located near Salisbury. It was much smaller than the camp we just left. It had only about six hundred people. It looked very similar to Tangero except that in Tangero, the huts were whitewashed, and here, they were just plain mud. The huts in both camps were covered with elephant grasses. Everything seemed so empty here, and it looked so poor.

(Note: Salisbury, Rhodesia, is now the city of Harare, the capital of Zimbabwe.)

We were assigned to huts next to a soccer field. Beside the soccer field was a huge baobab tree. I already knew about these giants from Tangero, but I still could not get over its size. This tree was even bigger. It was so gigantic that thirty men could not surround it with outstretched arms. A mandarin tree grew behind our mud hut. Our residential pathways were planted with citrus trees, mostly sweet, juicy mandarins and oranges.

They warned us there was a season of monsoons (tropical storms) but for now everything was quiet; there wasn't even any rain. It was so calm and quiet that it was almost annoying. We could even hear the buzzing of a single fly. I thought I would go deaf from this silence. Then all at once, it became so dark, it was scary. Black, heavy clouds moved quickly across the sky. They reminded me of cow udders ready to burst in a split-second. Suddenly, like a shot fired from a cannon, we heard the thunder and saw the lightning. The lightning was so bright, it was almost blinding. It pierced the sky to the right and then to the left. The clouds burst, and finally, the rain began to pour in unbelievable amounts. The ground was so hot that the water evaporated as soon as it fell and formed into a dense fog. In no time, huge streams formed that turned immediately into rivers and lakes. I didn't know if our mud hut would survive this storm, but to my surprise, the straw roof did not leak. After a few hours, the rain stopped, and the sunshine returned.

The bushes around the camp were alive with many different species of monkeys. One evening, three men, claiming to be hunters, wanted to show off how well they could shoot. They started shooting blindly in the direction of the bushes full of monkeys. The noise was so loud, it hurt our ears. Dust flew everywhere because it was so dry. The monkeys ran away, frightened by the noise. The hunters quickly reloaded their guns and started shooting again, this time deliberately aiming at the monkeys hiding in the palm trees and bushes. At the end of this shooting spree, one of the hunters had hit a baby being carried by its mother. There was a lot of screaming and squealing from the monkeys. The female monkey was crying loudly, clinging her dead baby to her chest. The rest of the monkeys, eager for revenge, immediately declared war on the hunters. They broke off coconuts from the trees and threw them at the men. Suddenly, from nowhere, a group of baboons joined the fight against the hunters. Now people came running, not knowing what had happened, but they soon found out. Because of the cruel and thoughtless actions of the hunters, they would be fined and severely punished by the British authorities.

At night in our settlement, there were hyenas, ugly dogs that snuck toward us, looking for something to eat. In time, they even get enough courage to show up in broad daylight. If one hyena found something, the whole herd of hyenas attacked it to get something to eat. They made terrible sounds as they barked their strange noises. The hunters, including my husband, immediately grabbed their guns when they heard the hyena noises. The hunters gave chase to the animals and fired their guns, trying to shoot them. I begged Joseph to be careful so someone did not shoot him, because in this noise, the hunters could easily shoot each other. The hyenas escaped, laughing that strange barking noise.

Unexpectedly, one day, I got a delightful surprise: a letter from my brother Tony. He wrote describing his entire journey from the time he left Siberia. Some of the details I already knew because we used the same trains to leave the camp in Siberia. He traveled to Basra, Jordan, Palestine, and Egypt. He was able to handle an army truck very well, so he was given the job of training young soldiers how to drive the big trucks. In 1943, he sailed from Alexandria, Egypt, to Italy and fought at Monte Casino. After the war, he moved to the United Kingdom. He settled in Wales, where he wrote me this letter. I wanted to see Tony, but I had to think of my own family. I was pregnant again and was so busy now; it was getting harder to take care of Jon. He was always getting into some kind of mischief.

One day, when Jon was about six years of age, he took the large magnifying glass out of our binoculars. He used the glass to set fire to dry leaves, grass, or paper, impressing his friends. He got the idea to climb up a telegraph pole, wanting to get a closer look at the sun to see if it looked larger with the magnifying glass. Once he was at the top of the pole, he looked at the sun through the glass. He immediately went blind, fainted, lost his balance, and fell in a heap on the ground, losing consciousness. I heard people screaming and running outside, so I left our hut and sped toward the crowd standing at the bottom of the telegraph pole. Someone said it was Jon. With my big pregnant belly, I tried to push my way closer to the pole. As I approached the child lying there, I saw it was my son, with blood streaming down his face and the magnifying glass embedded in his forehead above his left eye. His nose was also cut.

People helped me bring him to the camp hospital. The nurse washed the wound and immediately called the doctor. After he examined Jon, he told me there were no broken bones, but he would have scars on his forehead, eyebrow, and nose for the rest of his life, something Jon would always remember, his own souvenir of magnifying glasses and telegraph poles in Africa.

It was finally time for me to give birth to my second child. I had a really bad headache, so I went to the hospital. Two doctors examined me, a Pole and an Englishman. They deliberated among themselves, consulted other staff members, and finally decided I had complications and my birthing would be very difficult. They could not deliver my child at this hospital. They arranged for a Red Cross ambulance to take me to a hospital in

Salisbury as soon as possible. They assured me it was a first-class British clinic. I was carried on a stretcher to the ambulance. I suffered terribly all day Saturday and Sunday with labor pains. I could not wait for these pains to end. On Monday, January 27, 1947, after a very difficult birth, little Henry came into this world. He had long hair, twisted into a thick lock, and beautiful big eyes. The nurses smiled as they looked at him and said it was too bad I did not have a girl because he was so beautiful. While I was there, I lay like a queen in this exclusive clinic, and after two weeks, an ambulance returned me to my settlement.

All the nervous thoughts that had plagued my mind about my family came true: a letter arrived from my father. My parents left Tehran at the beginning of 1946. The priest who was my father's friend gave them the signal to leave on the last transport out of Tehran and suggested they leave together. They went by train through Baghdad and Aleppo and finally to Beirut. My parents were very happy about this turn of events in their lives. They lived under the care of the United Nations Relief and Rehabilitation Administration, an international organization dealing with the refugees of war. They were given a nice house and paid thirty-three pounds per month. Father wrote that from this sum of money, he had to pay the housing costs, but it was a very small amount, so almost the entire sum went into his pocket. They were living so well that they felt as if they were living in paradise. The city was surrounded by scenic hills covered with beautiful cedar trees. Everything was beyond enough, more than enough. They had plenty of money and plenty of food. My parents said they were happy and enjoying life. They even went on trips, visiting historic buildings left behind by the Egyptians, Greeks, Romans, and Turks. The only thing that irritated them was the fact that they lived almost exclusively among the Arabs and found it hard to get used to their customs, which were so very different from ours. Josephine was registered into a Catholic school, like almost all the other Polish children. In Beirut, there were two universities; one was American and the other French, but both were Catholic. There were several hundred Poles studying in these two universities.

Father knew Tony had settled in Wales and then moved to England. He had written to our parents to say he would like them to join him. My parents wrote that they had all the necessary paperwork to travel out of the country. In February of 1948, they left Beirut behind and joined Tony in England. I started to cry like a baby as I read their letter. They were tears of joy; they were alive, doing well, and happy.

Most times, when I'd give Jon some fruit, he gave it to a baboon who visited our settlement on a regular basis. Jon had befriended the baboon. They liked each other so much, they spent a lot of time playing games with each other. One day, our neighbor came out to hang her laundry, as usual. The clothes hung on a rope stretched between our hut and a baobab tree. I heard hustle and bustle and fussing noises, but I didn't look, because I was busy making pierogies and noodles with onions for our dinner.

Suddenly, I heard screaming, and our neighbor came flying into our hut, cursing and swearing that the baboon had attacked her. I left everything, grabbed a broom, and ran out into the yard to see what was going on. The baboon was sitting high in the tree, and as I looked at it, it shook its head, showing a mouthful of teeth, as though it were grinning at me. It had a bunch of bananas; it peeled them, ate them, and then threw the skins at the neighbor's freshly hung-up laundry. I knew she often teased the baboon; now the baboon was paying her back. I tried to explain to her that rather than curse the baboon to the high heavens, she should make friends with the creature, give it some fruit to eat, and she would not have any more trouble.

All at once, I heard unexpected noises coming from my hut and ran back inside. An ostrich had taken advantage of my absence to go inside in search of food. In a panic, the ostrich turned its small bald head and stared at me with its huge eyes. It surprised me. It seemed to assess the situation and apparently felt no threat. It did what it wanted, helping itself by swallowing all the food off the shelves and the table. Canned food, photos, anything and everything just disappeared into its beak and down its long neck. I looked around for the noodles and pierogies and saw they had disappeared. The ostrich had eaten everything. I was afraid of its hooves, so with the help of my broom, I moved slowly forward, step-by-step, urging it to leave our hut. Finally, after devouring everything else it found, it left.

The next morning, I did laundry, which in this climate dried quickly. I started pressing it with an iron filled with hot coals, as we did not have electricity in our huts (we had only three or four street lights at the intersections with electricity). Henry was asleep in his stroller, and Jon was outside in the shade of a baobab tree, playing with the baboon, giving him various commands and teaching him tricks. I was very busy, so I did not notice the silence, which usually meant trouble. Finally, when I realized I could not hear any sounds from my boys, I went to look at Henry and found the stroller was empty. I looked and saw another baboon running away with my baby. The baboon ran past Jon and his pet baboon and jumped onto the tree, climbing higher and higher among the branches and the leaves, disappearing into the dense foliage between the branches of the baobab tree. I was desperate, but I could not climb this giant tree. I cried for help, and immediately many people came to my aid, bringing fruit to entice the baboon down. But it did not leave the tree until later in the evening. We were all just standing under the baobab tree, trying to coax the baboon to come down. When it finally came down, most likely from hunger, it gave Henry to me.

The year 1951 began. We had many visitors: friends, cousins, and people dropping by to tell us they planned to move permanently to England. Apparently, it was relatively easy to get transportation through Khartoum, Sudan, to the United Kingdom. My memories of the excellent British hospital where Henry was born and the cleanliness and orderliness of the British colonies and, above all, the message from my parents about their departure to England motivated me to encourage Joseph to move there too. A further encouragement for us to leave was the fact that the native people were starting to rebel against the British, who ruled them with an iron fist.

And so we were set to leave for England. The journey was long, more than fifteen hundred miles by army truck, but the extraordinary landscapes compensated for our inconvenience. In places, the road was paved with asphalt, but mostly it was hard crossing in the wilderness on rutted wheel tracks, especially with two young children. After crossing the boundaries of northern Rhodesia, Tanganyika, and Kenya, we arrived at the border of Sudan. Once inside Sudan, the bush turned into desert sands. We were on the southeastern edge of the Sahara. People here lived in broken tents. We passed small villages and towns full of markets. There was no rain in this country except in June, during the rainy season, so people relied almost exclusively on the life-giving waters of the Nile. I saw huge expanses of cotton fields and was reminded of when I had worked collecting cotton in Uzbekistan for one pita bread a day as wages. I was told almost all of the harvested cotton was exported to England.

We arrived at our camp in Khartoum. I was happy to see it was nice and neat; the streets were well lit, and our accommodations were barracks, not mud huts. This place was where the British held Italian prisoners during the war.

As soon as we arrived in Khartoum, we registered ourselves to go to England. There was a very long queue, and no one seemed to know how long it may take for further transport to England. They asked us to be patient. We used our free time to explore the surrounding areas of Khartoum and later Egypt, Palestine, and the holy sites of Jerusalem. We learned that on November 29, 1947, the general assembly of the UN had adopted a resolution for the establishment of an independent Jewish state in Palestine. According to President Truman of the United States, the country of Israel was entitled to freedom. When we arrived in Jerusalem, Jon along with other children played in Jesus's tomb. Arriving at the Jordan River, we were blessed to find a priest standing in the river, baptizing children and adults. We joined this group, and all of us got baptized in the Jordan River, where John the Baptist had baptised Jesus two thousand years ago.

We continued sightseeing while still awaiting transport to England; this time, we went to the Red Sea. Jon was playing with other children on a bridge. Suddenly, I saw him fall into the water. People shouted that he was going under, and I knew he could not swim. A young man jumped into the water after Jon and pulled him from what would have been a watery grave. Jon looked like a wet rat. Again, I had to lecture him about disobedience. He was at the age where he got into mischief everywhere he went.

We left the camp in Khartoum after seven months. We had

lived in Africa for almost six years. Our journey to England started with about five hundred miles by truck to the port of Suakin. From there, we boarded a Dutch ship, the *Dundalk*. We sailed along on the waters of the Arabian Gulf. The waters were glittering, flat, and shiny like a mirror. As we passed close to land, we saw a road in the Arabian desert and were told it was the road to the very large port of Jidda. This port was very important because this was where Western countries traded with the Arabic world. Not far from Jidda were the two most important cities for the Arabs: Mecca, where hundreds of thousands of Muslims traveled every year to visit the shrine of Ka'ba, and the city of Medina, where they visited the tomb of Muhammad.

Before long, we approached the Suez Canal. Everyone was pushing their way to the bow of the ship, in order to see what the French and the Egyptians had accomplished building this canal, a work that took them one hundred years. Using the canal shortened our journey to less than half the time it would have taken if we'd had to sail around Africa. Our ship slowly and calmly navigated between the villages of Egypt on one side and Arabia and Palestine on the other.

Before we entered the Atlantic Ocean, we sailed on the Mediterranean Sea and encountered pleasant, cooler temperatures, making it much easier to bear. On the right side of the ship, we went around the British colony of the Rock of Gibraltar and then through the Strait of Gibraltar, and then we entered the waters of the Atlantic Ocean. The sky got cloudy, and the temperature turned chilly.

On the western horizon, after thousands of kilometers of travel, we finally spotted land. On the right side, we passed Spain and Portugal, then Spain again. After many more kilometers, we found ourselves looking at France. Soon, we spotted the coastline of England, our goal. We were getting closer and closer to the end of our journey.

We sailed past the estuary of the Thames River and passed East Anglia, continuing on to the port of Hull. We entered the port and were greeted by the English fog. I did not like this gloomy, wet weather. In fact, I wanted to go back to the sun, to the heat I was used to, but it was too late now. We docked at the port, and after we disembarked, we were transported to yet another camp called Keevil, an American base.

My dreams finally came true: I met my parents and sister Josephine again after such a very long time. I was disappointed that Tony was not with them, but after much hugging, kissing and tears, they explained that they were living at another American army base north of London. They told me Tony had lived in Wales but left for Alberta, Canada, to live with Aunt Sophie. They also said they were on a list to go to America. Father's brother had moved to Detroit before the war, while he was still a young man. I was so happy to see them again that it made this dreary English weather easier to bear.

Jon started school; his teacher was named Mrs. Rogers. He sat in the back of the classroom because he had never been to school in his life. He often ran away from school because he did not understand English. He could not understand what the teacher was saying or what was expected of him. The classroom was very confining to Jon, as he was used to being outside all day, playing with the native African Masai children and his pet baboon and birds. So of course, a truant officer came to our barracks many times and explained that Jon must attend school every weekday to get an education, even if he could not understand what was happening in the classroom. But Jon still continued to run away from school.

While we lived at the camp called Keevil, I decided to

divorce Joseph, who was very abusive, and move into the barracks where my parents lived. One day, we hurriedly threw our clothes into a pile as soon as he went to work. My sister Josephine arrived to help us; we moved without Joseph knowing we left.

While living at the camp near my parents, I talked to a new friend named Gorys, who was a justice of the peace, about Jon running away from school all the time. He told me the British government had set up special boarding schools for children who had lived outside the country. There, they could get an education and learn the English language. He helped me apply to the school, called Sheplebury in Stevenage. Jon was accepted, and I took Henry and Jon there by train. Henry and I returned to Mepal, leaving Jon behind at the boarding school. Unfortunately, Jon was only there a few months; after he reached eleven years of age, he was no longer entitled to attend Sheplebury. So my friend helped me again to get Jon into a different boarding school for boys. The new school was in Hereford on Buckingham Road. Jon was very well educated at these boarding schools and excelled at everything he did.

So England was not to be the last stop of my journey.

In August 1972, I arrived in the United States with my new husband. Jon had already left for Canada, and Henry worked in the Middle East.

Epilogue

Looking back over my life, I can definitely see the hand of God was on me and my family. We never would have survived without His help and intervention. It is because of this that I became a follower of Jesus Christ in 1999. This story reads like fiction, but it is all true; it really happened.

I cannot believe that I have lived to be in my 90's after all I endured. One of my favorite sayings is that "God does not want me up there yet". I guess He still has work for me to do while I'm here.

Perhaps that is why I open my home to anyone who needs a place to stay for however long they need it mostly to new arrivals from Europe and also to the homeless. I give money regularly to those I meet on the street and help my neighbors by cooking food for them or shopping for them or just taking them for walks. I freely give all I have to those who ask for anything, even if it means I go without. I know that today I have all I need: food in my fridge (when I don't give it away), clothes in my closet and plenty of shoes and boots to wear and above all a loving family.

Editor's Note

Katherine, the heroine of this story, is living in Hamtramck, Michigan. In January 2017 she celebrated her 93rd birthday.

Her son Jon lives in Windsor, Ontario, Canada. He is married and has 3 children and 1 grandchild.

Her youngest son Henry lives in Florida. He is married and has 2 children.

Tony passed away in 2013. He lived in Amherstburg, Ontario after leaving Detroit, Michigan.

Josephine lives in St Clair Shores, Michigan.

Stella passed away in 2015 and lived in Brantford and Toronto, Ontario.

About the Author

It is my honor to put into writing the past-life journeys of my mother and I. Coming from a care-free life lived with tribal people in Africa to a civilized life in England was difficult for me. Until age 10 I had no formal schooling. But I was eager for education and learned quickly. By age 21 I had already earned my London City Guilds degree in  building and construction, moved to Canada and opened my own construction company and was teaching special education at the high school level. I waited until I retired to be able to devote the time needed to write this saga. It is my hope that this writing will enlighten all who read it.

Printed in the United States
By Bookmasters